Game Fishing

Game Fishing

BOB CHURCH
GAME ANGLER OF THE MILLENNIUM

With contributions by Iain Barr, Mike Green,
Hywel Morgan and Dave Steuart

Foreword by Tom Saville

THE CROWOOD PRESS

First published in 2008 by
The Crowood Press Ltd
Ramsbury, Marlborough
Wiltshire SN8 2HR

www.crowood.com

British Library Cataloguing-in-Publication Data
A catalogue record for this book is available from the British Library.

ISBN 978 1 84797 059 6

Frontispiece: Bob Church caught several fish like this one when fishing in Canada. His team in the Commonwealth Fly Fishing Championship won the event. They travelled from the south to the north of Canada, fishing on Nimpo Lake, British Columbia, which is not far from Alaska.

Typeset by Bookcraft, Stroud, Gloucestershire

Printed and bound in Singapore by Craft Print International Ltd

Contents

Dedication

I would like to dedicate this, my sixteenth book, to three fine game fishermen now no longer with us except in memory. Firstly Geoff Clarkson, the most successful England World International team manager ever: I was proud to be in his team of five that won gold medals in England in 1987, and again in Tasmania in 1988. Also to two great salmon fishers, Hugh Falkus and Arthur Oglesby, who travelled south to check out the rainbow trout fishing in the reservoirs and small fisheries; I am pleased to say I had a great few days showing them Rutland, Avington and Church Hill Farm. A lot of our fishing was filmed for a set of videos, which was most successful. There, fishing lives on, because I noticed the old videos have now been re-released on DVD.

Acknowledgements

First of all thanks must go to the young, top reservoir fly fisher, Iain Barr, for taking us through his season's fishing month by month. Also to Mike Green, my regular fishing partner, whether it is for salmon, sea trout or pike; it is always well worth taking note of his approach and tactics. And to Dave Steuart, an old friend who has lived on the banks of the River Test for the last thirty-plus years. Lastly, the World Fly Casting Champion, Hywel Morgan, who has a remarkable style that you can study through his many tips on casting.

A lot of the small fly photographs were taken by Gavin Walding, and the natural insect photographs by Peter Gathercole.

I must thank my dear wife Jeanette for typing this manuscript, and for all her help and encouragement. Also Julie Emerson, because no Bob Church book would be complete without her lead-in poem.

Thanks again to The Crowood Press: this is the fifth classic we have produced together. And finally, thanks to Tom Saville for his kind Foreword.

Fishing: A Way of Life

Fishing is far more than just a
hobby; it becomes part of our lives,
It embeds in our hearts;
ensuring our hunter's instinct survives,
Silently beckoning and
demanding our time,
Holding us captive like
a fish on our line.
Inviting us to achieve our
ultimate goals and desires,
Needing our attention and
fuelling our fires.
Giving us equality with Lords and Sires.

Great is our passion when
we are casting our lines,
And the love in our heart
is hard to define.
Magnificent is our pride
when we achieve our goals,
Enriching our love and
feeding our souls.

Creative and varied with so
many methods and skills,
Oblivious to the elements;
attaining our thrills.
Adventurous and
daring as we seek out our prey,
Relaxing at home at the end of the day.
Sharing our passion and
gaining new recruits,
Enriching our lives with
our angling pursuits.

So many anglers with so
many hopes and dreams.
Enriching our desires on
rivers, lochs and streams,
Angling is a 'way of life' – at
least, that's how it seems.

Julie Emerson

Foreword

I started fly fishing in 1952, a few years after I had moved to the Midlands. How I wish there had been a book like this one! Living in Nottingham at the time, the nearest available trout fishing was in the Derbyshire streams around Ashbourne. The books were mostly about chalk streams – Skues, Turing and suchlike – which was not a great deal of help, and the weekly copy of *Fishing Gazette* was a hodgepodge of coarse/sea/game fishing. Casting tuition came from friends.

So my learning curve was slow and full of trial and error, and mostly the latter – and limited to the few venues I could get to. Although Tom Ivens' book on stillwater fishing had just been published, his Ravensthorpe seemed to be the impossible dream, all those miles away – besides which, it was private. During the first couple of years, four of us plucked up the courage to make an annual trip to EyeBrook Reservoir, which we fished most unsuccessfully, knowing so little about the different tactics needed.

Thus my fly fishing career tortoised along, and I gained experience as I went along. I managed to widen my river expertise on the Derbyshire Derwent, and the EyeBrook trips became weekly; I even managed to get a rod on the Aberdeenshire Dee! Thus the tortoise speeded up a little...

And then, suddenly it seemed, there was Grafham – and Bob Church! Bob was willing and able to share his expertise with us all, and everyone's learning curve took an upward turn.

And now, here's the book we've all been waiting for. In it Bob has assembled these modern-day experts to add their expertise to his own wide circle of knowledge: a veritable galaxy of angling stars. This is the book I needed all those years ago! Enjoy ... and learn!

Tom Saville
Bottesford, Leicestershire
June 2007

Dave Steuart (right) ghillies for Tom Saville on the River Itchin.

Introduction

Casting a Fly for Fifty-Five Years

I have been casting a fly now for some fifty-five years and more, and have loved every minute of it. I have tackled many species at one time or another, both at home and in foreign seas and rivers. There are just a few that I will not be writing about, but which I mention in passing to show you the variety of species it is possible to catch on a fly rod.

I went fly fishing for bonefish off Andros Island in the Bahamas, and found it quite easy, catching twenty-five on the first morning I tried it – though admittedly my fellow angler Peter Dobbs and I struck lucky, and it was a long time ago (thirty years). Then Andros Island in the Bahamas became more commercialized – but it put me off looking on this fish as trendy. I have caught specimen chub, barbel, zander, perch, bream, roach, rudd, carp, eels, tench and dace all on fly tackle. The pike I now recognize as a new 'game fish', my local River Nene producing good sport with pike on the fly. (*See* Chapter 12, Mike Green on pike and zander fishing.)

I am now seventy-two years old, but am still fishing from boat and bank for a full day, and I still visit all the major trout fisheries in the UK and Ireland. In the year 2000 I was voted 'game angler of the millennium' by the readers of *Trout Fisherman*, a great honour. My first articles were published in 1963, and I have done my best to present fly fishing for trout as an exciting branch of angling that every coarse fisherman should try.

In 1972 I was signed up by *Angling Times* to do a weekly page in their successful newspaper. This continued for twenty-eight years until the year 2000, leaving me with the record for the longest-running column. I had an influential position at *Angling Times*; the then editor Bob Feetham had

I have been casting a fly now for half a century.

excellent results, taking the readership up to 176,000 copies per week. At the time stillwater trout fishing was booming, and I was able through my column to help its popularity.

As the stillwaters increased in number I championed the cause to get all anglers out trout fishing, and as more and more coarse anglers tried their hand at fly fishing during the old close season – 14 March to 16 June – gradually the snobbery, which in times past had been quite prevalent in the sport, disappeared altogether.

My Career on the Competition Circuit

My career as an international competition fly fisherman included fishing in the Four Nations five times; I captained the team in Wales, winning gold on Lynn Brenig in 1990; then in 1992 I was made England manager – the event was held on Lough Melvin in Ireland, I was in the team again, and once more we won gold. Basically I was lucky to be part of a very good team of top fly fishers, and we travelled

The triumphant England World Team, who made two consecutive wins in the World Championships, this time in Tasmania's central plateau wilderness. Front left, our non-fishing manager Geoff Clarkson. Back right, the sponsor's representative, Dewars Whisay.

the world together for about fifteen years: New Zealand, Tasmania and Finland – north Lapland, Canada, Sweden, France, Belgium, Luxemburg, Iceland – I actually travelled round the world both ways just to go fly fishing.

From 1972 until 1983 I was unable to enter the eliminators because I was termed a professional, but in 1984 this rule was relaxed and I was accepted into the team: I had twelve very successful years on the competition circuit. I fished five times for England at World level, winning two golds, one silver and one individual bronze medal. When the Commonwealth captaincy was

passed on to me, the first three events were a hat-trick of golds for England, the venues Canada, Scotland and England.

My own career results were complete when I won a gold medal for our team of three – Chris Ogborne, Dennis Buck and myself – in the European Grand Slam; I had a further three individual bronze medals in this, my favourite event. Visiting Ghent in Belgium, and Dreux, south of Paris, also gave us some most interesting social experiences. In particular, this success at the higher levels culminated in an invitation to meet the Queen on the occasion of her fortieth anniversary at her garden party at

Outside Buckingham Palace, where the England gold medal fly-fishing team were invited to a garden party in celebration of the Queen's fortieth anniversary.

This is a golden rainbow, a subspecies of the ordinary rainbow. Fly fishermen like these because they can see them easily in the water. Bob caught this 8lb 6oz fish from Chalk Springs.

Bob with a 4lb 12oz tiger trout; this rare game fish is a cross-breed between a brook trout and a brown trout.

Small fishery specialist angler Alan Pearson with a UK Record Brook trout of 5lb 13½oz, from Avington Fishery.

Buckingham Palace, when all the British world champions in all sporting events were invited.

Throughout this period I was fishing in the west of Ireland, in Scotland and in Wales for sea trout and salmon. I also fished the river of 'giants', the Morrum river in southern Sweden. And then there was the incredible experience in Iceland of so many salmon and sea trout, also sea-run char and brown trout.

I will try and give you as much information as I can about all my favourite fishing places in my chapters in this book.

My Records Chart

The following chart is of my personal best caught game fish, all on fly; readers can draw their own comparisons with these, and perhaps make their own list. It is interesting to see how the size of the fish increases as the years roll by. Mine is up to date at May 2007.

- Rainbow trout: 27lb 2oz; England (2001)
- Brown trout: 13lb 12oz; England (2005)
- Brown trout ferox: 17lb 3oz, trolled; Ireland (2002)
- Sea trout: 11lb 4oz, worm; England (1975)
- Atlantic salmon: 28lb 2oz; Scotland (1985)
- Char, Icelandic: 3lb 2oz; Iceland (2003)
- Atlantic salmon: 45lb, estimated; dark red cock fish; Sweden (1986)
- Pike: 30lb 8oz; England (2003)
- Grayling: 3lb; Scotland (1997)
- Zander: 13lb 2oz; England (2007)

Frank Cutler with his bag of trout that gave him first place in the Classic, the event they all want to win.

There is also a list of rarer game fish; I come across these breeds from time to time, mostly at the smaller fisheries:

- Tiger trout: 4lb 8oz, crossed brown and brook trout; England (1983)
- Cheetah trout: 7lb 8oz, crossed rainbow and brook trout; England (1984)
- Golden trout: 8lb 6oz; England (1997)
- Blue trout: 7lb 2oz; England (1998)
- Brook trout: 4lb 8oz; Canada (1992)
- Brook trout: 3lb 4.8oz; England (1980)

Putting Something Back

Putting something back into fly fishing has always been my aim ever since I started to earn a good living from it, and I like

BELOW: Jeanette, myself, Grafham Smith, Tom Bilson and Moc Morgan started up the Ladies International teams for the four home nations. This picture is an early England team.

to think I have helped to get more people actually fly fishing than ever would have done otherwise. For example, the Youth International organization was the idea of the late Tom Bilson, Moc Morgan, Graham Smith and myself. I provided a decent cup for members to fish for, and it quickly became popular: proof of its success is that it is still running well today. Each year individuals up to the age of eighteen years from England, Scotland, Wales and Ireland, fish for the four Home Countries Championships.

The venues rotate around the best waters of the four countries. The Youth events are run in almost the same way as the seniors; this means that, if a youth is successful up to eighteen years old, he will transfer easily into the senior eliminators and should continue his success there. Examples are Jeremy Herrmann and Iain Barr; Iain writes the opening chapter to this book.

The Ladies International was started off in the same way by Moc Morgan, Tom Bilson, Graham Smith and my wife Jeanette and me; in the first year it was just England and Wales, then Scotland joined in, and then Ireland. As for the Youth movement, I presented them with a decent team trophy, a lovely rose bowl, and this has been fished for each year right up to the present day. My wife also gave a trophy known as the Otter Trophy, to be awarded for the biggest fish, and Graham Smith donated a third trophy, a bronze boat.

I run two separate events each year at Rutland Water; in April is the Frank Cutler Memorial competition, in which 110 fly fishers take part, fishing from boats. And during the first week in May, I organize the unique classic known by all the 'top end' fly fishers from all over the UK, Ireland and Europe as the Champion of Champions: it is for 100 strong seeded competitors, and is

Bob with a match-winning catch from Rutland Water; 24lb.

the event they all want to win. This competition takes place at Grafham Water.

There is no doubt that if you want to learn more about catching trout, join a club, and fish as many of their competitions as you can. You will pick up a great many tips from the person you are drawn with – I always enjoyed the camaraderie when fishing for England.

I have also fished in many charity fund-raising days at various fisheries – and in this context I would like to mention actor Bernard Cribbins, who gives these events a lot of his time. He is also a very good fly fisherman! Lord Roy Mason of Barnsley is another who has always been heavily involved with charity trout-fishing days, the proceeds from which have supported worthy causes such as disabled fly fishers' wheelie boats, and heart and cancer units.

The late Geoff Clarkson MBE: fishing at Grafham Water, with a brace of 4lb rainbows. This is at a team reunion weekend.

Bernard Cribbins and Bob Church after a day's fishing, auctioning off one of Bob's fly boxes for charity.

1 Reservoir Trout Fishing

By Iain Barr

I was privileged to have been brought into the sport of fly fishing by my dad, who fished the River Clyde in Glasgow as a teenager. My parents later moved south to the East Midlands, well within reach of many major trout fisheries, including the prolific Eyebrook and Foremark reservoirs.

Tackle has changed dramatically in those years. Bob Church Tackle was the first company to sponsor me in my quest for glory, and his very own Northampton rod accounted for many thousands of trout in my first ten years or so in fishing. This rod was stiff and very powerful, and tired the fish very quickly. Carbon rods have now advanced, and tackle companies, including Bob Church Tackle, are producing rods so light you don't know you are holding them.

Tackle plays a small part in fooling the trout to consume your fly. For me, it is the friendships I have built with people across the world. My current twenty-two caps for England have posted me around the globe, competing in World and European Championships with the finest of anglers, some of whom have become life-long friends. I have been lucky enough to win many major competitions, including the illustrious Bob Church Classic Trophy twice. I have been

Iain Barr before the start of a competition at Grafham Water.

16

Fifty motor boats are now all moored neatly ready for tomorrow's customers.

twice European Open Individual and Team Champion, also UK Brown Bowl Champion, and England team and individual silver medallist in the European Championships in Norway.

In this chapter I aim to share my success with you, and also the techniques, flies and methods that I use throughout a calendar year. As our climate changes, so does our fishing too, as the very life forms that the fish feed on change their habits.

Always remember, to be at peace with nature is an ideal in today's society; to catch a fish should be a mere bonus. And remember too: tight lines!

January/February – Enjoy Exceptional Winter Fishing

There is no mistaking that global warming is heating up our planet and in turn our lakes and reservoirs. Winter fishing is not how I used to know it – but there are still distinct differences between this and the other seasons, as water temperatures remain low. For example, there is a distinct lack of insect life to be seen in the air, which is normally such a good source of information as to what the trout are feeding on.

There is no doubt that a lure remains the fisherman's favourite choice of fly – though I have had huge success with nymphs, too.

Fresh from many variations on turkey meals at Christmas, the fly fisherman is hungry for some sport, and the trout are hungry for your flies, too. Many anglers pack their kit away in the garage or shed until spring arrives, but they are missing out on some fantastic sport. Although many large reservoirs may close through the winter months, there are many smaller fisheries that remain open all year round for the avid fly fisherman keen for that heart-stopping pull at his fingertips.

17

A selection of trophies won by Iain Barr.

Water Temperatures

Despite our warmer winters, our waters remain fairly cold and the trout stay dormant and reserved. Food is scarcer in the winter months and this can mean two things: the fish are less reluctant to chase, and they will readily take a correctly presented fly.

Colder water means it is generally very clear, as the water algae has died away, leaving us with crystal-clear waters. It is therefore essential to fish leader tippet such as fluorocarbon, a clear leader material that all but disappears when submerged in the water. I recommend an absolute minimum of 6lb breaking strength when winter fishing, but preferably 8lb – and if there are big fish in the lake then don't be afraid to step up to 10lb. Remember that it all but disappears, so you can get away with higher breaking strains.

Any winter sunshine will marginally warm the top layers of the lakes and reservoirs, and this warmer water is blown downwind in the top few inches. When this reaches the shore it is pushed back in a mildly turbulent manner, causing the warmer water to disperse and move out slightly from the shore. The strength of the wind will determine how far this warmer water will push out. I know that in wind strengths of approximately 20 knots this under-current turbulence can reach up to 80m (260ft) or so.

This marginally milder water encourages small winter larvae to hatch or come to life. At this time of year when food is scarce, any gathering of warmer water and insect life is sure to hold fish, and this is where you should be fishing in the colder months for consistent winter sport. On some days it may be uncomfortable, but a well wrapped-up angler will be rewarded. The warmer

A fine rainbow trout caught close in from the shore.

water will be close to the shore, so don't go wading straight in – if you do, this may cause it to muddy up due to the underwater turbulence, and the fish will move out.

The fish will be literally only a few yards out from the shoreline, so, knowing the fish are not far from the bank, it is imperative that you lift your flies out slowly at the end of the retrieve. Do this by slowly lifting the rod over your right shoulder, if right-handed, but keep hold of the line and wait until you feel it tightening. You are likely to witness swirls in the water where fish have turned away from the fly at the last moment. Simply cast the flies out a few yards, then slowly lift them out of the water again in an attempt to induce the take.

Although it may be more comfortable, try and avoid fishing with the wind off your back. This may make for an easier day's fishing, but equally it may prove fruitless,

as all the warm water is being pushed away from you. A left to right wind – when you stand on the bank and the wind is blowing from your left to your right – or a right to left wind may be productive, as warmer water is constantly passing you, but you won't get the accumulations that you would if the wind were blowing directly at you.

Fishing from the point of a small bay may be extremely productive, because here you will get the benefits of a cross wind, as well as the wind accumulating the warmer water in the edges.

Time of Day

The time of day can be crucial when winter fishing. I have fished many times during the winter with very little reward, only for there to be an explosion of life as the day warms up. The window of approximately 11:30–14:00 can be magnificently prolific

An early season favourite, the Cat's Whisker.

– though beware, as sometimes it can be as short as just one hour. Look for the start of small black midges hatching, and this will tell you that the day is warming up. The indication of these tiny offerings buzzing around your ears gives you an obvious sign of life. However, these insects have hatched from the lake bed and made the precarious journey from the bed to the surface. If the flies are in the air, then the fish have already started feeding on them below. It's time to make the correct fly choice.

Fly Choice

Although the trout may be hungry, they will be selective as to what they eat, so it is important to present the fly slowly at this time of the year when water temperatures are low. Lures will always be the most popular choice for most anglers during winter, as the slow movement, along with the movement of marabou tails, proves almost irresistible to any trout. My largest rainbow and brown reservoir-caught trout both came to a fly called the Cat's Whisker. This is tied using white marabou and a fluorescent yellow body with sink chain eyes tied in at the front. This is a prolific fly with an array of colours that the trout find irresistible.

I hear many anglers saying they had any number of pulls, but caught nothing. When fishing larger lures with long tails you will witness 'tail nippers', when the fish are grabbing at the tail without grabbing the hook. The temptation is to lift and strike, but you must resist this almost impossible urge to lift your rod: simply keep moving the fly. Some people say you must speed up the fly, but in the colder months a continuous retrieve at the same pace will induce the fish to engulf the fly. When fishing lures on their own, try small jerky movements to bring the fly to life.

The retrieve is probably the second most important thing after choosing your fly. An incorrectly presented fly can be as useless as fishing no fly. Remember the aim is to induce the fish to take the fly, so vary the retrieve until you get some interest, then continue at the same pace. Although lures in white and green, black and green or orange will arguably catch more winter trout, never ignore small nymphs. Once you see those small buzzers in the air, try small size 12 or 14 Buzzers on the droppers. I was catching steadily one winter on a lake using a black and green lure when a buzzer hatch started; whilst this hatch was on I never caught a single fish on the lure, but all proceeded to take the small Buzzers on the droppers.

The Booby

In all its various colours this fly arguably accounts for most lure-caught trout. The polystyrene eyes tied in at the front of the fly make it buoyant, and it is this buoyancy that makes it so irresistible. I visit many lakes and see trout anglers sitting down with the rod beside them, reminiscent of coarse anglers.

This can be a deadly method. Use a fast-sinking line such as an Airflo Di7 with a short leader of about three or four feet. Cast it out and let it sink to the bottom where trout will be feeding on bloodworm and other larvae seeking the depths for cover.

Your Booby will sink at the length of your leader from the bottom. Once it has settled, try short sharp pulls with long pauses in between: this will make the Booby dive and irresistibly rise back up, and it is this movement, of the Booby rising back up, that the trout find too tempting to resist. As the fish rise in the water layers, increase your leader length so your Booby is fishing higher in the water column. It is vital always to remember that trout can't see anything beneath them, including your fly, so if you are fishing this method and not getting any takes, then your leader may be too short and your fly is beneath them.

Before fishing this method, check that the fishery allows Boobies: some fisheries have banned them because the trout tend to swallow the fly right down their throats. If you are practising catch and release, then it is likely the fish will die. Always carry a set of forceps for such incidents.

Iain Barr Favourite January/February Rigs

Floating or intermediate line:
- Size 14 Black Buzzer on the point; size 14 Cruncher on the dropper; Cat's Whisker on the point.

Fast-sinking line:
- Single orange, or black and green Booby.

Top Tips

- Keep on the move.
- Fish your flies slowly.
- Don't wade straight in from the bank.
- Fish close to the margins.
- Don't be afraid to try nymphs on a mild winter's day.

March/April – Mastering Early Season Tactics

Many fisheries reopen after the winter breaks, when it's time for a fishing bonanza. This is a beautiful time of the year as the birds are calling their mates, frost can still be glistening in the grass, and the trout are extremely hungry!

As in the details for January and February, you should be looking for the warmest water, which will be in the cross wind or with the wind blowing directly at you. Late March or early April is usually when I venture out on to the larger reservoirs in search of some over-wintered trout. These tend to be sparser than in previous years, though we won't go into the reasons why; nevertheless, they can still be found – although you have to avoid the very hungry stock fish that are still naive to even the gaudiest of lures.

There are some very important things to remember when fishing sinking lines, and I aim to cover these in the March/April section. Many people think it is a 'chuck it and chance it' method, but there is so much more to it than sheer chance.

Fish Near the Shore

When boat fishing I tend to start my drifts approximately 40yd from the bank, and drift in. Most anglers know that the majority of early season fish are close to the shore, and this is true if the depths of water are right. As a general rule during the colder months of the season you should be looking for maximum depths of approximately 8 to 12ft. Even better, if you know the contours of the lake bed, try and fish over a shelf. Trout will patrol along a shelf as they feed in the shallow water, and have a bolt-hole over the shelf into the depths at the first sign of danger.

Fishing into the wind produces consistent sport in the early season.

Fishing your flies up and over a shelf can be absolutely devastating. One of the best methods for this is fishing the Boobies, because they can drop over the shelf and come over it without snagging.

To help you to understand the depths of a shore you may be drifting on to, try looking at the contour of the land: if the bank is very steep, then you could conclude that the contour continues into the water and hence it will be very deep close in. If the land is quite flat and uniform, then this may well continue below the surface, too.

Fishing across points of bays is usually very productive. When visiting any reservoir, if you are not sure where to start, it is worth fishing across any points at the mouth of the bays. Such points are created by built-up silt as two currents meet and drop their sediment. This sediment provides the perfect conditions for larvae to hatch in; and where the sediment has built up, there is also a shelf on either side, which

offers the perfect feeding ground and bolt-hole at any signs of danger.

Fishing the Drop

When trout reach a reasonable size and are put into a cage to grow, they are fed on pellets that drop through the water layers to them. Previously trout pellets used to float, and trout always used to look up for their food. I am convinced this is one of the reasons why very few trout are seen rising in the larger reservoirs now, as they are used to feeding below the surface almost from birth. This instinct of feeding below the surface on food dropping to them is in them almost from the day they are born, so when a fly drops through the layers without any artificial movement I am convinced the memory of pellet feeding instigates a take.

When fishing a sinking line of any description you should be anticipating a take on the drop as your flies slowly fall through the water layers. However, when allowing your flies to drop, you should count them down

Fish across points of bays for the chance of a fish like this.

in seconds, as this will help you calculate at what depth the fish are feeding. Depending on what fly-line sink rate you are using will help you dictate the depth. A Di6, for example, sinks at 6in (15cm) per second, so for every 2sec count it has sunk a foot (30cm). So imagine you have cast out your line and allowed it to sink for 18sec, then it tightens up on the drop, you know that fish took at approximately 9ft (3m). If you get several more at this depth, then this is probably their cruising depth. As the day warms you may notice that the fish come up in the water column, and if you start getting takes at 6sec, then you know that they are 3ft (90cm) down, and so on. If the fish came up to just 3ft down, the Di6 could be arguably too fast, as the flies would be dragged below the feeding level too fast.

The Retrieves for Fast-Sinking Lines

Many anglers do what I call the robot retrieve, a repetitive retrieve that often fails to induce the take. Trout will follow the fly all day on some days if it's a monotonous retrieve. Variation is the key, and one of my favourite retrieves is to do three long, slow pulls, and then three slow figure-of-eights, and the trout will often intercept the fly when you start the long pulls after the figure-of-eights.

In recent years many competition anglers are pulling lures faster than you can imagine, and it works. I have fished alongside fellow anglers who have been making the boat shake they have been pulling so fast, and have been catching. I had been pulling what I thought was fast, but was just getting follows; when I quickened the pace, I started catching. To get the fastest retrieve possible, lean forwards, if fishing from the boat, and thrust the arm with the rod in as far forwards as possible. With your other hand, reach forwards and pull the line and throw it back as far as your arm can reach. Repeat in this manner as fast as you can, and if your arm does not hurt and you keep getting follows, then you

> **Top Tips**
>
> - Vary the retrieve of your flies.
> - Look for drop-offs or shelves.
> - Look for uniform depths of about 8–12ft.
> - Keep changing flies.

are not pulling fast enough. I have come off the water after competitions and my arms have been hurting for several days after. The water temperatures remain very low as we still suffer frosts at this time of year, so it's important to fish your flies slowly on a sinking line. For the early boat season I use the Airflo Di7 line.

A fairly new retrieve that appeared in the last decade or so is the 'roly-poly' retrieve, sometimes known as 'milking the cow'. You place the rod under your armpit, and hold it firmly by clamping your arm tight against your body. You then grab the line and pull it down using both hands repetitively (this is where 'milking the cow' came from). Although this is a great method for varying the retrieve by speeding it up and slowing it down, and also a good method for creating very fast retrieves, I find the hook-up ratio very low. One tip I can give is this: don't be tempted to lift the rod up, but keep pulling the line until it truly locks up, *then* lift the rod. This retrieve is a last resort for me, however, and one I don't recommend.

May – A Buzzer Bonanza!

May can often be prime time, and arguably one of the most productive months of the calendar. Many lakes and reservoirs have been open for a month or so, and are still full of relatively freshly stocked fish. Not only that, those trout that have survived the winter months and the early onslaught will be feeling the pinch in their rationed bellies, and will readily take a fly.

In May many anglers still choose to throw lures in the hope of a limit of trout. For me, May can offer some of the best nymph fishing of the year if the buzzer hatches are happening, and with our planet warming, May is often prime time for a buzzer bonanza. Although you can have buzzer hatches most days of the year, if conditions are right, it is May when they can be most prolific. During the winter months the buzzers that hatch are often much smaller in size and almost always black. In May they can often be like mini birds, as buzzers over 1in in length appear in their thousands! The buzzer forms approximately 90 per cent of the trout's natural diet, so there is no more important method to get right than fishing the buzzer: it truly is the most sensual and exciting method to fish. Such stimulation at your fingertips as the line tends to slowly tighten, or a tightening to awaken any angler who is off guard!

Anglers often see cloud-like formations of flies over trees or buildings, swarming and drifting in the lightest of breezes like clouds of smoke rising skywards. These are almost always hatches of buzzers. Another indication of a buzzer hatch is to watch the migratory swifts and swallows. Seeing these sweeping gracefully through the skies will indicate a buzzer hatch.

Look for the Hatch

When fishing a lake or reservoir such as Foremark or Eyebrook, arguably two of the best buzzer fisheries in the country, the swifts and swallows not only tell you *when* the hatch is happening, but also *where*. Only a fool thinks that buzzer hatches happen all over the lake – you can be spitting them out of your mouth at one part of the lake and counting them on one hand at the other end. The larvae need a soft shallow bed to lay their eggs, and where one part of the

*A fine-looking rainbow caught on a
Buzzer while fished static.*

lake may offer this, the other end may be too deep, or it may have a clay bottom and insects will not lay their eggs here because it is too hard.

Birds will often cover the skies, flying majestically hundreds of feet up high – then within minutes they are gliding just inches above the surface at incredible speeds, turning like high-speed bikes on a double chicane: the hatch has started! The fact that the birds are now hunting on the surface means that the buzzer has achieved its perilous journey through the water – but it then faces more trauma as it reaches the skies.

So, once you have arrived at your chosen venue, how do you know what colour, weight and size of Buzzer to use for a fantastic day's sport?

Choosing the Right Size and Colour

Once you have arrived, take a look in the margins of the lake and there you will find the remnants of the 'evening before' hatch.

Look for the buzzer 'shucks', the cases from which they emerge, because this will tell you the precise size of the pupae in the lake. If you find no adults to indicate the colour, just take a look in any glass window or spider's web nearby. When arriving at any venue I am always on the lookout for the signs of a hatch. Grab a buzzer in mid flight and check its colour by opening your fly box and simply matching the colour of the natural fly to the artificial one. Look closely at the natural insects, and look for the coloured cheeks or possible blood-stained abdomens. Imitate these with a crisp packet or a red butt Buzzer to increase your catch rate. Not only are you imitating the natural more realistically, but the crisp packet and red butt give the trout that 'target zone' they often find irresistible.

Size is not as critical as the colour, as I tend to offer a larger mouthful to appeal to the trout's greedy nature. Be careful though, because if the Buzzers are very small – for example a size 16, and you try a size 8 –

then they are likely to ignore it, as it is out of the ordinary. Stock fish will readily snap it up, but Buzzer fishing is when I catch most of my better quality fish, so slightly bigger is often better – but not too big.

Fishing the Correct Depths

Being a competition angler, none of my Buzzers are artificially weighted, they are simply tied on various hooks with differing amounts of varnish to get the weights I need. The depth is critical when fishing the Buzzer. Natural buzzers start their precarious life in the lake bed, and slowly ascend to the surface before reaching maturity – and the waiting birds. The fish will follow the hatch through the layers. Many times I have been catching fish on heavy Buzzers, only to take them on adult dry fly imitations an hour or so later. It is imperative that you change the depth of the Buzzers as the hatch progresses. In late April when the larger waters are still cold, try starting with heavier Buzzers tied on size 8 or 10 heavy wire grub. Buying varnished or epoxy Buzzers will add weight to them, and help you get them down to where they need to be.

The depth you are fishing your Buzzers can be controlled in several ways. The obvious one is the weight of your flies. If it

Iain Barr's favourite Buzzer.

is early season and water temperatures are low, try using heavy wire Buzzers coated with varnish: their slim profile ensures a quick trip to the lake bed where the trout will be waiting. As the fish follow the hatch nearer the surface, change the dropper flies to lighter patterns. There is no rule to fishing Buzzers in a buzzer hatch – popular flies such as my Cruncher or Diawl Bachs make excellent substitutes.

The Washing Line

Not just something to hang your clothes on! I believe this method was designed by anglers from the south of the UK. It is a fantastic set-up for suspending your flies in the top few feet by using a Booby and a team of nymphs on a floating line. Some anglers use a Booby on the point and one on the top dropper and fish nymphs in the middle and suspend them there; others use just one Booby on the point to gain more depth. The depth of the cruising trout should help you decide whether to use one or two Boobies: if they are in the top 2ft (60cm) I would recommend that you use two Boobies, but if they are generally below 3 to 4ft (90 to 120cm), then I would opt for one Booby on the point.

A typical set-up for a washing line would consist of a Booby on the point, a Cruncher and Diawl Bach in the middle, and maybe a hopper on the top dropper if you fish four flies.

This method is very popular with the competition anglers, and they keep refining it. A large-eyed Booby will hold your flies higher in the surface, but more and more anglers are now fishing smaller-eyed Boobies to allow this to sink slowly with the nymphs. The England Loch Style team used this to great effect in 2004 when we caught most fish during the international, but were pipped to second by weight. The Booby almost flutters as the nymphs slowly drag it down, and more fish take the Booby when it is like this as opposed to riding on the surface.

The exact tactic was to tie a heavy grub hook Buzzer just 3ft (90cm) above the Booby, as it was felt that the fish were about 6ft (2m) down and we wanted the Booby and nymphs down at that depth as quickly as possible without racing through the layers.

The Bung

This style of fishing is a relatively new method to grip the trout fishing scene, and love it or loathe it, it is simply deadly. The reason there are so many antis in the sport of traditional fly fishing is that it is almost mimicking float fishing. Instead of maggots suspended below the float, trout anglers suspend flies below the bung. The bung can be made of basically anything that floats, though the most popular are large polystyrene shapes, often fluorescent in colour to make them easier to see. Others use tightly compacted deer hair, poly yarns or even a cluster of cdc feathers. I confess to not being a fan of this prolific method, but I do not shy away from its devastating effects. There is no better way to suspend your flies at any one depth completely static. In May when the fish are feeding heavily on buzzers and usually quite deep, it has to be worth a shot.

The Bung Set-Up

Tie your chosen bung at least 3 or 4ft (90 or 120cm) away from the end of your floating fly line. In April I suggest that your first dropper fly is 6ft (2m) away from the bung, and the point fly a further 3ft (90cm) away. If you fish three flies below the bung, then tie the third 12ft (3.5m) away from the bung. Having three flies at varied depths will help you identify the cruising depths of the fish. Obviously if you catch five trout at 12ft down, then this is their cruising depth. But don't just stop there, adjust your leader so that your first dropper is at 9ft (2.5m), your second at 12ft (3.5m) and the third at about 14ft (4m). Doing this will bring your previously redundant droppers closer to the feeding zones of the fish, and increase your chances of the fish seeing your flies.

Fishing New Zealand Style

I discovered this method of fishing whilst fishing the 2001 World Championships in Lysksele, Swedish Lapland. I had heard of it many years before and I know it had been around for some time, but I had never seen it used or mentioned so much as it was in this event.

What is it?

I had previously always used conventional droppers for tying additional flies to my bung cast until I discovered this method. What the New Zealand anglers started doing was to tie their additional flies beneath the bung, or dry fly that was used as an indicator, by tying the leader around the bend of the hook to the next fly. Could they not thread the eyes, or had they had other thoughts behind it? It was clever all right! In the World Championships they were using it by fishing a dry fly on the top dropper, then tying a small nymph to fish a foot or so below it by joining it to the back of the hook and not a conventional dropper. This style soon took to the domestic trout scene and anglers started using it for bung fishing.

The Advantages

Fishing this style puts you in immediate contact with every fly on your cast, from the point to the top dropper. There are no extra dropper lengths that have to be tightened by the trout before you make contact. Fewer knots and less nylon dangling from your leader makes it harder for the fish to spot – even the most resilient of fish are easily fooled. Knots in droppers are a thing of the past with this method, and we have all been smashed at dropper knots that have become weakened. No more 'granny' knots appearing on your droppers, which weakens the strength of your tippet material. It is quicker to tie a fly on, rather that having to tie in dropper knots. I used the New Zealand style to great effect on Rutland Water one year when the fish were on the fry. I used a floating fry with a small Diawl Bach tied just 2ft (60cm) below the fry. Some fish were fry feeding, but I noticed some were 'head and tailing' and were definitely not feeding on the fry – they were feeding heavily in the energetic Corixa in amongst the fry.

The floating fry was acting as my bung, and the Diawl Bach was the suspended nymph, and by using this combination I had two food sources covered in one cast. I caught some cracking fish that morning, both on the floating fry and the nymph. Don't be fooled into fishing the bright grenade-type indicators when a fly quite capable of catching a fish can be used.

These are some examples of New Zealand-style rigs to try:

- Klink hammer dry – Cruncher
- CDC shuttlecock – Cruncher
- Floating fry – Minkie
- Floating fry – Diawl Bach

When to Use the New Zealand Method
There is no doubt that this method is very successful and has some huge advantages, but when would you choose it over a conventional leader/dropper set-up? It is best suited for when you are fishing slowly, for example nymphing, dry fly fishing with a suspended nymph, or the floating fry and Minkie combination. If takes are going to be subtle and you need to be in direct contact, then this is definitely my first-choice set-up. It still works when pulling lures fast, but isn't always necessary if the lures are coming back at incredible speeds, as there is very little slack line anyway.

The dry fly and nymph combination method is extremely popular on the rivers, and has vastly increased my catch rate with grayling and trout from streams and rivers. The cream of the sport on rivers – John Tyzack, Jeremy Lucas and Simon Robinson, to name just a few – almost put this rig up as second nature, and catch devastating numbers of fish using it. It gives you the best of both worlds, with the grown-on fish slurping down the dry, and the hungry smaller fish attacking the nymph. The most popular dry used is a klink hammer tied with a large 'post' to help you see it bouncing down the river, or cdc dries, which also stand out. I learned this method from these river experts, and just adapted it to lake fishing.

Leader Length
Adjusting your leader length is another great way to control the depth you are fishing at. If you are fishing a leader below 15ft (4.5m) then your flies will not sink as deep as someone fishing a 20ft (6m) leader. To compensate for a longer leader, just fish a heavier fly on the point. Many competitors fish the same flies as me, and I even give them my flies, but they fail to catch at the same rate because the leader lengths are different. Next time you see someone pulling them out, don't just look at the flies, but look at his leader length too, as this can make a massive difference to the depths you are fishing at. The breaking strain of leader tippet they are using will also affect the depth you are fishing at; thus someone fishing 10lb tippet will get their flies deeper than someone fishing 6lb tippet of the same length.

Casting Distance

I'm often puzzled why anglers insist on throwing a long line when buzzer fishing, especially from a boat. It can sometimes be needed when fishing from the bank, but it is not important when fishing from the boat. I catch plenty of fish on the drop when fishing Buzzers, and this is at the end of the cast, and if you are casting into the horizon the chances are you are going to miss it. Short lining of no more than 15–18yd gives you much more control, and a better chance of not missing takes. To give yourself a huge advantage, grease up the last 2 to 3ft (60 to 90cm) of your floating fly line with Mucilin, and watch this as an indicator. You can't do this at 25–30yd, but rest assured you will see more takes before you feel them.

Midge Tip or Floating Line

I am an avid fan of the midge tip fly line. This is a floating line with a 3ft (90cm) clear intermediate sinking tip. Only when the fish are nymphing very near the surface, and takes are very subtle and I need the aid of the end of the fly line, will I use the floating line over the midge tip. However, most of the time I will fish the midge tip. I fished alongside a fishing friend and watched him catch seven fish on the midge tip line to my none on a standard floating line: I simply got no takes to his seven, even though we fished identical flies. It was this day that convinced me there was a difference, and there definitely is. I have won numerous competitions on the midge tip line when it has clearly outfished the floating line.

I believe the 3ft (90cm) clear tip makes a huge difference to that of a standard floating line. Many people question how such a short tip can make such a big difference, but my results prove it. The first difference is the angle that the midge tip gives your flies. The sinking tip gives your flies more of a uniform ascent as opposed to the floating line. One of the major differences, and the reason I will fish the midge tip over the floating line, is the hook-up ratio. Halfway through a European final I switched from a floating line to the midge tip: I was hooking approximately one in four takes on the floating line, but when I fished the midge tip I hooked almost all of them. I believe the submerged 3ft tip acts as a weight that helps set the hook on impact of the take.

The Loop

In May the takes can be very subtle, and you hardly feel a thing at your fingertips. However, by watching the loop of fly line between the rod tip and the surface of the water you will see the take before you feel anything at your fingertips. As you see the loop lifting, simply lift into the fish. Other takes may be more savage and can end in the leader breaking if your rod tip is too low to the surface. I recommend fishing the rod tip just an inch or so above the surface to start with, but if you witness savage and aggressive takes, lift the rod tip about 2–3ft (60–90cm) from the surface. The slack line between the rod tip and the water surface acts as a buffer and will prevent breakages. It also works as a great indicator, as the loop lifts off the water when the fish speeds off with the fly.

The Retrieve

The retrieve is probably the next most important thing to the actual fly. There really are only two ways to fish a Buzzer: one is static, the other is stop! They are best fished with a cross wind and allowed to drift naturally round. When bank fishing, choose a cross wind, or when boat fishing simply cast across the wind. Be sure to turn your back and not twist, otherwise you will end up with terrible back pain! One of my other favourite ways to fish a Buzzer is to give them a slow pull, then pause for 8–10sec, then repeat; this allows the flies to ascend and descend through the water

Ripples will be easier to spot in a flat calm. Remember, if you see ripples at the rod tip you are retrieving too fast!

layers just like the naturals. As the natural buzzer pupae rise from the lake bed to hatch they often realize the air temperature is too cold, and descend back down again. Fishing your Buzzers with a long, slow pull, then a good pause of about 10sec, gives fantastic coverage of all the depths and is probably one of my most effective methods for Buzzer fishing, especially in water over 8–10ft (2.5–3m).

I see many anglers retrieving Buzzers too fast – even a steady or slow figure-of-eight is just too fast when they want it static. I have witnessed teammates catch nothing as I pull them out around them, simply because they are moving them. For best results keep your line tight, and if your floating fly line is causing ripples on the surface, or the line is moving at your rod tip where it meets the water surface, then you are fishing it too fast. In the year 2005 I had ten fish in the Lexus competition on Rutland Water on the Buzzer in less than a couple of hours, and did not feel one of them take. All were taken by static fishing, and watching the line move at close range. I could have counted on one hand the number of fish caught by the boats that swarmed around me and my partner, who was on eight or nine at the time. We both immediately noticed they were retrieving too fast, even though it was a slow figure-of-eight. Static *means* static, but many people feel the need to retrieve their Buzzers. Stick your hands in your pockets if you get the urge to retrieve the line!

The Hang

Many anglers only associate the hang with lure fishing, but it is just as deadly with the

Hold the rod high to hang the Buzzers on every cast.

Buzzer: the slow lift of the rod and the pause imitates the natural perfectly as it wriggles its way to the surface then pauses for a rest. Very slowly lift your rod and pause much longer then you would with the lures. Keep the line tight and watch for it moving, and you will find most of the fish will be hooked in the roof of the mouth.

The hang method can be fished several times throughout the retrieve, and not just at the end. During your retrieve simply lift the rod and hold it there, and do this several times throughout the retrieve for extra bonus fish. I have had some fantastic fishing on the hang with deep Buzzers. Notably I recall a day on Draycote when the fish would only take the Buzzer on the hang. When fishing the Buzzers deep and hanging them, then slowly lifting them, this imitates the ascent perfectly. On this particular day this was the only way I could catch them: with static retrieves and fishing the drop, nothing happened – but the moment I hung my flies almost vertical below the boat, the rod tip buckled over. Time and time again this has proved the only way to connect with the fish, especially when they are feeding deep on the Buzzers.

Iain Barr Favourite May Buzzer Rig

Size 10 Black Crisp Buzzer on the top dropper; Plains Cruncher size 10 on the second and third droppers, and a size 8 grub hook Black Crisp Buzzer on the point.

June/July – High and Dry

Fishing the dry fly is one of the most exciting types of fly fishing because all the fishing

Top Tips

- Match the colour of your Buzzer to the naturals.
- Fish your nymphs static.
- Hang your nymphs.
- Grease up your fly line.
- Watch the loop for movement.

is visual: you can actually watch your imitation being swallowed by an unsuspecting trout. As a general rule the perfect conditions for dry fly fishing would consist of a mild day with a gentle breeze with good cloud cover, but I have had some magnificent dry fly sport in complete flat calm and sunshine.

June and July offer the fly angler prime time dry fly fishing: our reservoirs and lakes have warmed up, and the fish are now feeding nearer the surface. Any substantial hatch will instigate a rise, as the adults lie vulnerable on the surface, usually laying their eggs in their short lifespan. Buzzers remain the main dries, but any surface-laying insect will become immediate prey.

Wind Lanes

As a rule, from May onwards, when fishing near the surface, but more so with dry flies, always look for wind lanes when boat fishing. These are obvious flat strips of water that often expand across the whole lake or reservoir. There are many theories for why these are formed, which we won't go into here – but one thing that is true of them is that they always hold feeding trout. The flat calm strip is caused by tight water tension on the surface, and this traps any floating insect tight in its grasp. This larder of food is a magnet to the trout, and free drifts across the middle of a lake along a wind lane can produce masses of trout to the dry fly. Try and avoid your boat drifting in the middle of the wind lane: rather, drift down the side of it, because when you go back round to drift down it again, the fish in the lane haven't been spooked. My personal best bag of eight trout weighed 29lb 10oz, caught from a large reservoir and all in a wind lane using my favourite Iain Barr Competition Big Red. This dry fly accounts for probably about 80 per cent of my dry fly-caught trout.

Another place to look for fish feeding off the surface is by a bank with the wind coming off it. Any insects caught in the prevailing winds inevitably end on the trout's table as they lie helpless on the surface. Look for long grassy banks or banks lined with trees, both of which insects tend to inhabit.

Knowing What Type of Dry Fly to Use

With over twenty-seven years of fishing experience and watching trout rise, I have learnt to tell from the trout's different rise forms at what hatching stage the fish are taking the fly. The well-known 'head and

Iain Barr always uses a red dry fly as his first choice – his very own Competition Big Red.

tail' rise form tells me the fish are taking the adult fly that is riding high on the water's surface. A swirl seen at the surface tells me that the fish are taking the emerger that is breaking its way through the surface film. A flattening of the water on the surface indicates that the fish are taking the nymph a foot or so down.

Knowing these rise forms will help you decide which fly to choose. If you see the head and tail, then you need an adult dry fly such as the Big Red or Shipman's Buzzer. If you see a swirl at the surface, then dry flies such as the Iain Barr CDC Hoppers or Cul de Canard Shuttlecocks should be used. These are emerger-type dry flies that hang half in the surface and half in the film, and the fish tend to take these with much more confidence.

Many anglers fishing dry flies get many swirls to the fly without the fish taking. This is because the flies are sitting too high on the surface. When adding gink to the fly to make it float, only add it to the top of the fly and not all over; this will ensure that the fly sits more in the surface instead of high in the wave. If your fly is sitting proud on the surface, then it is probably sitting too high and the fish will swirl at it without taking it. Moreover, most hackled dry flies that are tied the standard way by winding them around the hook, and not in a parachute style, are likely to sit too high in the surface. Try trimming any of the hackle that sits below the shank of the hook so there is just hackle sprayed over the top. When this is ginked up the fly will sit right in the surface film, and this will make it an easy target for any feeding trout.

A common mistake people make when dry fly fishing is to cast too long a line. However, this only results in 'lining' fish and pushing them further away from you. Simply shortline your flies about 12yd maximum in front you. This gives you several advantages:

- You can see your flies more easily.
- You can lift the line off more easily and cast to a rising fish much more quickly.
- With just a short line there is not much added 'line weight' when lifting into your fish, which will help prevent hooks straightening.
- You can get your fish in more quickly without causing too much commotion.

It is also important to fan cast your dries by covering all the water in front of you, and never repeat the same cast consecutively. If you imagine a clock face in front of you, cast at the nine o' clock position, the 10 o'clock position, the 11 o'clock position, then the 12 o'clock position, then repeat. Many fish will take a dry fly within a few seconds of it hitting the surface so I generally leave it for no more than about 5–6sec, and cover the next bit of water. Contrary to this is if you are targeting a particular fish and are trying to intercept its path by leaving it on its route. Watch the path a trout is taking as it rises freely, then cast in its anticipated path about three or four yards ahead of it. This distance can be reduced if there is a big wave, or increased in a flat calm.

I see far too many anglers lifting too soon or too late when a trout takes a dry fly off the surface. You may have heard of the 'God Save the Queen' scenario: by saying this when a trout takes your fly, the theory is that you will end in a solid hook-up. This is not quite true, however: on a certain day, maybe, but every day is different. You may miss the first few fish of the day as you strike too soon or too late, but by watching the fish take the naturals around you, you will be able to gauge their pace of taking the fly.

Each strike should be different, depending on what type of dry fly you are fishing. If you are fishing a dry fly that is riding high in the surface, such as a Shipman's Buzzer, for example, then a pause before the fish goes down on the fly is essential. However, if you are fishing an emerger-type dry such as a CDC Hopper or Shuttlecock, then you need to strike immediately you see any movement. Emerger-type dries sit slightly sub-surface or in the film, so the fish barely has to break the surface to take it – so always strike on the slightest of swirls.

Whilst fishing in the Loch Style International on the infamous Loch Leven in Fife, Scotland, during practice the team witnessed big fish moving in no more than 3ft (1m) of water. They were feeding on tiny black buzzers in the margins. Most of the team had left them, considering them impossible to catch. However, a key thing to remember is this: if you see fish rise, then they are feeding, and if they are feeding, then they can be caught with the right approach. As the fish were in very shallow water, nothing other than a dry fly would do. My first colour of any dry fly to go on to my cast is always red: it doesn't matter if there are green flies, black flies or spotted pink flies on the surface, I will always fish a red dry to start with. Only if they refuse this will I try other colours.

An emerger-style fly like this Hopper should be used when you see small swirls on the surface.

I approached the shallows with fellow international Phil Dixon, and proceeded to cast a size 16 red CDC Shuttlecock into the feeding area. On the very first cast a 4lb bar of Scottish silver supped down the dry, then all hell broke loose! A few more followed before the disturbance seemed to disturb the others. I have had an identical experience on Eyebrook, taking over thirty trout on a size 16 Red CDC, and once took thirty-seven on Stocks Reservoir, all on the Big Red. So when you try the dry, always try the red first!

Dry Flies on an Intermediate Line

I believe most of my success has come down to my trying something different. One of the strange things I do is to fish dry flies such as my hoppers on sinking lines. I tend to use them quite regularly on slime lines just a few feet down below the surface. You would all have witnessed trout splashing at dry flies on the surface in an attempt to drown them. They do this because they can feel vulnerable when breaking the surface, so take the fly a few feet down where they feel comfortable. With this theory in mind I tried fishing hoppers on an intermediate line. I actually first qualified for the England National team having fished hoppers on a slime line, as I was missing too many when fishing them dry on a floating line.

The advantage of fishing these dries on an intermediate line is that you can actually cover two methods with one cast: you can fish them dry when you first cast them out, and then fish them wet after allowing them to sit there for a short while. For best results fish them wet with a slow figure-of-eight. Another favourite method of mine with the submerged hoppers is to fish a Booby on the top dropper, with hoppers behind it on the slime line. The Booby will attract the trout, and they will often take the droppers instead. I won the Foremark Open, catching twenty-two trout in two hours, on this very method.

Top Tips

- Try a red dry fly first.
- Don't strike too soon.
- Use Frog Hair copolymer for your tippet.

Tackle Requirements

The only time I make a switch from my fundamental lure or nymph tackle is when fishing dry flies, and I swap my Loop #8 rod for a Loop #7. This softer rod with its fast tip allows me to cover fish very fast, and accurately – but importantly it isn't too stiff, which otherwise may result in the lighter wire hooks used on dry flies straightening out. The #8 Loop rod remains soft enough for dry flies and allows me to bring them to the net quickly during a competition – but for pure pleasure fishing you can't beat the #7 for dries.

Another fundamental difference is the leader tippet I use. For pulling lures and fishing nymphs I would use Frog Hair fluorocarbon, but for fishing dries I would use Frog Hair copolymer; its lighter properties ensure it does not drag the fly down as fluorocarbon would. However, due to its lighter properties it floats, so would need degreasing by using the product called Fullers Earth: keep applying this as and when you see your leader floating.

August – The Tough Month?

August can be a daunting month, and is often referred to as the 'dogged' month. Some fisheries reduce prices to attract more anglers in these hard times – but they need not be hard! With water temperatures soaring as the sun relentlessly beats down on our lakes and reservoirs, things start to change. However, because the water temperatures are rising, it doesn't mean the fish don't feed: if they stopped feeding they would die, so they have to eat. Food items can be prolific in August, as the big buzzers tend to die away, and offerings such as damsels, small green buzzers and pin fry appear. So although August may be called the tough month, it is just as fruitful as the rest, with the right approach.

The Damsel

The first time you are dazzled by the dancing blue 'neon-like' adult damsel fly is the time to imitate the nymph. Adults are often seen locked in courtship as they dance above the reeds and water edges, and rest assured, if the adults are about, the nymphs are being eaten below the surface by the trout!

The damsel is fished throughout the whole year, and will be taken as a lure before the real imitative patterns start to work in late July through to August.

When hatching, the damsel nymph swims quite quickly to the bank side or protruding reeds. Here it creeps out and soon hatches to become the winged adult. Fishing in these shallows is where you will catch some trout. The nymphs seem to have an inbred fear of trout as they immediately head for weed cover after birth. They are generally found in the warmer shallows of the lake, but have been seen in large weedbeds in open water. Look to fish around weedbeds for almost guaranteed success, or in shallow uniform water depth of approximately 4–8ft (1–2.5m). Or obviously, if there is a gathering of adults in one area, try here with the nymph. You occasionally see trout leaping trying to catch the adults, but in over twenty-seven years of fishing I only ever recall catching one fish with an adult damsel in it.

How to Fish it and with What Retrieves?
I would opt for a slow intermediate when fishing damsels, to avoid line 'wake'

as you will be fishing the fly with jerky movements. The nymphs will not win the award for the fastest swimmers, but they will win the award for the best tail wigglers! This is crucial when retrieving in the attempt to imitate this butt-wiggling motion. After casting along the chosen weedbed, allow the nymph to sink to several feet. The natural often swims a few feet, then rests, so the best method to imitate this is to do a long pull and pause. However, my best retrieve, which considers the wiggling tail, is to do a slow figure-of-eight and 'kick' every third or fourth figure-of-eight, and add in a pause every 5 or 6sec for deadly results. This motion kicks the tail into life and often induces a take. Always lift the fly slowly out of the water, as this is an effective time to hook the trout because the fish attack the escaping nymph.

Which Lines can I Use it on?

There is no given rule for this, and although you are often trying to imitate the natural in less than 8ft (2.5m) of water, competition anglers catch them on fast-sinking lines, more often than not the trout are taking these as a lure and not a natural nymph. A slime line would be my first choice, or a floating line or midge tip line would be more than good enough.

Green marabou damsel lures can be lethal through August.

Many of the top Damsel patterns have gold heads, and this helps with the 'tail-wiggling' motion with the slow figure-of-eight and kick method described earlier. This should be fished as the point fly, as this will turn your cast over more effectively.

Pin Fry

Pin fry can be the scourge of many trout anglers, and hours of frustration may be spent chasing these hoover-like manoeuvres of the trout. The coarse fish in our reservoirs produce millions of young as they hatch in their millions across our lakes and reservoirs and this is bumper crop time for the trout. Some anglers get confused as to what the trout are feeding on, as the pin fry are so small and people often confuse them with daphnia feeders or snail feeders.

The first clue will be the vast surface activity of the trout, and they are likely to be in shoals making the most of this bounty. The second clue is that it often starts in isolated pockets across the lake or reservoir. The final clue is that if you are casting at surging fish all day and are catching nothing, then it is likely you are fishing for pin fry feeders. I get countless emails and phone calls describing this very thing, and you can almost hear the frustration from the angler.

Some of my best bags of fish have come from pin fry feeders, including an impressive eight fish limit of nearly 29lb in a matter of an hour or two. The surface activity was immense as shoals of rainbows hounded the tiny pin fry.

Imitations

There are very few flies that accurately imitate a pin fry, but you can get close. What you have to remember is that your fly is literally one in a million in most cases, so by getting an exact imitation you are probably reducing your chances. You have to get a fly that stands out in the crowd.

One way to do this, and always my first choice, is to fish something slightly bigger than the naturals. Most anglers' first choice is a sparkler Booby, but mine would be a size 12 plain Cruncher. The pin fry are a very pale brown and almost transparent in colour, and there is no better colour than a small Cruncher to match this. This fly is bigger than the naturals and looks like it: it is not too big to scare the fish and make it look too unnatural, but just big enough to appeal to the trout's greedy appetite! Secondly I would have a size 12 Glo Head Diawl Bach on the cast with a fluorescent red head. The red head makes it stand out from the crowd, yet it is still small and drab enough in colour so as not to spook them. I would fish a second Cruncher, and a size 12 small Booby on the point.

Depth Control

Pin fry feeding almost always happens in the top inches of the surface, so it's important to keep your flies in there to have any chance of catching these pursuing trout. By adding a small Booby on the point you are effectively hanging the flies in the top few inches of the surface. By keeping a steady retrieve the flies will remain high in the water and increase your chances of catching one of these fish. Remember the fish can't see downwards, so if you

The bright red head helps it stand out in the crowd – a red Glo Head Diawl Bach.

are catching nothing, the first question to ask is 'Am I going beneath them?'. My first choice of Booby would be a size 12 Hare's Ear Booby as it is again light brown in colour, and the wake of the Booby coming across closely imitates a scampering pin fry. A steady constant retrieve of a fast figure-of-eight will keep your flies high in the surface and cause the Booby to make enough disturbance on the surface to attract the trout.

Cast Set-Up

Usually I would suggest keeping your flies a minimum of 5ft (1.5m) apart or 6ft (1.8m) if you can manage. In the case of pin fry feeding it is better to have them closer together to increase your chances of catching the fish. I would suggest fishing all three or four flies on a leader of approximately 14ft (4m) at the most. The more flies you have in the zone of the fish when they are herding pin fry, the better. Because the fish are so high in the water their window of vision above them is very small, and you have to increase your chances as much as possible to get the fish to see your fly.

Once you have your cast set up, the next most important thing is accuracy. The closer the fish is, the more accurate you are likely to be, so let the fish get within a comfortable casting distance before making your cast. I tend to fish 'blind' up to 10yd in front of the boat, and as a fish rises I can lift off and be on it in a second or two. Always try and cast your *flies* at the fish, and not your line: many anglers hit the rising fish with their line, and not the flies, and this spooks them. Also, by casting your flies across their path, as opposed to casting at them and bringing the flies away from them, you will increase your chances of catching them.

These are my favourite flies for pin fry feeders: Cruncher; Glo Head Diawl Bach; Hare's Ear Booby.

Daphnia Feeders

August may be known as one of the toughest months of the fishing calendar, but it can be explosive. Daphnia is a tiny water flea that lives in our waters in the UK and is a very important part of the trout's diet. It is almost impossible to see with the human eye until it clusters in large underwater clouds. Trout hoover up this excess food with consummate ease: they feed almost like basking sharks, because as they swim they take in thousands of these tiny fleas. They may be tiny, but they are extremely high in protein, and this is why the trout feed so heavily on this tiniest of crustaceans. If you use a marrow spoon to find out the contents of the trout's stomach and you find an orange or green mush, then this is daphnia!

Imitations of Daphnia

Daphnia are far too small even to contemplate imitating, so the next best thing you can do is to try and match the colour. Without any doubt various shades of orange are the best, with shades of green coming a distant second. The Blob fly took the fly scene by storm in the late 1990s, and it has revolutionized lure fishing. I have created my own types of Blob to catch the daphnia feeders, and I have yet to find any other fly that touches the Blobs when

A perfect rainbow trout taken deep using an orange Booby.

fishing for daphnia-feeding trout. The Blob is basically a ball of fritz on a hook tied in the brightest of oranges, pinks and dark colours such as black. However, just adding some fritz to a hook does not make a good Blob pattern. The number of turns of fritz on the shank is critical, as is the angle to which the fritz is sitting. The Blob is so effective because when it is pulled fast, the air trapped in the fritz is released out the back of the fly causing a bubble trail immediately behind the fly. However, it can be just as effective fished slowly, and this is when it best imitates daphnia. I won the Bob Church Classic Trophy for two consecutive seasons by fishing two Blobs on a fast-sinking line with the slowest of retrieves. The fish I caught were all stuffed with daphnia.

Where to Find Daphnia

With daphnia being so small and like a cloud, it's location is very much dictated

It doesn't have to be a big lure to imitate pin fry – this subtle Cruncher is the perfect match!

by the wind direction. Wherever the wind is blowing, this is the next destination for the tiny water flea. Strong winds push this tiny crustacean across the lakes, and it is after a strong wind that you find the biggest clouds of daphnia on the windward shore. You may think that there is a tinge of colour in the water, so scoop some into your hand and take a closer look, as it may well be daphnia. And I can guarantee that if there is daphnia, then there are trout, too! With big clusters of daphnia you may see ducks feeding near the surface on it.

Daphnia is almost transparent, and does not like the sun penetrating through it. With this is mind, the following rule should be followed when fishing for daphnia feeders. If it is sunny the daphnia will dive to the depths where the sun does not penetrate, and this will vary depending on the clarity of the water. Water temperatures do not affect the depth the daphnia will be at, so whether it is the depths of winter or the height of summer, if it is cloudy the daphnia will be high in the water, and if sunny it will be deep. It is arguably the most crucial of tactics to find the correct feeding depths of the trout. The daphnia will be in an almost uniform line at their chosen depth. In other words you are unlikely to find daphnia at

This two-tone Blob would be hard to beat when fishing for daphnia feeders.

2ft (60cm) below the surface and then find it at 15ft (4.5m) down also. It is therefore important to keep your flies at the cruising depths for as long as possible. One of the best ways to do this is to fish two Boobies on a sinking line. Unless the fish want the flies at super speed, I would opt to fish two Boobies. Due to their buoyancy they will not drop through the feeding layers too fast, whereas a Blob may well be dragged through too fast.

Mixing Nymphs with Lures

August is a great month for mixing your lures with your nymphs. People often ask me why I fish a team of nymphs with a lure on the top dropper, or even the middle dropper, and not the point. People say, surely your lure should be on the point? But who made up that rule? There is a logical reason for fishing it on the top dropper. Trout usually chase the fly from behind, and more often than not you will get more follows on most days to a lure than you will get them taking it, especially brightly coloured lures at this time of the year. When trout chase your lure and decide not to take it, they usually turn away from the fly. If your lure is on the point of your cast and the trout turns away, there is nothing left for it to see. With my set-up of the Blob on the top dropper, any fish turning away at the last minute will have three trailing nymphs behind it that it has to pass on its way back down. Also it has to pass this team of nymphs to get to the Blob on its first initial investigation. Therefore, I have increased my chances sixfold of catching it, because it passes three nymphs to get to the Blob, then it passes them again if it turns away from the fly.

I won the Lexus European Open Championships with this very method by using two Cat's Whiskers with two Crunchers in the middle on a Di7. Many people associate nymph fishing with lines in the top 6ft (2m) or so. However, the nymphs hatch from the lake bed, so why not fish them on fast sinkers, too? On this particular day the fish were feeding about 15ft (4.5m) down and the water was fairly cloudy, so I opted for two Cat's Whiskers, which stand out well in murky water at depth. I put my two nymphs closer to the lures than normal, because if the fish saw the Cat's Whisker, I wanted them to see the Crunchers, too.

Although I had very few fish on the Cat's Whisker, they were drawing the fish in. The spacing between the flies played a critical part in my success, as my partner for the day copied my tactic. He had a greater distance between the lure and nymphs so the fish were seeing the lure and ignoring it, but they didn't see the more enticing imitative nymph in the cloudy water.

Don't Fish Bright Colours Together
If fishing lures, I always separate bright colours at least 12ft (3.5m) apart. I believe the fish are spooked if they see too much monstrosity together. Always separate a team of lures with nymphs or the highly popular Cormorants. When pulling two Blobs I will predominantly use two Cormorants in the middle unless the water is crystal clear. If it is clear I will use two nymphs, or if I feel the fish are really nervous I will fish just two Blobs 16ft (5m) apart.

The Cormorant is a subtle pattern that does not scare the fish, and the Pearly Goose Cormorant is by far my best Cormorant pattern, as it has accounted for many of my larger fish over the last two seasons.

Top Tips

- Count your flies down.
- Hang your flies every cast.
- Be prepared to fish very deep.
- Try a team of nymphs with a lure.
- Place the nymph closer to the lures in murky water.
- Keep bright lures at least 12ft (3.5m) apart.

Iain's favourite dropper between two Blobs.

An orange Booby is ideal for daphnia feeders if they want the fly fished slowly.

September/ October – The Months of Plenty!

After the longer summers we are experiencing the fry season getting later and later in the year. However, don't worry, the bonanza goes on just the same, it's just that we have to wait that bit longer! The coarse fish in our lakes and reservoirs spawn and lay thousands and thousands of eggs in the summer: these are known as jelly fry or pin fry. They feed on the rich source of food in the lakes, and rapidly grow into 3-4in fry. The trout seem to have some sensor in them that winter is imminent, as a fry frenzy starts! These are exciting times! Although I thoroughly love my nymph fishing, this time of year brings a new excitement: it's big fish time! But to challenge the potential monster trout you may come across, you need to ensure you are geared up for the job.

Choosing the Correct Tackle

The Rod

Fry time is big fish time, fact! Losing any fish can be soul destroying, but losing that fish of a lifetime could be heartbreaking. So it is important that you up the 'muscle' in your kit to be prepared for that extra-special fish. I seriously recommend a minimum of a #7/8 rod, but if you have one, even an #8 or #8/9. For this you need the line to go with it, so choose the correct line to balance the rod. I use an #8 loop fly rod or even an #8/9 bone fish rod! I tend to fight my fish hard, as I have a theory that the longer they are in the water, the more likely they are going to stay there, so I need a good 'pokey' rod to bring them to the net. A stiff rod is also necessary, as the flies you are using tend to be heavier, such as leaded Minkies, for example, or heavily sodden, floating deer hair. The larger fish, especially brown trout,

You need to be tackled up for monsters like these during fry time!

have much harder inner mouths, and it can be difficult to penetrate the hook, especially with a softer rod. I have fished with many anglers who 'bounce' fish off because they are using a soft rod with large fry patterns tied on heavy wire hooks. Don't fall into this trap by using a #6 weight during fry time, because it could cost you a trophy fish.

The Line

Having chosen your rod wisely, you need the line to match. When using heavy rods I recommend going one line heavier than stated on the rod. Thus if I am using an #8 rod, I tend to use #8/9 rated lines, especially at fry time; this will help you cast heavier flies and prevent the rod from 'collapsing' when casting. Many anglers, including myself for some time until I realized why I was missing too many fish, choose the wrong type of fly line when fishing for fry feeders. Due to the hardened mouths of grown-on fish, especially the brown trout, you need to really drive the hook home to ensure it is set firmly in the fish's mouth. I recall missing fish after fish on a large floating fry. The fish were clearly taking it and I lifted into every one and they barely stayed on a few seconds. This happened on too many occasions, and having pondered on the matter for several weeks after, I was still questioning why.

Then by chance on one visit I used an old floating line, and caught almost all fish on the very same fly. I soon realized that it was because this old line had very little stretch in it, and this was helping me set the hook; the other line had too much stretch in it for the larger trout I was hooking with this big floating fry. Based on this finding I now use the Airflow Sixth Sense lines with no stretch when fishing for fry feeders. The original floating lines from airflo come with minimal stretch so may suffice as I have used these over the years. Takes can be subtle, or so aggressive that you nearly lose

your rod. The non-stretch line ensures that the hook is set and that there is no 'stretch' when the fish takes. Non-stretch sinkers should also be used if fishing large fry lures below the surface. I have missed many big fish due to using a line with stretch when using larger hooks for fry feeders. But not any more!

Leader Material

Choosing the tippet material is also crucial. I wince when I see many anglers going fry bashing using just 6lb or 8lb leader material. With a non-stretch line and the chance of a big fish that will hit you like an express train, I wouldn't dare fish below 10lb. I use the Frog Hair in 10lb or even 12lb, and no less; anything below this and that mantle-piece trophy fish may just break you.

The Flies

Flies can be kept to a minimum, and mostly I tend to use my leaded Minkies, Minkie Boobies, sparkler Boobies and Humungus. I am also a fan of the floating fry, and although nothing may be showing, this will bring up the trout – it is such an easy mouthful for them as it lies in the surface imitating a dead fry. The fish tend to herd the fry into a frenzy, then attack them, leaving stunned fry in the surface – and the floating fry is the perfect imitation for these! I fished alongside a fellow angler and was catching a few on the Minkies on a medium sinker, but sport was slow. Although nothing was to be seen, he tried a floating fry and caught six huge trout in no time! So next time when you are fry bashing, ignore the floating fry at your peril!

Other useful flies to have in your armoury are the silver and gold tubes and the traditional appetizer. Fishing sparkler Boobies at this time of year can be either very frustrating or very rewarding. Trout in this season are in aggressive mood and are used to chasing dashing fry across the surface. One

The sparkler Booby is a great fly for 'plopping' across the surface.

A leaded Minkie like this is hard to beat during fry time.

of the best ways to imitate these is to rip a sparkler Booby across the top like an escaping or injured fry on the surface. Pulling a Booby on the floating fry may result in the sheer frustration of fish chasing without taking the fly.

Choosing the correct line to pull Boobies across the top is all decided by how long the fish are willing to chase before they get fed up. I have fished on occasions when fish have chased the Booby across the top for almost thirty yards, and other days when they chase it for just a few. There is a saying in the competition world of 'you can't weigh follows'! This is true, as many anglers talk about fish chasing their Booby all day, but only have one fish to weigh.

The trout are obviously interested in the fly if they are chasing it, so when you witness follow after follow, change your line to a higher density to make the Booby dive under. If the chases are short, then I would recommend fishing a fast sinker such as the Di7, as this will drag the fly below the surface quickly and encourage the fish to take. If they are chasing the fly for a long way but only fishing slowly, I would opt for a Di3 or Di5. The other option is simply to fish a smaller-eyed Booby – these are

becoming a firm favourite in the competition world!

Where to Locate Fry Feeders

Before you venture on to the lake, think of where structures such as boat moorings, pontoons and large weedbeds are situated, or basically anything that will give fry cover. Another clue is to look for seagull activity. When competing, I tend to look for cormorants, as these may indicate where the trout are; when Buzzer fishing I look for swifts to show me where the hatch is happening; and when fry bashing I also look to the sky. Bombing seagulls and diving grebes tell me where the shoals of fry are: and where the shoals are, I guarantee the trout will not be far behind.

Seagulls are not diving birds and can only pick up fry from on or near the surface. If you see seagulls bombing, then the fry are clearly near the surface, and if you see diving grebes in the same area as the seagulls, then this would indicate that there are also fry deeper. In this particular situation I would suggest that the trout below are herding the fry to the surface, then attacking them, whilst at the same time making the fry easy targets for the aerial birds also.

I experienced this last year when watching seagulls bombing and trout crashing the surface. Anglers all around were fishing floating or slime lines, and I saw very few rods bending. The clue was how long the trout could be seen for, and the fact that the grebes were in the same area. The grebes were diving and coming up with fry after about 20–30sec or so; this told me that the fry were actually quite a few feet down, and the trout were simply chasing them to the surface. The trout were swirling near the surface, taking the lethargic fry and heading back down to their cruising depth. Don't be fooled to casting at rising trout that simply show once and then disappear, with a floating line or floating fly pattern.

In this scenario I would opt for a fast-sinking line but fish Minkie Boobies. You may question why, if the fish are deep. If a fish does herd fry on the surface and I cast a Minkie at it, then it has very little chance of attracting the trout amongst the thousands of naturals. However, with the Minkie Booby I can 'plop' this across the surface to attract the trout's attention immediately. Also, as they sink, they drop through the layers much more slowly and therefore stay in the fish's window for much longer.

The Retrieve
Fishing the drop is important, especially when fishing leaded Minkies at this time of year. As the Minkie hits the surface it will make a 'plopping' sound that the trout are immediately attracted to. I have studied trout taking my flies for years, and can assure you they are lightning fast – they can take a fly and spit it out before you can even think about reacting. I once watched a fish follow my orange Blob to the boat and swirl around it. After cruising around it for several seconds it took it and spat it out at such speed that I didn't have time even to think about lifting the rod to set the hook. The same can happen to you when fishing Minkies after they plop and hit the surface. To maximize your chances of catching these, after casting out your flies make sure you get a tight line immediately,

Magnificent grown-on brown trout feed frantically on the fry to fatten up for the hard winter ahead.

as the fish may take it within seconds of it hitting the surface.

To make your fly stand out from the crowd try an erratic retrieve by slow pulls followed by short jerky pulls. This kind of retrieve will better imitate an injured fry and make it a target for the trout. Short, slow pulls with a pause in between is also a great retrieve, as this allows the mink fur to pulsate in the water.

When fish are feeding deep on the fry and you are having to use sinking lines, don't forget to hang your flies. Too many anglers associate the hang with pulling Blobs on a fast sinker, but it is also crucial when fishing for fry feeders. Hanging a Minkie is like offering a stunned fry pattern in mid-water, and this is easy pickings for a trout and absolutely lethal!

It is important that you make the most of fry feeders whilst they are 'on'. I have had some explosive sport and taken four or five magnificent trout in an hour or so, only for it to die away completely so you wouldn't think there was a trout in the place. They exert vast amounts of energy chasing this high source of protein, and they can only do it for so long before requiring a much needed break. Another reason is that they are simply too full. I have caught a trout of just 3lb and counted some forty-three small decaying roach fry inside it, and I still don't know how it intended to fit my Minkie in its stomach.

If you have seen fry activity in front of you and it has slowed down or stopped completely, try fishing away from where the activity has been happening, and fish a small fry imitation with a very slow retrieve. Even the fattest of trout would find it hard to resist an easy meal!

Another method now becoming extremely popular is rudder fishing. A metal rudder is attached to the stern of the boat and used to guide the boat down the wind at some incredible speeds. Anglers use

A typical fully finned, fry-feeding rainbow trout taken on an Iain Barr-leaded Minkie.

Iain Barr with eight fish he caught at Rutland Water, including brown trout and two 5lb rainbow trout.

various sinking rates of fly line, and practically tow large silver and gold tube flies behind the boat. This was once known as fishing 'Northampton style', the very town Bob Church now lives in! I am not a fan of this method, and I believe this is one of the main reasons for the demise in over-wintered trout in many of the large popular reservoirs such as Rutland Water. Despite the falling numbers of over-wintered trout appearing here, it still accounts for most of the biggest fish caught from the lake. If you want to catch a double-figured trout, then this is arguably one of your best chances of doing so.

Daddies on the Menu

Although September may be the start of the fry-feeding frenzy, there is a certain gangly creature that always features high on the trout's agenda: the crane fly, or 'daddy long legs', is certainly a food source the trout do not ignore. They start to appear in August, but it is in September and into early October that the daddies start their danger-thwart journeys, bouncing across the waves of our lakes and reservoirs. Strong winds with a previously wet night constitute prime daddy long legs conditions.

The perfect big 'daddy'.

They tend to come to life at night, and I haven't seen many feeding frenzies on them in the day except on a few occasions; but I have spooned trout when they have been stuffed on them. I have concluded that the trout mainly feed on them after dark, as this is when they are plentiful – but only the daftest of trout will refuse one during the day.

The Best Place to Fish with Daddies

Picking the perfect bank for fishing daddies couldn't be easier. Quite simply pick the bank with the wind coming from behind you, preferably with long grass. This ensures that a steady supply of these fumbling terrestrials is being fed to the trout lying in front of you. If fishing from a boat, start your drift from such a bank, and drift across the lake. As with other dry fly fishing, look for wind lanes forming across the lake's surface, and head for these.

Dance in the Grass!

Daddy long legs love the long grass, so don't feel too embarrassed to go dancing in the grass to encourage the clumsy terrestrials to take to the air and ultimately fly on to the lake. You may well be surprised at the numbers of these flies lying in the grass behind you. As they land in the water, ensure you cast your naturals into them and wait – and it won't be long before they are taken for their natural counterpart. Don't cast a full line into the water: start by fan casting in the margins, then slowly cast further each cast.

Rise Forms

There are two distinctive rise forms to look for, and these are a giveaway that the trout are feeding on the daddies. The first and most obvious is a very splashy rise. The trout are not actually taking the fly, but it is an attempt to drown it before sipping it down as it lies in the film. When fishing daddies, if you see a splash at your fly, try not to strike into the fish, because it is likely that you will strike into thin air, as it was an attempt by the trout to drown the fly. If you are unsure if the fish has taken the fly, try a strip strike, when you literally strip the line back fast with one long pull. If the trout has the fly in its mouth, then you will feel the tension and you should lift the rod. If it hasn't taken the fly, then there is a chance it will attack it as it moves away from it. If you get too many splashy rises, then your daddy long legs is sitting too high, as mentioned in an earlier section. Trim away excess hackle, add gink to the top of the fly, and try again.

The second rise form is the slowest of head and tail rises. A daddy long legs is a large meal to a trout, so it needs to roll over it comfortably to ensure it gets it, especially if it is tumbling across the waves at speed.

The Sunken Daddy

If a fish splashes at your fly and you miss it, this is a missed opportunity. Being a competition angler and trying to refine all methods so they are the most effective and efficient, I rarely now fish a dry daddy long legs. The trout splash at them to try and sink them, so they can take them more comfortably below the surface – so why fish them dry in the first place? I recall fishing a European International Team final. I had practised several days before, and spotted the occasional daddy long legs on the surface, and now and again a fish taking them – but they had them in their stomachs when I spooned the fish I had caught. There was a good breeze, and this helps drown the daddies.

I set up with a team of two daddies on the top and point with two nymphs in the middle. I added a little gink to the daddies so they would fish dry in the surface film for approximately 20sec, then the nymphs would drag them under. I took seventeen fish during the match, and lost half of that

again as I went on to barbless hooks. The point to note was that I hardly saw a fish take a daddy long legs, but by finding them in their stomachs I knew they were feeding on them. Almost all the fish took the daddy long legs, and all took them when they were sub-surface. The wind had picked up during the match, so more daddies were drowning in the tumbling waves, which made my sunken daddies the perfect imitation. So when you are fishing and you see daddies about, try a wet one first.

Daddies appear when fry are abundant, but I have caught plenty of large trout whilst fishing for fry feeders. One of my best methods is to fish a floating fry on the point with two wet daddies on the droppers. You are offering two of the trout's favourite food items in one go, which they can rarely resist!

Corixa Feeders

On reservoirs such as Chew Valley the corixa is high on the trout's list of diet food, and these tiny submarines play an important part in the trout's nutrition in these later months. The rise forms to these probably vary more than any other food the trout pursue. You may see splashy rises; head and tails; violent eruptions at the surface, or probably the most common – the flattening of the surface followed by a small swirl. This is most common, because the corixa makes a bolt to the surface for a gulp of air before heading back to the weeds.

Where to find Corixa Feeders

Corixa like the shallow water, preferably with good weed cover. Here it is not a long journey to the surface for a gulp of air, and they have the cover of the weed to dive back into. I look to fish in depths of about 6–8ft (2–2.5m) as a maximum, although they can be found in slightly deeper water. In this depth the best line of attack is the floating line.

Patterns to Try

I have seen many conventional patterns trying to imitate corixa, but I find that small drab nymphs, maybe with a small bit of flash in them, is the best line of attack. Flies such as Diawl Bachs, Crunchers or Hare's Ears would be hard to beat, and always my first choice. I have fished many matches on Chew Valley and caught good bags of fish fishing along the weedbeds of Villice Bay and Herons with small nymphs tied on a size 12. Although competition rules don't permit it, on leisure days I have had some good success on leaded nymphs: the lead gives the fly an instant attraction as it plops into the water and dives fairly sharply, just like the naturals.

The Retrieve

The retrieve is probably the most important thing to remember when attacking corixa feeders. Wearing your polarized glasses, watch the naturals in motion, as it really is very interesting: they appear from nowhere as they make that dash to the surface. Some get to the surface and hang in the film, and this is generally when you get the 'head and tail' rises taking them; others dash to the surface for a split second, and then dive immediately back down again. However, their journey is not a smooth one: they make short, darting movements, and often not in a straight line, and this is when you witness explosive eruptions from the trout. This is also the clue to your retrieve.

Once you have cast out your team of nymphs, allow them to settle to just above the weed. Like all fishing below the surface, make sure you keep a tight line as the flies drop, because the trout may see your falling nymphs as an easy meal. Once they have reached the required depth, retrieve them with 2–3in, sharp jerky movements for about 5–6sec, then pause and repeat the process. Once your flies are nearing the boat it is important that you hang them to imitate the corixa in the most natural way. I catch over 50 per cent of my corixa-feeding fish on the hang near the boat. I came 5th in an Open European Championships on Chew Valley fishing the corixa: I fished a team of Crunchers and Diawl Bachs over some shallow weed, and used the tactics

---

Top Tips

- Beef up your tackle.
- Look for signs of fry-feeding activity.
- Never lift into an aggressive splash.
- Grease the top of the fly, not all of it.
- Twitch your nymphs for better results.

A Gold Cheek Cruncher in a size 12 makes the ideal corixa pattern.

above to take some cracking rainbows, with most coming on the hang near the boat to the Gold Cheek Cruncher.

November/ December – Don't Pack Your Tackle Away!

It amazes me how the number of anglers out fishing tumbles during and after October. But November and December can be fantastic fishing. For many years my dad and brothers used to fish Rutland every Boxing Day, and almost always caught our limits whilst others tucked into more turkey! Only family commitments prevent us doing this, but I still try and venture out over the Christmas period. The trout are still living and still need to feed, and you will be surprised what food is still available through these winter months. Fry can still be plentiful, corixa bountiful, and small hatches of buzzers continue to hatch as the day warms up.

Big Fish on the Midge!

I recall fishing a large reservoir with ice around the edges, which I shattered as I stood with my feet in the water's edge. The reservoir was full, grass piercing the water's surface several yards out from the water's edge. In amongst this grass, tiny black midges were hatching, and large trout up to 5lb were taking advantage of them. I cast at plenty of these, but took only one fish on a large black tadpole – yet these were feeding fish, just waiting to be caught! I went home on that Saturday night and tied some size 16 black shuttlecocks, and went back first thing in the morning. As I arrived I could see fish rising, and I couldn't tie my flies on quick enough! Frost glazed the grass and a mist hovered over the lake – but these fish were feeding! I caught my limit before lunchtime of eight fish up to 5lb on the tiny shuttlecocks. I came home and told stories

of my amazing morning's sport – but when I returned the following week, the fish had gone. There were no small midges to be seen, and the fish had moved into the deeper water.

One of my favourite flies for this time of year is a plain black tadpole. I tend to fish it on an intermediate line, with long, slow pulls for best results. Try adding small

---

Top Tips

- Fish your flies slowly.
- Try dark-coloured lures.
- Keep fishing!

Iain Barr has a good catch here, but he is checking up on how many fish some of the others in the competition have caught.

nymphs on the droppers, and beware of fish hitting these on the drop. I like to fish this into the wind, so add a small piece of lead to your fly, or try one with a gold bead.

The Final Cast

I am often asked why I am so successful in fly fishing. In fact I don't do too much different from all those anglers around me. The only thing I do is think about everything I do. Sometimes I do things adversely different just to experiment, and it is this experimenting that brings up new ideas. Furthermore, the competition circuit reveals new tactics, patterns and tackle year in year out, so why not enter more competitions?

Flies and lines are chosen for a reason. The retrieve is chosen on the day to best suit the fish, and the area to fish is often dictated by the wind. All these require a little bit of thinking about, so it's not just a chuck and chance when you go fishing. Next time *you* go fishing, try thinking about your choices, and question yourself as to why you have made the decisions you have. Also think about each fish you catch, and the ones that you didn't, because all this analysis will help you build a better understanding of the prey you are seeking. Above all this, there are some basic fundamentals to remember. Fishing is an art, and a pleasure. We cast out our flies, and retrieve them in anticipation of the line going tight. That exhilaration at your fingertips keeps us coming back for more.

The queue of anglers waiting to weigh in at Grafham Water after a big competition.

I have learned so much from highly skilled legendary anglers such as Bob Church and Dave Shipman, my idols as I grew up with the sport. I progressed through the ranks of England Youth Fly Fishing to the senior teams, and have had the pleasure of captaining my country in my chosen field. It is honours such as these that make me proud – and being able to fish in some of the world's most amazing settings makes me realize how lucky I am. However, wherever you may go fishing, be at peace,

enjoy the sport, and if you catch nothing, so what: it just means the fish are there for you to catch and enjoy next time. I am sure that some of the delinquent children in today's society could benefit from our beloved sport. The tranquillity you experience, the world at your feet with nature happening around you, would, I am sure, reach the toughest of hearts. Above all, let's keep out sport going: let's encourage others into this fascinating and tranquil pastime of ours.

The sun setting over Rutland's Lax Hill.

2 Learning Night Sea Trout Fishing

By Bob Church

Lessons Learned from Cyril Inwood

When it comes to night fishing for sea trout, my mentor was the late Cyril Inwood. I was very fortunate to know Cyril quite well. I first met him in 1963 on the opening day of Pitsford Reservoir; I fished from the bank with him all day and we caught a lot of trout, fishing catch and release after keeping the limit catch.

So years later, when I wanted to try for sea trout with the fly, it was to Cyril and my other old friend, the late Frank Cutler, that I turned. Cyril and Frank would take the last two weeks in July as holiday, and they would go with their wives to North Wales, where they shared a four-berth caravan. Staying close to the lovely Betsy Coed, really all Cyril and Frank wanted to do was fish the River Conway for sea trout and salmon. Never mind sunshine for their

Bob Church began fishing with Cyril Inwood in 1963.

Frank Cutler was Cyril's regular fishing companion. Frank was a great all-rounder, winning gold medals at coarse fishing and trout fly fishing in the home countries events.

wives, they prayed for rain, which would bring in new fish.

During the sixties and early seventies this river produced some very big sea trout for Cyril, and for Frank in particular. I drove to Wales for a weekend with the idea that Cyril was going to show me how to go about catching some big sea trout – and he did, too. Quite unexpectedly I met his grandson Mark 'Spike' Harrison, and as I got to know him better I used to talk about his granddad, and would tell him what a good fisherman he was. Mark told me he had Cyril's own handwritten account of his sea trout tactics and catches, all in an old blue duplicate book. It concentrates on night fishing – which is when you catch the big specimens.

At the time of writing sea trout have suffered a series of setbacks during the last ten years: there have been fewer sand eels in our estuaries, and the sea trout have had to endure a much greater burden of sea lice. An unfortunate consequence of confining salmon in salmon-rearing cages is that they play host to millions more sea lice;

then when a repellent is put in the cages to repel the lice, they drop to the estuary bottom, where the unfortunate sea trout are suddenly covered in them. The distress caused from less food and the leech-like, weakening effect of too many sea lice has depleted stocks. However, happily they do seem to be making a comeback on some of the worst affected rivers that I fish.

I have seen some very large sea trout caught in the River Morrum in southern Sweden – two in fact at 22lb 8oz. The best our party managed was 12lb, caught by cricketer Alan Lamb; I had one of 8lb 4oz, and was happy with that – but this was day-time fishing.

I have caught lots of sea trout in my time in the UK, and in particular from rivers and loughs in Ireland. Drifting traditionally in a boat we have had great sport in the West of Ireland, in places such as Lough Furnace, Upper Lough Feeagh, Lough Costello, Lough Innagh, Lough Kylemore Abby, and the upper Lake Ballynahinch system.

Fishing Lough style I have caught plenty of sea trout just using a floating fly line and

This Danish angler caught the second 22lb 8oz sea trout from the River Morrum. Unfortunately he gutted it before I could get a photo – but even gutted it shows its impressive size.

This 5lb rainbow is the type of fish the late Cyril Inwood was used to catching.

a three-fly cast. Stripping fast across the waves, then stopping and teasing the 'bob fly' static for a few seconds works best for me. I like a Daddy Long Legs on either the point or sometimes the top dropper; also a must is a blackfly: the old fashioned Bibio is still good, and there are some useful variants with small, fluorescent red pieces in the body. I have done well with a Heather Fly, too, complete with knotted red legs, six of them. A fly I first tied for the browns of Rutland Water called 'Goldie', is a marvellous sea trout fly for loughs and rivers. I nearly always have one on to make up the three-fly cast, along with the Daddy and Black Palmer.

In Scotland there are times in rivers when I and my friends have caught on small-size 14–12 dry flies, usually in the evening. I had some good catches on the Spey tributary Avon, and also on the Aberdeenshire Dee. The best flies were Black Gnat types or Greenwell's types, variants of those basic old-style flies. In other words, the standard patterns still work well, but if you liven them up with a scrap of modern materials here and there, they do seem to perform better.

Following Cyril's Advice

Let's now turn our attention to some of the fundamental details of Cyril's advice on tactics, flies, and his general approach to catching sea trout at night, when the big

Yet another 20lb sea trout is brought into the official weighing room of the River Morrum.

specimens come out to play. It is the ambition of most sea-trout fishermen to catch a big one – by which I mean 10lb plus. Cyril always said he was lucky to have some of the best sea-trout fishing companions anyone could ever meet: Welshmen who fished the River Dovey, and from whom he learned a great deal in the fifties and early sixties. Also being a reservoir fly fisherman gave him a good start, because he could cast a good long line. On many good spots you need to cast right to the other side of the river, dropping your fly under overhanging branches covered in summer leaves: this provides a safe resting place for sea trout before they become more active after dark.

Cyril always maintained that to catch a fish of 10lb and over is definitely the thrill of a lifetime, and you would never get a better fight, pound for pound, from any other species of fish. Certainly when I caught an 11lb 12oz fish recently my mouth was completely dry at the end of the battle – and I am an 'old hand' at it! There is just

something about sea trout that captivates you, to the point where I lose sleep over them and then find it hard to keep awake – I often do this for two weeks at the end of July every year.

There is no greater thrill than to tighten into a big sea trout and see the rod arch over against the sky, while at the same time the reel check is screaming and the line hissing through the water. Then you feel the line splice clink its way through the rings, and it's still going now, some thirty metres away. Next you hear a big splash as he jumps three feet out of the water, and you are then able perhaps to start recovering a bit of line – and all this in pitch blackness! Though by now your eyes will be used to the dark, and provided you don't panic or foul the line or some underwater snag, in fifteen minutes or so he will be ready to net. And with the torch shining on a magnificent fish, that whole moment will be with you forever.

You can start trying for these big fish when the water warms up around the end

Nigel Collins lands a good sea trout from the middle reaches of the Wear. This is Nigel's own river, and he says it is fast improving for sea trout and salmon.

of May, although you must have the right conditions – following a flood would be a perfect time. Sea trout don't like mist on the water, or thunder, rain or moonlight: they like a warm, dark night, though we never seem to get enough of these. But don't waste your time in poor conditions, as I did.

High water is hopeless, too, even if it is clear; the sea trout will not take if the flies are coming round too fast and too high. The fly must come round slow and deep, just inches off the bottom. In high water I have tried putting lead shot on my leader, but they still will not have it, although I know the fly is near to them.

Most sea trout writers tell you to fish the tail of the pool, yet most of my big fish have come from the deepest part. By a big pool I mean one that is about 165ft (50m) long and about 10 to 12ft (3 to 3.5m) deep, because the big fish will lie here in the daytime. Sea trout like trees and bushes overhanging the river. Look for this type of pool to fish in the evening, so as to get to know it if you intend staying after dark.

The stream will be slower in the deep pool. Sometimes when the fly is swimming slowly round with the current you will find a shelf there, and this is a good place for a take. I like to fish the same pool every

Study the pool in the day, so you know the best wading and landing spots after dark.

Bob Church with his best sea trout to date, an 11lb 4oz specimen from the River Test.

year, as I am learning all the while, and my results get better and better with time. In the end, my mind has an underwater map of the whole pool bottom, and if any sea trout are in, I know where they will be lying and I know the right flies to catch them on.

The smaller fish come on the take first, then after midnight it gets darker – the blacker the night, the better. Keep a lookout for rising fish just before dawn.

Tackle

Rods, Reels and Lines

Cyril would use two fly rods, one 10ft, the other 11ft. These carry different line ratings: a 7/8 for the lighter work, and a 9/10 for heavier loads, with bigger tandem flies/lures. Of course Cyril was using silk line and split cane rods in those days, so I am just bringing them up to date. So the fly rods would obviously be carbon – your reservoir fly rod would do – and of course the weight forward; and plastic fly lines replaced the silk ones long ago. Cyril

This Danish angler gave me the choice of spot, so I picked the obvious point with a fast flow into the big pool. He fished in the little bay in slack water and caught this fine 16lb 8oz sea trout on the Morrum.

Jeanette shows her expertise once again by netting this lovely sea trout of close to 5lb from the drifting boat on Lough Kylemore Abbey.

Alex Behrendt weighs in a 9lb rainbow for one of his lady syndicate members. This is where it all began for the small water followers: it went under the name of Two Lakes.

When I took Ron Randall to Avington for the first time, he caught his limit too quickly, and as he was my guest I purchased another day permit for him. He caught a second limit (four), but this time a 15lb rainbow was amongst them. My four fish are on the left, the best one 12lb.

would be amazed just how many reels we carry around with us nowadays – but I am sure he would have loved the Slyme slow sinker.

For his reels and landing net, all his notes say a big reel and a big net with 100m of 30lb breaking strain backing. His net was a Gye salmon net: these are still about, but their crude, wide netting splits the tails and fins of any fish you would like to return; so buy a big net for the job, but make sure it has fish-friendly, narrow, soft mesh netting – then if you want to return a fish, you can do so without it suffering harm. (I use my journalistic licence to modernize Cyril's antique tackle.)

Waders

Waders, whether thigh or chest, should have studded boots to ensure a secure footing – most river bottom stones are slimy and uneven, and it's easy to slip over and fill your boots, which can leave you very uncomfortable for the rest of the day or night. So keep away from cleated rubber soles, just make sure the sole and heel have plenty of studs in, then you will wade confidently without slipping.

A wading stick on a sling around your neck is a very good aid when in the middle of the river. It doesn't get in your way because the river's flow holds it in a downstream of your body whilst you are not using it – though when you *do* need it, as I did a few times last season, it's a godsend.

Fly fishing after dark – always take care.

3 Sea Trout Fishing: Flies, Tackle and Tactics

By Bob Church

Tackling Up for a Night's Fishing

The Silver Doctor fly takes some beating. I always start the evening session by using a size 10; it's not dark enough for the big ones until midnight. Cyril used flies on the cast, to which he would add three or four maggots (if these were allowed), and if you can't get maggots, a piece of pork rind cut very slim with a razor blade will do – Cyril considered it looked like a big maggot, but without the wriggle. With this set-up it is usually possible to have a lot of fun to about midnight with sea trout up to about 6lb; and you can add a few nice brown trout to the list, as the large browns also feed best after dark. After the clock strikes 12am, I put on a size 4 salmon fly or tandem lure, and these I fish until dawn.

Make your own leader casts with 8lb or 10lb nylon (I suppose it would be fluorocarbon if Cyril had been alive today) – naturally the 8lb is used with the smaller flies, and the 10lb with the larger ones. For very big sea trout 12lb or even 15lb modern fluorocarbon would be better.

Cyril also observes that during the hours of darkness these fish don't seem to worry about thickness of line as they would by day. The bigger fish have harder mouths, too, so you need a sharp hook and the stronger line so as to strike it firmly home. I have often hooked eight big sea trout when conditions were right, but finished up landing only five of them – they are so powerful, and fight pound for pound harder than salmon, or indeed any other fish.

Just in case you get fed up and pack up, you should have two torches in your bag because you know how easily they can let you down. Also, a change of fly may require a torch, to take the fly out of the

Good size browns feed well after dark while sea trout fishing.

fish's mouth, and of course to see how big he is. This should be done with your back to the river or behind the hut, because you should never let the torch light flash over the water – even lighting a cigarette could frighten the fish, and these sea trout spook quite easily. Finally, remember that it gets very cold most nights, so take a litre flask of tea or coffee.

A Good Night's Fishing with Cyril

We have everything in place now, so Cyril will take you out on one of his good nights and tell you how he fishes – though first make sure you leave nothing obviously valuable in your car before locking it, otherwise you could get a broken window and your kit stolen – such is life these days. It is worth mentioning that we arrive at the pool at twilight time only because I know it so well. Never wade an unknown pool at night, but check it over in daylight first; find out where to get into the river safely, where to wade, and where to get out or land a sea trout.

The rod is set up with an eight- or nine-weight fly line, floating, then 9ft of 10 to 12lb leader nylon, as Cyril would have used; though I imagine he would have liked fluorocarbon better, so we will overrule him and use the modern fluorocarbon. Then he tied on a number 4 Blue and Silver home-tied fly. Sometimes I use a dropper and the standard old patterns – Alexandra and Peter Ross work well. You will need a big landing net on the water's edge, but put it somewhere you can easily play your fish to.

This is Cyril's account of what he calls a 'red letter night':

'One or two salmon and the occasional sea trout had been jumping; I just sit and wait, watching the river all the time. I look at my watch, five past ten, too early yet. The birds are still twittering away in the bushes, the owl in the big tree behind me hoots once or twice, he is answered from another tree on the far bank of the river. Then a pair of mallards glides into the pool, landing with a splash.

Gradually the birds stop as they settle down for the night. Then we hear a big splash, this time from a good sea trout; I spot the place next to a big rock. Several smaller fish have moved up to the head of the pool. Then another big fish crashes out of the water. I look at my watch: 10.45pm – right, I think that is dark enough.

I am eager to get out now and begin to fish. The signs are good, with quite a few fish active. I am fishing the two-fly method with 12lb line. I put three maggots on each hook, then get into the water so as to be able to cover the head of the pool with a comfortable cast. I wade very gently and quietly, but still manage to spook the mallards, which fly off.

Nearby, a sea trout moves under the bushes/small trees. I pull off a few yards of line and cast out down and across, holding my rod tip near the water; I wait as my line comes round with the current. My left hand is holding the line tightly. As the flies are coming round I flick the rod tip a little up and down, and that tells me where my line is. I feel two quick knocks, but whatever you do in this situation, don't strike, because the next thing that will happen is a sharp tug – and then I strike. A sea trout of about 2lb splashes about before I net him.

I cast out again and feel two more knocks, but nothing happened, so I have to change the maggots as that first fish had squashed them. After that I catch another two, one of around the pound, but the other a nice fish of 3lb 8oz.

I then move down to the tail of the pool, leaving the middle undisturbed. I catch two fish in the tail of 1lb 4oz and 1lb, also a brown trout of about 12oz. I look at my watch again to see it is fifteen minutes to midnight – time for a cup of coffee and a sandwich.

It's now midnight, and I pick up my heavier rod, which I made up earlier. I get in the water about three-quarters of the way up the pool. Wading out very carefully, I cast a line under the far bank. I don't retrieve. but just let the current swing the fly line round. If I do touch bottom with the fly I will help it round with a fast figure-of-eight retrieve.

Working my way steadily down the pool, a big fish moved near the far bank, but having fished the pool well as I thought, I was surprised to reach the tail of it without a single knock.

I once more came out of the water and back to the hut and had another coffee; at least it keeps you awake. I could not quite make it out. Water was a perfect height, a lovely warm night, fish were moving fairly regularly. Perhaps the stream was a bit faster than I had thought and my fly is not down enough. So I rub my leader down well to degrease it; for this I use a mixture of Fullers Earth and washing-up liquid – I always keep a small pot of this in my pocket.

Out once more, and I make for the spot so I can cover the last big rise. First cast, bang I was in: I knew he was a decent fish, and played him carefully to the waiting net. I slowly waded to the bank to despatch the fish, a fine specimen of 6lb 12oz.

Now it was all happening, and the next good cast was a beauty of 8lb 4oz, then 5lb 12oz, then a 7lb fish; after that I had two more fish briefly on and off – then, as may be expected, the pool was completely dead. Four fish in five casts for 27lb 12oz: I was very pleased with myself, and the adrenalin was keeping me wide awake.

Time now was 2.30am, and I emptied my flask for my last drink and the final onslaught. It was just beginning to get light, and I sat taking in the scenery. But I knew from my experience that now was a good time for a 'really big fish'. I had rested the pool well and, sure enough, there were a couple of big fish at least, still splashing about in the middle of the river. I checked the point of my hook to make sure it was good and sharp, and got into the river again, obviously just upstream from where the big ones were showing.

I cast out, letting it all come round slowly, keeping my rod low over the water once again, ready for a quick strike. I very slowly kept moving a few yards downstream after every cast. It was around twenty minutes of this when I connected with something very big, the take was so vicious and the fish ran about ten yards, then spectacularly leapt well clear of the water, hitting the cliff-like, eight-foot high bank on the far side of the river – and as he dropped back, he came off. I had never experienced a sea trout doing that before or since.

I had had a good look at the fish, which was anything from 12lb to 14lb. Anyhow it didn't seem to disturb the others because they were still moving. So I tested my hook point once more: it was OK, and I was cursing my luck. Working down the pool again, I saw my line lifting, then the tug, tug, tug and I struck into a good sized, very heavy fish, and again he leapt out and dropped back with a crash. I had dropped my rod tip near to the water, then raised it again allowing for the jump and therefore keeping in better contact with the fish.

Now it went off on a fast run, as the reel's check screamed. He looked a good 10lb plus in the second or two that I saw him. I gradually edged downstream and out on to the bank where my big landing net lay – and of course I had selected the best, even bank for this, with no obstacles around.

I managed to turn him, bringing him back towards me, then he came up on top but bolted off again, heading for the roots of a tree which were well out in the water. I then had to put extra pressure on, which I hated to do with sea trout, but I knew if he got to the roots he would break me anyway. I managed to turn him again and the hook held but it made me sweat a bit.

The fight lasted for twenty minutes; it would have made a super film – who said fishing is slow and boring? I tapped him on the head twice, then took out my spring balance and weighed him: 12lb 4oz, an excellent fish.

It was time to pack up. I was now feeling tired, but well pleased with the night's work. The only snag was walking back to the car, with waders, all the kit and 58lb 12oz worth of sea trout. This was one of my red letter nights, though I have had plenty of bad ones too, usually owing to water rising, or mist and moon. I know you don't want to read about those, or my blank days and nights; it's bad enough suffering them, let alone reminding oneself – as long as you know what causes them.

Some nights just the big fish are on. One such night gave me just two fish of 13lb 10oz and 9lb 8oz; these were the only two takes of the night. I had another night when I had six big fish on, but only landed one, at 8lb 12oz; that's how your luck runs sometimes. I think sometimes they take the fly just with the neb [the hard bit at the front of the mouth], and others the fly in a good mouthful.

Sometimes you only get a slight knock, which can be a big fish. Never be afraid to use big flies or lures; big sea trout are not too particular. I know big sea trout feed on their own fingerlings and salmon parr and minnows, but I don't think they are any different from big cannibal brown trout in various waters throughout the country.

I suppose although I am a sea trout fanatic I am also a bit of an all-rounder, inasmuch as I cannot fish for sea trout all year round.

So in the winter I match fish on the rivers and canals with reasonable success. I can get comfort and pleasure really from any sort of fishing.

So although we can catch sea trout in day time, I am firmly convinced that the best possible time is at night, and I have pursued this theory with success over a number of years. I was perhaps fortunate in being tutored by some of the finest sea trout anglers in the country on the River Dovey.

I had a natural fly-fishing background as I was a pretty good reservoir fly fisher, and this was a great advantage. I could cast well, sometimes having to miss trees that overhung the river on the far bank; as the fish lay beneath them, that was where you had to drop your fly without hooking the branches.

Being able to tie my own flies was another good help, as I fine-tuned some well-known standard patterns of both sea trout and salmon flies. Catching fish is a form of hunting that sounds innocuous, but this night fishing is not without its hazards, and any intending devotee would be well advised to heed the advice I can give him.

I am addicted to visiting the same river for a fortnight each year, simply because knowledge of all the pools and runs is invaluable. I could probably make a map of the river bed of the particular stretch I fish.'

Now although Cyril mentions the River Dovey, I know for a fact that the River Conway was where a lot of his big sea trout came from, in a pool called Harvard's. Cyril continues:

'Sea trout are cunning, without doubt, and the "whoppers" only achieve their size by being more cunning than their fellows. Noisy wading, flashing lights, or anything of a disturbing nature will ensure a lack of response from a big sea trout. The times and conditions that are ideal are few and far between, so don't spoil your chances by being clumsy.

Just last summer produced a lovely 14lb 12oz sea trout for me and, old hand that I am, while playing this fish I had it going through my mind that I would lose it, a fisherman's crisis no less, knees were trembling, arms aching and my mouth parched dry. The reason for this sudden nervous attack was that I doubted the integrity of my tackle as the splicing of my backing crunched its way through the rods rings. But this is the feeling that draws me back year after year to do battle with these giants.

From May onwards you are in with a chance of a decent early sea trout. For day time fishing, stick to the deepest part of the pools, moving from spot to spot. A pool about fifty yards long is very good if it is about twelve foot wide, as fish will shoal up in the deepest part of such a pool. I have never succeeded in fast, high water.'

A More Humorous Night

With the reader's indulgence, Cyril prefers to describe one of his more humorous nights, and although he laughs about it, it was rather scary on the night.

'This particular night was the first of my holiday. I arrived at the farm and parked my car, and made sure it was securely locked up. A few words with the farmer, and I was eyeing with some trepidation a field I needed to cross, with three rams in it and a cow with a new calf. But another field after that came between me and the river, and in this one were some cows and a very large black Galloway bull. They were all respectfully given a very wide berth, despite the farmer's bland assurance that the bull would not hurt a fly.

A deep satisfaction filled me as I reached the pool, and I enjoyed savouring all the memories that came flooding back as I gazed at it, but in particular the overriding anticipation of what was to come. But sadly, a sudden sharp rise in the water forced me out: it was too high to continue. I packed up, and had some uncomfortable moments before I returned safely to my car through the two fields, my torch stabbing the darkness trying to find a black bull on a very nark night. Have you ever tried it?

The following night was perfect, so I set up two rods as usual, one of 10ft, the other 11ft. I chose two nets for landing fish on this night: one very big, which I left on the bank in the best spot for landing a very big one, and the other I clipped on my belt – it is still a reasonably good size, as I have netted a 20lb salmon in it.

On these night sessions I am usually entirely on my own, and bearing this in mind, I make sure I have everything to hand. I am likely to have two torches in case of a failure, a pair of scissors on an extending pin clip, a hand towel, leader sink and the usual flask full of coffee. I put three or four marker sticks on the water line so as to tell at a glance if the river rises again: you can get caught out wading across to a shallow, then the water rises and you can't get back. Take care, especially if there has even been rain in the hills. On this occasion conditions have settled, so it should be all right.

The water I fish has the luxury of a fishing hut, and all extra gear is left in it. As before, I start with my 10ft fly rod and fish two flies, as I am allowed to put maggots on the hooks here, so putting three on each fly. Just gone 10pm by my watch, and I was eager to get going after missing out on the previous night. Then came the first heavy splash as a big sea trout jumped in mid-river. But do you know, I finished the session with a blank?

Farther downstream, on another night a fisher had just two takes for 23lb 2oz for the brace, with the largest at 13lb 10oz: on another occasion I hooked six big fish and only landed one, of 8lb 12oz – such is the varied luck, for and against, involved in sea trout fishing on a dark night.'

Cyril's best sea trout was 18lb 8oz; he also had one of 16lb 7oz.

Finally I would like to say to any fellow sea trout angler that the road to substantial catches of big sea trout is, given reasonable conditions, applying knowledge of the sea trout habits gathered over the years, to persistent hard work. May I close with this assertion: 'a night-shift worker usually draws a bigger wage than a day worker'. Enough said.

Epilogue to Cyril Inwood

When Cyril was sixty years old he unfortunately caught Weils disease while fishing his beloved River Conway. He had just a small cut on his hand, and he must have touched the grass where a female rat had left a urine scent trail; the pathogens entered his bloodstream and almost killed him a week later. I remember visiting him in Northampton General Hospital. He was fighting the disease very well, and assured me as he lay there looking almost yellow: 'Doctor McQuade has told me he will get me round. I've promised him a good sized salmon every Christmas while I can still fish.' The doctor had five salmon that I know of.

Doctor McQuade gave him about five years to live because he had bad angina, a side effect of Weils disease being that it affects angina sufferers badly. During that time we fished quite a lot together. He always wanted me to drive because he had this premonition that he would collapse at the wheel of his car. So I would drive his Morris Oxford, or I would take my Austin Cambridge, two great cars of their time. He told me a lot of his secrets during those five years, almost as though he didn't want his fishing skills to die with him. And Cyril did in fact die at the wheel of his car, on his way to fish Eyebrook reservoir.

Cyril Inwood was indeed the master. Here he shows his catch of six salmon on the right and five sea trout on the left.

Bob Church's List of Sea Trout Rivers and Loughs

The following are sea trout rivers I have fished with success, and they are all still worth trying, as far as I know.

- River Tweed
- River Teviot, where my wife caught a 10lb 8oz fish
- Also its tributary the River Till, which is very good
- River Spey, and its tributary the River Avon, which is excellent
- River Test: I have caught lots of sea trout here over the years, including my personal best at 11lb 4oz
- River Towey
- River Dove
- River Conway, Cyril's favourite where he caught sea trout on the fly to 18lb 8oz
- River Ness
- River Findhorn
- River Aberdeenshire Dee
- River Morrum in southern Sweden, with very large sea trout (see my references to it); the first two fish I saw caught went 22lb 8oz each
- River Hitara in Iceland.

This beautiful 18lb sea trout was caught by Isaac Kristian, the guide from the river of giants, the Morrum in Sweden.

Now to that other great sea trout sport: catching them from a drifting boat in the traditional style. The West of Ireland loughs are still quite good, despite the sea trout's problems when in river estuaries. Lough Furnace and a favourite of mine, Lough Feeagh – known as the Burrishule Fishery – are at Newport; all the following loughs are in either Galway or Mayo:

- Lough Innagh
- Lough Kylemore Abbey and its upper lough: I had a good evening's sport here with Carol Neal, with plenty of fish up to 3lb, catch and release. Earlier in the day my wife Jeanette boated a fine sea trout of near 6lb
- Lough Costello: we had good catches here, and returned all of them
- Lough Corrib
- Lough Beltra
- Lough Conn, and finally
- Ballynahinch Castle and Lough Carrow More.

4 Casting

By Hywel Morgan

I must say, when Bob asked me to contribute to this book I felt proud to be helping a man who is a legend in the sport of angling. He was an innovator with regard to the products he produced, and a true leader in the revolution of large reservoir fly fishing. I hope my section on casting will help all of you who read this book.

Hywel Morgan, aged eighteen months, walking down his back garden in the village of Pontrhydfendigaid with a fly rod in his hand.

At the tender age of eighteen months, I was introduced to my first fishing rod. This is not a big surprise to most who know my dad, Moc. I can't think of a time when I was without a fishing rod when growing up – it was only when I went to secondary school that I encountered other sports, which I became quite good at.

My Personal Career and Achievements

I can't remember my first fishing lesson, but my earliest recollection is fishing the Teifi Pools for wild brown trout: Dad would carry me to the lakeside as I was too small to walk through the reeds, and then leave me there to fish while he fished around the lake and then came back to quite literally pick me up. For this I will be eternally grateful, as fishing has taken me all over the world, and has made me great friends from all walks of life; furthermore, always travelling with the old man enabled me to have lessons from the true 'greats' of the angling world. My first step on to a casting platform was under the watchful eye of the then British champion Lionel Sweet, who always asked for a volunteer to help in his demonstration; as dad was the commentator then, I was the pupil at the young age of four years.

After this I fished extensively throughout my youth for wild browns and sea trout, and it was only by accident that I became

Hywel at a very early age fishing at the Teifi Pools in mid Wales.

At the Royal Welsh Show, Lionel Sweet gives Hywel (aged four) his first casting lesson.

closely involved with the art of casting. Two of my friends were interested in casting, and were competing at the CLA Game Fair; they insisted I have a go, but I wasn't really interested in putting a piece of wool into a ring, and couldn't see the point of it – until I won the competition and received a £15 tackle voucher, which, if my memory serves me right, I spent in Bob's stand.

After this I practised all through the winter, hitting hoops in the back garden, and became known as the 'garden fishermen'; but the practice certainly paid off, and at the next year's show I won all the prizes in the junior section on day one, all the prizes in the Open Professional on the second day, and all the trophies on the last day. This continued for three years until the

judges at the CLA asked me not to enter the competitions any more. At that time I was only sixteen, so I decided to find other casting competitions.

The British Casting Association was my next step, which at first I found totally alien. Casters were using 16wt rods and lines to achieve distances I never thought possible with a fly rod. This was an exciting time when I did a lot of learning, and through the teaching of Jack Martin (former World Champion) and a lot of practice, I started to win some of the British casting events; however, I was still far removed from both European and World standards. To achieve this objective I took six months out of my life and practised six days a week, six to eight hours a day. This was incredibly boring, but

CLA trophies.

it worked, and in my first competition of the year I won most of the events, and in doing so set many new British records. After this I won the European Casting Championships in Berlin in 1987, and the World Games in The Hague in Holland in 1993.

After achieving this, my thoughts turned back to fishing, as all anglers would always say to me 'You can cast, but you can't catch fish!' After winning gold in Holland I was fortunate enough to qualify for the Welsh team going to the World Fly Fishing Championships held in Norway the following year. This was a baptism of fire, as I had not fished in the home internationals for years, and going to the 'Worlds' was a totally new experience: there were twenty countries, all fielding a five-man team with a reserve, and to say the fishing was tough was an understatement. One particular lake was renamed the 'Graveyard' because it only produced five fish between one hundred anglers, all of whom fished it for three hours each! But things went well

Hywel standing in the number one place on the podium at the World Casting Games held in The Hague in Holland in 1993.

for me, and by the last session I was sitting in seventh place, with only one river boat section to go.

All the anglers ahead of me, bar Pascal from France (who had already won gold), were on the Graveyard, and no fish had been caught in any morning session. I remember Russell Owen, our captain – who at the time was reigning World Champion – coming up to me before the last session and telling me not to panic, and to stick to the game plan. I was drawn to fish with a Czech, and anyone who knows anything about fishing will understand why I was very nervous: being in a boat on a river with one of these guys could mean a severe pasting! The only problem you have when deciding where to fish is the language barrier, but after some ten minutes of sign language and pointing, it seemed that both of us wanted to fish the same area, which was just fifty yards away from the start point.

Our problem was that every other boat wanted to fish there as well, but I did have one trick up my sleeve – or should I say

in my tackle bag – and that was six miniature bottles of 'Famous Grouse' whisky, which I offered to the controller to get us there first! This worked well, and we were put in the spot we wanted. And I couldn't have dreamt of a better start, because as the anchor was set, I cast out and hooked a fish on my first cast! This was a great way of calming me down, and within fifteen minutes I had taken another four in the boat.

Meanwhile my Czech boat partner was nymphing in the bow with a floating line; however, he had only 4in (10cm) of line on the surface of the water and he wasn't catching, so he changed to a sinker – but again, with only about 4in of the line actually going into the water. But in no time at all he landed four fish and lost another three – and as the saying goes, 'Well, if you can't beat them ...' So I changed tactics and started doing the same as him: but for me, it was to no avail, and after thirty minutes I remembered Russ's words and went back to the game plan. This enabled me to have seven fish in total at the end of the session. That bus ride back to the team hotel was the longest in my life, but it was worth it, and when the results were up I found I had secured individual silver.

The following year I was captain of the Welsh team in the 'Worlds' in Ireland, a fantastic event and brilliantly organized; sadly, the only thing that can't be organized is the weather and the fishing, though I am proud to say that we won silver as a team. One of the best ever teams I have fished in is Wales' squad for 2000: we had strength in depth and fished for each other – but again France proved too strong, as they have on numerous occasions. Nevertheless, silver on England's home water was fantastic for a Welshman!

Since then I have fished many a time for Wales in the Home Internationals, but the one that stands out in my mind is the match held on Brenig in North Wales in 2004. At 6am on the morning of the match I had a phone call from the wife telling me our second child had been born, a 7lb 3oz baby girl! The problem was that she was in a hospital two hours journey away, so if I were to go and visit them I would not have been back in time for the match. But before I even asked, my wife said that she had done her job, and now it was time for me to do mine and win gold! I would like to thank all thirteen of the Welsh boys that day, because if we had not won gold I would have been in big trouble!

Casting Techniques

Enough of my past, let's get down to the business of casting. This can be the most frustrating barrier to get over when you start to fly fish. Done properly it is poetry in motion and looks effortless; done badly and it looks painful. After one demonstration one member of the audience commented

Hywel holding the cup after Wales won gold at the 2004 Home International Fly Fishing Competition. Hywel, who had earlier learnt that he was a father again, was the top Welsh rod.

that I could nearly make the rod and line talk. Just remember, keep practising. The one thing I will say is that the more relaxed you are, the smoother and easier the casting will become; whereas the tenser you are, the more it becomes difficult and the more you upset the rhythm of the cast.

The Way You Stand

The first thing to look at is the way you stand, and there are two schools of thought here: the closed stance and the open stance. The closed stance is great for short, accurate casts: this is right foot forward for the right hander, and vice versa for the left hander. In the open stance it is left foot forward for the right hander, which lends itself for distance work. But when you start, don't get bogged down in detail, just have your feet shoulder-width apart and your weight evenly distributed between both feet.

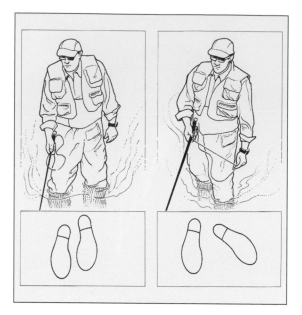

Beginners should stand with their feet shoulder-width apart, with their weight evenly balanced between both feet.

The Way You Hold the Rod

The next step is to hold the rod comfortably, and you can use any grip as long as it suits you. The traditional grip is thumb on top, or you can place your thumb to the side of the handle with your first knuckle going up the back of the rod. This is the grip I use when distance casting, as it gives you more leverage and enables you to put more power into the cast (but more of that later). Another way is to put your index finger pointing up the side of the rod, which a lot of anglers like as it enables them to obtain straighter casts. But the most important thing is to be comfortable, as this will make the casting smoother and more relaxed. How to hold the arm is easily explained, because by just dropping your arm by your side and bending at the elbow you automatically get into the start position for casting.

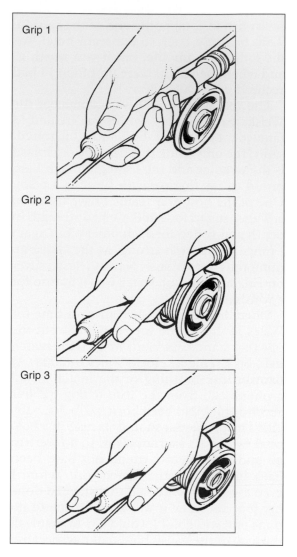

Grip 1 is the traditional grip with the thumb on top. There are two alternatives: thumb at the side (grip 2), and the index finger pointing up the rod (grip 3).

The Roll Cast

To start the cast, just feed out some 8–10yd of line outside the tip ring, which is easily done by just moving the tip of the rod back and forth while leaving line out. Once you have done this, lift the rod into the upright position and tap the rod forwards. This is

The roll cast.

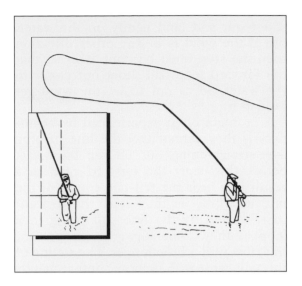

The overhead cast showing the stop position.

the roll cast, and can get you out of trouble whenever something goes wrong.

The Overhead Cast

The overhead cast should always be started with a straight line from the tip of the rod, all the way down to the leader. Then start slowly, thinking of it as acceleration to the vertical with a pause, and then the same thing on the forward cast: start slowly, and speed up to your stop position. The stop position is always dictated by the wind: if it's from behind, then you stop the tip of the rod early, which will allow the line to

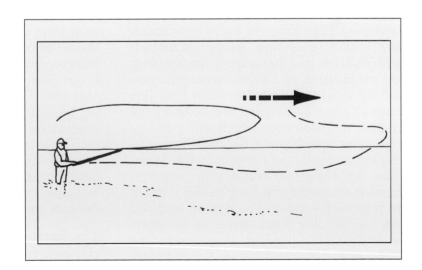

The overhead cast showing the forward stop position.

shoot out and land gently on the water, but if the wind is in any other direction then the stop must be done later so that the forward loop will shoot out closer to the water, so as not to let the wind get hold of it.

A problem often experienced by beginners is they cannot feel the line turning over/straightening out on the back cast before they start the forward cast; as a result you hear the tell-tale sound of the line whipping as they start the forward cast, caused by the line still being in a loop as they come forwards. To prevent this, just wait a little longer. The timing of this will come with practice; unfortunately you can't do this by counting, as the pause depends on how much line you have in the air: the longer the line, the longer the pause.

Obtaining More Distance

After you have accomplished this – and it might take a little time – the next step is to try and obtain some more distance. To do this you have to load the rod a bit more, and the easiest way of doing this is to introduce the single haul, which is when you pull the line with the non-casting arm as you are accelerating the rod into the back cast. This is easy to do, as both hands are working the same. As you slowly lift with the rod, you slowly draw the line with the other hand, and as you accelerate into the back cast you speed up with your line hand. This will increase the bend in the rod on the back cast, which will give you more line speed going backwards, resulting in more rod load for your forward cast. The one important factor with your line hand is that after you have pulled it down to your side, it must remain there, and you release the line from there; at no point should your line hand travel up to meet the rod, because this will release the rod load, as slack line is allowed to run through the

rings: this will result in the total collapse of the cast.

The Double Haul Cast

The ultimate casting technique is the double haul, which will add great distance to your cast (*see* opposite). However, it can be very difficult to learn as both hands are working at different speeds, and if your rod hand cannot take care of itself without you thinking about it, then you should practise until the rod hand is automatic so that you can concentrate on your hauling hand. Once you have done this, then the next step is to forget about the single haul and think of the first haul on the back cast as a short sharp pull (think down and up), no more than 12–18in (30–45cm); this will enable you to get the hauling hand back up to meet the rod at the top of the back cast in preparation for the forward cast. If the first haul is too long, then you will never get it up to meet the rod, and you might suffer from slack line between the hauling hand and the butt ring.

Once both hands are together at the upright position, start the forward cast with both hands moving forwards together; and as you start to load the rod under the weight of the line, draw the line hand away from the rod. Both rod and line hand should be travelling at maximum speed just before release. Jack Martin told me when I was learning to cast with tournament gear that if I had a watch on the wrist of my hauling hand then I should break the strap off on the final delivery, and if I didn't then I was not hauling hard enough. I know with fishing gear you don't have to pull so hard, but still the hands need to be travelling as fast as possible without overloading the gear you are using.

The Extended Double Haul

Once you have mastered the above, the next step is what I call the extended double haul,

Short, sharp pull of the line downwards.

Both hands meet at the top of the back cast.

The left hand accelerates away from the rod hand.

Release the line at maximum speed.

where on the back cast instead of stopping the rod just after the vertical, you let it drift as far back as possible. In ideal conditions the rod can be placed nearly horizontal: this allows far more rod loading room, as well as opening up room for a longer haul. This is ultimate double haul, and needs to be practised a lot because your timing has to be perfect: the line will be travelling so close to the ground on the back cast that if you are just off, then it will end up on the grass behind you.

To do this cast you do have to change your body position slightly, because it will enable you to drift the rod more easily, and allow you to keep the cast smooth. This position is known as the exaggerated open stance, and comes from tournament casting, which does get the best out of every outfit you use. For a right-hander, place your left foot pointing slightly to the left of where you are casting: this opens your hips to the cast and enables you to use them at the start of the forward cast. The best comparison is with a javelin thrower, who will start the forward motion with the hips rotating first, then the shoulder, and then the arm comes through; the only difference between this and a caster is that the javelin thrower has a run up and the caster doesn't, and he lets go of the javelin at the point when the caster turns the tip over.

Salmon Casting

Salmon casting is probably the hardest technique of all to learn, or so everybody

The single spey cast. The anchor point is to the right of the angler and upstream of where he is casting.

thinks, but in fact the basic casts such as the roll cast and overhead casts are far easier to learn with a two-handed rod than with a single-handed rod. This is because the lever you are using – the rod – is far longer, and you are using two hands, and it takes less effort to make the whole thing work.

When I teach anglers to use a salmon rod the first step is to get them to use both hands in the opposite direction. I first start them casting overhead, as this is the easiest way of getting them to use both hands. So as you are pulling your top hand up towards you for the back cast, the bottom hand should be pushing away. For the forward cast the top hand pushes away from the body as the bottom hand pulls into the body. This should be repeated several times so that both hands get used to moving in opposite directions – and once you feel it is working well, try to swap the hands over and have your weaker one up the rod; this will stand you in good stead as you try and learn the more advanced casts needed to fish for salmon.

The Single Spey Cast

The next step is to learn the roll cast, as this is the start of the mythical spey casts – which in fact are only roll casts with changes of direction. The old roll cast was taught to me many years ago at a CLA Game Fair by Arthur Oglesby, and he would say that you draw the rod up slowly into the 1 o'clock position, wait for the belly of the line to settle and create the D loop; then his actual words were, 'Now try and break the rod!' which to a twelve year old was a great challenge! I never did it, but it certainly made the roll cast easy.

Once this has been achieved, then you must move on to the jump roll, as this is the first and most important part of the single spey. If you are practising this on moving water before you start, just drop the tip down to the water so that the line goes tight, and when you move the tip the line will move; then lift the rod to 10 o'clock, and sweep it to the side, then back into the roll cast position. What you are trying to achieve with this is to lift the front part of the line and leader and place it in an anchor position diagonally to the side of you. This will take some practice, and the best way I have found to do this is to practise on grass by placing a rod tube down by the side of you, and trying to place the line on top of it every time.

Once the above has been achieved, then moving to a single spey is easy, because the only thing you do differently to the jump roll is that as you sweep the line into position, you turn your body at the same time. This results in the line being placed in an anchor point further to your right. The important thing when you are using the single spey when you are fishing is always to watch where your fly lands, and always place it downriver from where it landed, otherwise you will cross the line and end up in a tangle.

The Double Spey Cast

This cast is seen by many as the most difficult of all salmon casts to learn, but in fact it is far easier than the single spey, because with the single, you, the angler, have to dictate the anchor position, but with the double the cast will do it for you. To execute this cast, first drop the tip down to the water to obtain a straight line, then start lifting the tip upriver – you will end up with your arms crossed over each other – then sweep around following the line on the water all the way round to the roll cast position, before doing the forward cast.

I hope this 'whistle stop' tour of casting helps you catch more fish! (See also my website www.hywelmorgan.co.uk)

5 Sea Trout

By Mike Green

About the Author

Mike Green is a retired optometrist who started fishing some sixty-two years ago when he was four years of age. He enjoys most branches of the sport, including sea angling, and has fished for trout, sea trout and salmon, bonefish, and many species of coarse fish. His favourite species are the predators, namely pike, zander, perch and chub, and pursuing these with a fly rod is his idea of paradise. His fishing career has taken him to some breathtakingly spectacular places both in the British Isles and further afield, including Alaska, Canada, New Zealand, the Bahamas, France, Spain, Egypt and the Seychelles. Mike has a real passion for fishing, and this is clearly revealed in his contributions to this book.

My Pursuit of the Sea Trout

Pound for pound, very few freshwater fish fight harder or more spectacularly than the sea trout, and their pursuit with the fly rod must rate as one of the very best experiences in the sport of angling. When fresh from the sea and 'in the mood' they can be so easy to hook – and yet, when conditions do not suit them, you would swear there wasn't a fish in the whole river! Takes can vary enormously from a ferocious pull that threatens to rip your arm off, to a gentle 'happening' that is hard to describe, almost ethereal in nature. At times, in the pitch black of an overcast starless night, I have been concentrating hard on making smooth, quiet casts and slowly 'figure-of-eighting' as the fly was swinging gently round in the current, when 'something' has happened. It's perhaps as though a tiny twig or other debris has almost imperceptibly touched it, yet the ensuing reflex strike has met with the solid resistance and head-shaking power of another good sea trout. Little could be more exciting than experiences like this!

Sea trout are often caught 'by mistake' on flies intended for salmon, usually (but not always) in the rough water at the head of pools; I have myself caught, and have witnessed my friends catch, some really big specimens on 2in salmon autumn tube flies on the River Tweed. Invariably, however, those fish were very coloured, having been in the river for some time, and were almost always returned.

The quest for sea trout tends to be a night-time activity as a rule, and there is no doubt that fish are most active in the hours of darkness. Hugh Falkus, in his well respected book on sea trout fishing, said that you should not start fishing until it is too dark to see your fingers at arm's length. However, there are always exceptions to every general rule, and in fact I have seen times when the fish have been charging about (and taking my offerings) in the gathering dusk, then turning off completely as real darkness has fallen. It could be, however, that this was due to a fall in temperature, as sometimes they can be very sensitive to such things.

The Fish Itself

I could be wrong on this point, but I believe there is no genetic difference between a brown trout and a sea trout. If this is so, the latter is simply a brown trout that goes to sea in order to enjoy better feeding than he would have found had he stayed in the river. In the case of salmon it seems to be fairly well documented where and how far they go during their marine life, whereas as far as I am aware, the movement of sea trout, once they leave the river as smolts, is more of a mystery. I have heard it said that they tend not to move far from their own estuary, but I am not at all certain whether or not this is the case.

When they return to the river of their origin, as with salmon, nature shuts down the need to fill their bellies with food. There is, however, a definite difference between the species in this respect, because whereas salmon almost never have food in their digestive tracts, the stomachs of freshly caught sea trout often *do* contain a certain number of insects, tiny fry and suchlike. This is especially the case when they have recently moved into the river system from the sea. As time goes on, and they spend longer in freshwater, I believe that their stomachs tend to shrink as the amount of food that they ingest decreases, and this would explain why they become harder to catch as they become more 'stale'. It also lends evidence to the theory that fresh-run sea trout will eagerly crash into large fry-imitating flies, whereas when they have been in the river for some time, the angler may fare better with much smaller insect-representing flies. You could also argue that

the longer the fish remain in the river, the more they may be reminded of their early days as parr and smolts when they were eating small nymphs, flies and crustaceans. This is pure conjecture, however, and nobody knows for sure!

Early Experiences

As far as I can remember, my first encounter with sea trout (on fly, anyway!), was again on the River Helmsdale. I was told by Jimmy Mackay, the then proprietor of the Navidale House Hotel, that, as I was on Beat 5, I should not waste the opportunity of fishing the Craggie Bend at dusk. He assured me that sea trout were running the river, and many of them would be intent on making their way up the Craggie Burn where they traditionally spawned. I duly made my way up to the aforementioned pool armed with my 7wt trout rod and an 8lb leader with two Teal Blue and Silvers, size 6, which, I was promised, would 'do the trick'!

The evening was perfect, warm and calm, and the water was clear with that peaty tinge common to most rivers in that part of the world. The presence of sea trout was not in doubt, because as soon as I arrived, the V waves and swirls were everywhere. The majority of the action seemed to be in the smoothly flowing tail of the pool below where the Craggie Burn joined the river, which, looking back, is what you might expect of fish looking to run the burn under cover of darkness. I started just above the burn mouth, and first cast had an arm-wrenching pull followed by several solid 'thumps' from what was obviously a decent fish – which then inexplicably came off! (How they do this, having seemed so firmly 'on', has never ceased to fascinate me.) But I had little time to be disappointed, as those fresh-run trout attacked my flies like tigers! I was astonished at the sheer power and aggression of the takes, and the acrobatic athleticism of their fight. It was thrilling fishing indeed, and a night I shall never forget!

I ceased operations when I had caught six fish, all of more or less identical size at a fraction under 2lb – and quite impressive they looked at breakfast time, laid out on a large silver platter. The Teal Blue and Silvers had worked 'like a dream', and, naturally, became my first choice sea trout fly. It is still a very good bet to this day, though I later discovered what I feel is a much better one. Nevertheless, the Teal Blue and Silver caught sea trout for me on the Helmsdale, Cree, Beauly, Nairn, Conon, Ewe and Ness in Scotland, and also the Mawdach, Conway and Dovey in Wales.

I had a really memorable night on the River Ewe, which runs its short course from the famous Loch Maree to the sea at Poolewe in Sutherland. My good friend Willie Armstrong from Inverness somehow wangled me the opportunity to fish there for a night with him, and though he took to his car for a sleep, I persevered through the hours of darkness, and managed to catch (and release) a hundred fish before dawn! I must stress that the great majority of those fish were 'finnock' – small sea trout between 8oz and 1lb – though amongst them were half-a-dozen lovely trout between 3lb and 4½lb. Nevertheless, it made for another unforgettable memory, which I have never come remotely close to equalling since, and certainly never will now. The river must have been totally alive with fish that night, and I was lucky enough to be there to take advantage of the fact. (I wish I still had that degree of stamina today!)

Another little event that I clearly remember was at the end of a week I had on the Scottish Blackwater and Junction Pool on the Conon. The water was low, the sun hot, and the fish stale and very hard to tempt.

(My twin boys were four or five months old at the time, which makes it thirty years ago – frightening thought!) Anyway, I tried early and late as the only possible chance, and managed to catch and release a coloured salmon from the Blackwater. That was my only fish until the end of the last day, when I tempted a nice 10lb salmon by stripping a tiny size 14 black and yellow 'Tosh' in desperation as the light started to fade.

Encouraged by this success, I decided to have a go at two or three large sea trout I had spotted jumping right at the tail of the Junction Pool, just above the road bridge. I had never fished that part of the pool, and it was quite a bit deeper than I had anticipated. (Looking back, I should have had an exploratory wade down there in the daylight!) Anyway, I edged my way out as far as I could – rather apprehensively! – and cast my Teal Blue and Silvers out into the darkness. The flies could not have travelled three yards when everything tightened with a vigorous pull, and I eventually netted a 4lb silver beauty of a sea trout, followed shortly after by another, slightly smaller at 3lb! The thrill of a solid take from an unseen fish somewhere out there in the darkness has to be experienced to really be appreciated, and I was quite proud of my display of the three lovely fish at breakfast, on a difficult week, and felt that I had earned them.

The Haslam

On one occasion when I was fishing on the Conway with Roy Thomas, he showed me a fly tied for him by Frank Cutler, and which had worked spectacularly well for himself and Cyril Inwood in the early days. It was introduced to me as the Haslam, and I liked the look of it immediately; I soon had some tied up, and never really looked back. Apart from when I am fishing the sunk

One night's catch by the author. At that time it seemed that the huge runs of sea trout would go on for ever. Sadly, however, they seem to be much more of a rarity these days, for whatever reason. (Harvesting sand eels for fertilizer probably hasn't helped!) Nevertheless, looking at this picture makes me feel slightly ashamed of killing so many fish.

line (of which more later), the Haslam is almost always on my cast, either as point fly or dropper, and over the years has caught many hundreds of sea trout as well as some lovely brownies to 6lb. It was my 'killer fly' on what I regard as my best ever one-night catch on the River Ness: fifteen sea trout, five of which were over 4lb (*see* photo), and it has caught me my best ever sea trout of 7lb 8oz. If this is not enough I have also taken several salmon 'by mistake' while sea-trouting in the 'gloaming' on the wonderful

Haslam! At worst it is a cracking pattern that I can heartily recommend to any game fisherman.

I was invited with Malcolm Patrick, my dentist and good fishing friend, to fish an evening on the Tamar in Devon by a charming fellow called David Pilkington. David was the local sea-trout 'hot shot', and had designed a fly known as the black/blue 'Bumble', which had done stalwart service in the tempting of many fine sea trout. He looked at my Haslam, a pattern new to him, with politeness, but suggested his Bumble would perhaps be a better bet. Being totally confident in the Haslam, naturally I kept it on. We met up at 1.30am for a debriefing, to find that Malcolm had caught two, David three, but the magic Haslam had caught twelve! I believe David now has one or two of this great pattern in his fly box, and I would suggest you would be well advised to do the same – indeed I would go further and say that if the fish won't look at it, then there is likely to be precious little else that *will* tempt them!

For those who can't wait any longer, here is the pattern:

Materials:
- Tag   Silver wire
- Body   Black silk
- Tail   Golden pheasant crest feather
- Throat   Blue hackle or squirrel hair
- Wing over   Black squirrel with mallard
- Cheeks   Jungle cock

Method:
The diagrams overleaf correspond to the numbered list of instructions.

1   Secure the single hook (usually size 12 to 6) in the vice, wind on the black thread, and tie in the silver wire, as shown.

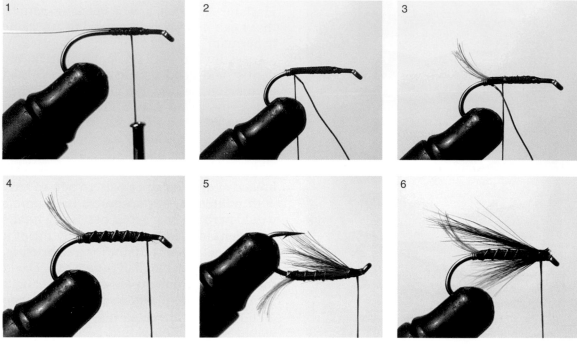

Tying the famous Haslam. See text for instructions.

2   Make three or four turns of wire to form the tag, and secure.

3   Tie in the golden pheasant crest feather tail, making sure that it sits nicely upright.

4   Form a nice even body, either with the tying thread, or alternatively with black silk or wool, then wind the silver wire over, making five even spiral ribs.

5   Turn the hook upside down in the vice, and trap in the blue throat at a length about two thirds of the way to the hook point.

6   With the hook upright once more, tie in the black squirrel under-wing, and the brown mallard over-wing, carefully ensuring that the ends of the wing fibres marry up nicely with the tip of the tail feather.

7   All that remains is to add the jungle cock 'cheeks'. Make a whip finish, and varnish the head, firstly with clear, then with black varnish for a shiny professional effect.

And that's it, a simple fly to tie, and one that can be devastatingly attractive to sea trout. Please do give it a try.

While on the subject of flies, one summer on what was at that time my regular two weeks on the Laggan Beat of the River Ness, the water was 'on its bones', and the

A selection of M.G. sea trout flies: 1, 2 and 3: Haslams. 4 and 5: Blue Zulus (good dropper flies). 6 and 7: Teal Blue and Silvers. 8 and 9: Peter Ross. 10: Surface Muddler. 11: Frank Cutler's original Haslam lure. 12: Surface Muddler. 13–16: Sunk lures for late night sunk-line fishing.

chances of a salmon just about nil! Willie Armstrong, the then owner of the stretch, said to me, 'You won't need your Haslams this time. Use tiny black flies on 12 and 14 hooks, that's all they will look at.' This proved to be the case. My father and I caught no salmon that time (I didn't even try for them!), but I did catch seventy-eight sea trout for the two weeks, and almost all on the tiny black flies suggested by Willie. The ones I tied were simply a peacock herl body kept short (low water style), and eight or nine black squirrel hairs for the wing; very effective they were, and worth remembering for low water conditions.

It was interesting, by the way, that on that trip I rowed all over the beat, and although it was low and gin clear, I hardly saw a fish. However, at dusk, out went the little black flies under the trees, and 'wallop', they were there all the time! It's just amazing how they can hide during the long, hot, bright days.

Basic Tactics

Sea trout fishing tends to involve two different approaches according to the time of night: the first involves late evening until midnight, and the second 1am until dawn.

The first phase of the sport is the one with which most anglers will be familiar. During daylight hours the sea trout will have been hiding away, either in the fast water at the head of pools, or perhaps in the shade of overhanging trees and vegetation; but as dusk gathers they become more active. They start patrolling around in the smooth, gentle water in the middle and tails of the pools, crashing about and sometimes swirling and slashing at sedges and hatching insects. If they are there, and the conditions favourable, you should certainly see signs of their presence.

A floating line is invariably used at this time of the day, and if I feel that the fish are fresh from the saltwater, I would generally follow the advice of the late great Hugh Falkus and use a large, silver-bodied lure on maybe a 2 or 4 long shank hook. A big 'Silver Blue' was Hugh's first choice, but to be honest I think it matters little. A wily ghillie on the River Ness, whose reel I often heard screaming with fish after fish in the July darkness, showed me his favourite lure: it was a 1in stoat's tail black tube fly, which he said was all he ever used, or ever would use. He certainly had his fair share of sea trout, and more than once I saw the bottom of his boat completely covered with those silver beauties. (The fact that he then took them up to the pub and exchanged them for whisky is another story!) The point is, that in the right conditions of warmth and darkness, fresh-run sea trout will eagerly attack almost any pattern of largish fly.

The 'right conditions' brings me to another extremely important point, which is that I don't know of any other fish so sensitive to atmospheric conditions. In the distant past, being rather keener than I am these days, I would fish regardless of the weather: wind, rain or cold, I would be out there, often until dawn – but after countless fruitless such episodes, my considered conclusions are these: mild, dull, still, overcast dark nights are *ideal*. But if, as dusk approaches, it starts to rain, the temperature suddenly drops, the moon comes out, a wind gets up, or, worst of all, a mist comes on the water, go home and have a large scotch! I know there is always a chance while your fly is in the water … but I can *never* recall catching a decent fish in any of the above-mentioned conditions, and I would go so far as to say that you would be wasting your time to continue.

And when the fish 'go off', they leave you in no doubt because the river goes completely dead – no splashes, no 'V's, no rises, nothing. Part of the reason may be that they don't actually *need* to feed, but are (we think) acting on instinct. At sea they do much of their feeding at dawn and dusk when the prey fish can be approached more readily, and the memories of those gorging sprees remain strongly embedded in their minds. In other words, while conditions suit, they just can't resist attacking something that presents an easy target, and reminds them of the sort of food they were eating in salt water.

When inhibited by atmospherics, however, they just switch off, keep their mouths closed, and live off their fitness, strength and body fat. The longer they remain in the river, the more this tends to happen, and the harder they become to catch, even in seemingly ideal circumstances. Annoyingly, on the odd occasion when everything seems perfect, they just don't want to know. You go to the 'hot spot', present your fly as perfectly as you know how and – they totally ignore it! But that's sea trout fishing at times, I'm afraid, and you either have to 'take it on the chin', or fish for something else!

Even when you are enjoying a good catch, and getting some sort of action every few casts, suddenly everything seems to change. You may get a couple of 'on and offs', then an odd 'tweak' – and then the river goes completely dead! You can't mistake it, and persevere as you may, for a while, at least – but it's over!

At this stage my advice is to cease operations, and follow one of two courses: either go home, have a whisky and then to bed; or have a cup of strong coffee in the fishing hut, rest for an hour, then set up (or pick up) your other outfit, and get back to it! This brings me to phase two of the plan, namely 1am until dawn.

This stage of the sea-trout fishing saga has, I must admit, always fascinated me. The action is invariably quite a bit slower, but the rewards can be electrifying. Almost always a sinking line is used, the density of which is determined by the depth and flow of the river. The fish are now settled and have taken up position close to the river bed. They are not now actively looking for food, but are basically having a rest. Nevertheless, a large, lightly dressed lure travelling slowly and steadily across their noses can still induce a positive response, and that response is not only nerve-tingling and heart-stopping, but can also result in the capture of the biggest fish of the night.

I have lost count of the number of times the ambience of the situation has completely enveloped me. I have been concentrating so hard on leading that fly gently around in front of the fish, the darkness has seemed to sharpen my senses to the point that I have almost imagined myself to be the fly – at risk of sounding 'airy fairy', at times like this it has seemed to me that I could actually *feel* the presence of the fish (strange things happen in the dark!). Then, in the midst of all this attentive fishing, has come the solid thump of a taking fish, followed by complete mayhem

An early session M.G. sea trout catch by the author on floating line and Haslam fly. The largest fish weighed 7lb exactly.

as a big angry sea trout has screamed off downstream.

I find it hard to describe the intensity of the excitement that grips you at times like this. It is certainly not for those with a weak heart, but surely must rank as one of the most breathtakingly wonderful experiences in the whole of angling! There is the powerful head shaking as the fish tries to eject the hook, followed by a series of runs, cartwheels and leaps while the ratchet on your reel screams in protest! It is well worth persevering with the sunk line tactics for such a reward, and I would urge you to keep at it, despite no obvious signs of fish. That next cast could be the one!

As to the lure itself, I would advise something about 2in to 3in long, with a silver body, a black or badger lightly dressed wing, and a red or blue throat hackle. You can use two size 4 or 6 long shank lure hooks in tandem, or possibly a small treble as the 'stinger' or tail hook. Don't be too fussy – as I once read, in my very early days of trout fishing (in a book by the great Tom Ivens?): 'It ain't what you fish, it's the way that you fish it!'

Another consideration is *stealth*. I have mentioned above how sensitive sea trout are to atmospherics. Well, perhaps I should go further and state that they are extremely sensitive to *everything*! Much of my sea trouting on the River Ness has been from a boat, either on my own, or with one of my twin boys. When fishing together we have always tried to behave like Apaches, with every movement slow and gentle, and taking great care not to drop a priest (or anything else) in the boat. Remember that the fish are relatively close, and the quieter you are, the better, and invariably in suitable conditions we have nearly always done well. I recall a late night session with son number two, James, when he caught six lovely sea trout all between 2lb and 4lb, and topped by a cracking 6lb brownie!

Don't make a sound, don't make a ripple, is the best advice I can give you, because sea trout are not stupid!

Bait/Fly Combination

I have heard it said that there are times when sea trout will only take a fly whose hook is adorned with two or three maggots. It is usually legal to do this (though I would check first), and I have to say that on a couple of occasions in the past I have given the method a good try, and caught fish. There is, however, the inconvenience of carrying the wriggling little brutes somewhere on your person, and another big drawback is that maggots are not particularly tough, so unless you cultivate an extremely gentle casting style, you will find that every three or four casts they have disappeared and fresh ones have to be added to the hook. Personally I find this too annoying for words, and perhaps even more importantly, I really do not believe that the addition of 'bait' to the tail of the fly makes any meaningful difference. My assertion is that a well presented, well tied sea-trout fly will catch all the fish anyone should need. I have not used maggots in this way for many years now, and have caught plenty enough good sea trout to keep me happy. Try it if you fancy to, by all means, but I expect you will come to the same conclusion as I did. Have confidence in your fly, fish it as well as you can, and be stealthy – and you will catch plenty of trout!

The Surface Lure

This is another 'string to your bow', and one that I am far more enthusiastic about!

Most reservoir trout fishers will be familiar with fishing muddler minnows or 'poppers' for rainbows, ripping them across the waves and watching those exciting bow waves as fish roar up behind the fly. Well, the surface lure for sea trout is basically an extension of the same idea. It can be devastatingly successful on dark calm nights (the darker the better), and really heart-stopping when they take it with a sudden savage swirl. This is not always the case, however, because although the lure is literally on the surface, sometimes the line tightens without any visual warning whatsoever, and suddenly you find yourself attached to your quarry. How the fish manage this feat I am never quite sure!

Whether or not they actually take it, the surface lure is a good way of establishing if the fish are there, because they will usually at least come up and have a look at it. You may see a 'V' wake coming up behind the lure, or a sudden splash at, or just behind it; but I would say that, as with rainbows, for every one you actually hook, another three or four will show themselves in this way. Unlike rainbow trout fishing, I have not found it successful to strip the fly, but rather to fish it 'down and across' in the same way as a normal fly, and slowly 'fig-ure-of-eight' it as the line swings around in the stream. What you are trying to achieve is an imitation of a large insect or small creature making its way steadily across the surface. It can be very exciting and, like the sunk line technique, will often entice the biggest fish of the night.

Not a huge fish for some rivers, but a really nice one for the River Ness, and my personal best sea trout at 7lb 8oz, as described in the text.

Conclusion

I would like to finish this chapter by recall-ing one of my most memorable episodes sea-trouting with my twin boys on the River Ness. They were in their early teens and both good fishers. I sent them out in the boat together while I took my chances wading, and we were to meet up at mid-night for a whisky in the hut. It was Satur-day evening at the end of a great and suc-cessful week. It seemed to take forever to get dark, but eventually I waded out like a heron and made a cast. Five seconds later I was playing a 2lb sea trout on the dropper fly, a blue Zulu, size 12. That fight totally ruined my leader, and at 11.30pm I nearly gave up and called it a night. However, I knew the boys would fish it to the bitter end, so with headlight and spectacles I made another leader with just one fly, a size 12 Haslam (of *course!*) on a long shank size 12 hook. I waded out again as carefully as I could, and cast out into the darkness.

Almost immediately my arm was nearly ripped off by a savage pull, followed by several big crashes and long shattering runs. I said a quick prayer that this one would not come off, as it was obviously a 'belter'; and after a long battle, I was relieved to see a substantial silver flank slide over the rim of my net. It just had to be a sea trout after such an aerial display, and a shine of my headlight into the net confirmed the fact – 7½lb of silver per-fection! What a terrific end to the week! As I arrived back at the hut I could hear the boys rowing back up the beat, so I hurriedly put the kettle on, put the two-pounder on the usual sheet on the floor, and the big one on the table. The lads burst in, saying 'Not bad, we've had four fish up to 2lb. Any luck yourself?'

'Yes, I've had a nice one,' I replied. They glanced down at the two-pounder in the customary place and said, 'Yes – nice one!'

'No, not that one – this one,' I laughed, pointing at the table. Their faces were a picture, and we had an extra large one that night!

Lastly, if I have passed on any useful ideas to regular sea-trout addicts, or encouraged any fishers who have not yet tried this won-derful branch of our sport to give it a go, I shall have achieved my aim.

Tight lines to one and all!

6 Salmon in the South of England

By Dave Steuart

Dave Steuart's first salmon. Caught from the 'Royalty Fishery' on the Hampshire Avon at Christchurch in 1951 when trotting for barbel with maggots. The fishery manager, Brian Parkinson, gaffed the fish, as all salmon were killed in those days.

About the Author

Dave Steuart is an all-rounder who fishes for every species of fish when the opportunity arises, whether it is coarse fishing, game fishing or sea fishing, at home or abroad. Even so, he is one of those few anglers in Britain who has managed to catch hundreds of salmon from the South of England. Due to the pressure of work he was only able to fish once, or sometimes twice in a week, but has nevertheless from South Country rivers twice caught over fifty salmon in a season, and once over sixty – even though on many of the South Country salmon beats, where a rod is let on one day per week or one day per fortnight, many of the rods consider they have done well if they end up the season with just half a dozen fish. But what fish they could be in the 'glory days': they could be 20lb, 30lb or even 40lb, and there is still the possibility of 30lb salmon from southern beats; and even though the spring runs of salmon have declined so drastically in the major southern rivers, there is still the chance of a very big fish coming to the landing net. In Dave Steuart's early days it would have been to the 'gaff', as nearly all salmon caught were killed; however, nowadays most salmon are returned to the rivers, a policy that will continue until the species is less vulnerable to extinction, and so the net is the necessary landing tool.

(Cont.)

(Cont.)

Dave Steuart was one of the first anglers to return all his fish to the river: because the species was becoming scarce as compared to his early days of salmon fishing, he began returning every salmon he caught in 1990. He wrote an article in *Trout and Salmon* to support his views that salmon could be returned safely to rivers, and this article was quoted by the NRA at a salmon seminar in Winchester, when it asked anglers to do the same. Returning salmon has now become almost standard practice in the South. Yet even this season (2007), a few salmon over 30lb have been taken from southern rivers. Dave Steuart never made the 40lb mark, but he got very near it with a fish of 39lb, and took many fish topping 20lb. It was many years ago, in 1966, that he caught his first thirty-pounder.

From southern England he has caught salmon from the Dorset Stour, the Hampshire Avon, the Test, the Itchen and the Fowey, but he has increased his knowledge of the species with catches from Cumbria, Scotland, Ireland, Canada and Alaska. He has also increased the sizes of his catches, with the Canadian and Alaskan Pacific species to 51lb. Although he is nearly eighty years old, he is still catching a few Atlantics from the South Country rivers.

In his chapters Dave Steuart describes the problems salmon have to overcome just to make it to the sea and back in order to feed up and propagate, for the very survival of the species. The natural problems are many, but the salmon has survived them for thousands of years. Man's interference with the 'balance', however, is something else, and only time will tell if the salmon can overcome the ways of human evolution.

The Incredible Migrations

Homing

Practically every angler, and most certainly salmon anglers, will have a general idea of the incredible lives of salmon, and how they travel from their feeding grounds off Greenland to their respective rivers where they spawn. They will know that the resulting offspring will make their way to the same areas to feed until maturity, probably sexual maturity will start kicking in, and they too will then follow the same routes as their parents back to where they were born, whether to Ireland, Britain, Europe or the Americas. That is how it should be; but it isn't as simple as that.

There are many dangers on those journeys. Apart from the predators at sea large enough to tackle a salmon, since man started exploiting the Atlantic feeding grounds and some migration routes, he has made enormous inroads into the populations of salmon by over-harvesting, and many thousands of tons of salmon, millions of fish, have been removed from the sea, and therefore have no longer returned to their rivers of origin to fulfil their purpose of propagation. Although the Eskimos had known of the feeding grounds off Greenland for over 200 years, and as long ago as 1955 a fish from Ireland was recorded off Sukkertoppen (a tagged fish?), they did not realize the commercial possibilities until the Danes showed a real interest around 1964; by 1967 it was reported that 1,350,000 salmon had been killed off Greenland that year.

Since the Danes and Eskimos started their commercial ventures, and the Faroese long-liners also exploited the salmon resource, various 'buy-outs' of the North Atlantic netting interests, and 'quotas', did limit catches, and as it was also evident that the over-harvesting was resulting in a

A 26lb salmon from the River Test. One of many hundreds of salmon Dave has caught from that river.

reduced 'take', some of the netsmen were amenable to the conditions imposed, for compensation!

There is also hope that one of the greatest dangers to the species while at sea, drift netting, is now almost eliminated. The biggest problem for *our* southern populations of salmon was the Irish drift nets, but as I write this in March 2007, there has been jubilation among salmon anglers, because after a long battle between the Irish government and the angling fraternity – notably Orri Vigfusson of the North Atlantic Salmon Fund (NASF) and Brian Marshall of the Wessex Salmon and Rivers Trust (WSRT) – the Irish drift nets are now banned. It is difficult to give enough praise for the work these two men and their organizations have done over many years to accomplish this, along with others of a similar persuasion. All salmon anglers owe the organizations devoted to the welfare of the species a great debt.

Unfortunately I believe the Faroese started fishing commercially again for salmon in the year 2000, and another problem is the unregulated Atlantic Salmon Fishery by nations not under the North Atlantic Salmon Conservation Organisation. Also, man being man, there will always be illegal drift nets and other forms of illegal netting, and I have seen reports of illegal drift-netting by the Danes; and when one considers the length of some drift nets, which I guess is only possible because of the invention of nylon, it is amazing that anything survives. I don't know if it is true, but in 1992 I read of a Japanese net that was *63 miles (100km) long*. The boat, the *Sumiyoshi-Maru*, was escorted into La Rochelle by the French Navy and heavily fined. France only allows drift nets up to 1.24 miles (2km) long. However, now that the number of drift nets is less, things should be looking better for the mature salmon on their way to the spawning beds, and if that was their only difficulty, they would – but there are several more dangers that they must overcome.

As the mature fish arrive at their estuaries, predation by seals is a huge problem, and this has doubtless been exacerbated as a result of media intrusion, which supports the perpetuation of all pretty-faced creatures in spite of their predation of more useful species. I appreciate that one could argue that seals have as much right to live as salmon, but as seals have no predators around our shores they do not fit within a balance of the ecology without an occasional cull. The increase in the seal population is staggering. The estimated number of seals around our shores in 1954 was 20,000; by 1988 it had risen to an incredible 90,000. According to DEFRA the seal population of the United Kingdom is at present 30,000 common seals and 115,000 grey seals, which just demonstrates the seal's resilience in view of the fact that at one time it was considered the disease phocine

91

A nice fresh fish caught from the River Test in the pool in front of his house, situated on the side of his 'Abbey Mill Fishery'.

distemper virus (PDV) might have reduced its numbers considerably. The number of homing salmon taken by seals doesn't bear thinking about.

Homing salmon do occasionally get lost and turn up in rivers that are not those in which they were born. I live on the banks of the River Test and have owned a small stretch that had a good salmon run thirty years ago when I bought it, and among the hundreds of fish taken here we have had fish that have been tagged in both the Avon and Frome. I look upon these fish as nature's deliberate mistakes. If salmon only ever returned to the rivers of their birth they would never have spread their species

from their original source. Authorities tend to refer to the genetic purity of the salmon of a river, and consider that it is essential to preserve it. I am not so sure, and the fact that fish occasionally run the wrong river is a natural way of spreading genes. Also, over many decades, man has spread the genes from various river sources to our southern rivers, and to my belief, very successfully. Does the amazing regeneration of the River Tyne salmon have a mixed gene pool?

Perhaps here is a good place to say that my knowledge of southern rivers is mostly confined to the Test, Itchen, Avon and Stour; I don't know the rivers of the South West so well, although the couple of times I fished the River Fowey my methods worked well enough. The River Test and the River Itchen are Sites of Special Scientific Interest (SSSI), and the River Itchen is also a candidate Special Area of Conservation (cSAC).

Another of nature's survival techniques is that the return of homing salmon is spread over a period, sometimes several months. Thus if there were a natural catastrophe and all the fish in a river were wiped out, the next lot of salmon to arrive would ensure the continuation of the species.

Those salmon that have arrived at the estuary having survived or escaped the dangers of the sea journey, and the seals, what then? At the mouth of some rivers are various forms of netting that all take their toll: some are legal, some not, but they all deprive the river of fish that would, or should, produce progeny for the future survival of the species. A few decades past, before man increased the dangers to the salmon at sea, there were so many returning fish, and such successful spawning over clean gravels, that it was possible to crop the returning fish in goodly numbers; but now that the number of returning fish to our southern rivers is greatly reduced, it is not a practice that should continue until

The 'third of the season', caught just downstream of the house in 2001. This fish, 14lb 12oz, was returned, as by then, Dave had long been returning all salmon caught.

Another Test fish from years past when they were killed. Dave's Alsatian poses quite proudly.

stocks rebuild to sustainable levels. And that includes the catches of anglers. The EA admits that the salmon of the Test and Itchen are *not* at sustainable levels and therefore the species is in danger of disappearing from southern chalk streams.

As an example of progressive understanding of present problems, in 1996 WSRT started negotiations with the Avon netsmen at Mudeford to sell all of their catch to them to be returned to the river or retained for broodstock. The Avon netsmen must be applauded, as they have fully cooperated in the efforts made to save the salmon in the Avon, and, one hopes, any fish that may still wish to run the Dorset Stour. This is still an ongoing situation. But further than that, I believe all Avon salmon anglers voluntarily return their fish to the river.

So salmon have entered the estuaries on a high tide, and with good levels within the river systems are eager to run up the rivers; but there are difficulties here, also. As salmon are cold-blooded and take the temperature of the water in which they find themselves, it needs to be warm enough for their metabolic rate to be sufficient to enable them to have the energy to swim upstream, and even more important, to have the energy and ability to surmount any obstacles in their way. They will enter rivers willingly enough in almost freezing temperatures, but the river temperatures need to be above 40°F for them to easily ascend the obstacles they will need to pass on the upriver journey.

Barriers to salmon migrating upriver have unfortunately been with us for a few centuries. Since man first dammed rivers

Dave poses with a 22-pounder caught with one of the crank-handled rods he used to build, to be used with multiplier reels.

Dave caught plenty of salmon from the Dorset Stour. Two fine fish.

and streams, installed fishing dams, built mills and hydro-electric schemes, and impounded water, the salmon has had to battle against obstacles to its progress to the spawning grounds that were not naturally there. In some cases suitable fish passes have been placed within the barriers, but in many instances they have proved to be inadequate. As man requires more and more water for his modern lifestyle, abstraction, dredging and the lowering of water tables have between them denuded river systems to such an extent that what may have been an adequate pass for salmon to negotiate twenty or thirty years ago, is no longer suitable, and should be redesigned and rebuilt.

Unfortunately, the political will to improve fish passes here in the South by the various authorities has, in my opinion, been sadly lacking. For many years – indeed through most of my lifetime – it has been known that fish passage in some southern rivers has been extremely difficult; but to many, the authorities appear to have been reluctant to act to improve fish passage, even though they have had the power. We have a stretch of water nicknamed 'Dead End' because it is not possible for fish to pass sluices at the top end of the stream. Before I owned the water there were many salmon taken from it, but since I have owned it we pass as little water as possible through the sluices so that fish are not encouraged to enter. I took a couple of salmon from it when I first owned it, but have not fished it for over twenty-five years. I have arranged with the authorities to net and remove upstream any salmon, and at one time they moved sixty. I asked for a fish ladder to be built, but it was

A nice fresh fish from the River Itchen when using the centre-pin reel.

The River Fowey in Cornwall provided Dave with this fine fresh fish caught in December, a river noted for its 'back end' run of fine fish during the last few months of the year.

suggested to have a full-width baulk across the stream to raise levels and ease the pressure from the sluices. There is sufficient bank height to have two of these baulks at different levels, as an old-fashioned ladder, but it is probably fifteen to twenty years since the original suggestion, and nothing has come of it, although it has recently been mentioned again by the EA.

It is within the instrument of law that, 'Fisheries should be maintained, developed and improved.' Unfortunately, if that interfered with other authorities and their plans for development, agriculture, drainage, or whatever, those authorities sanctioned to deal with fisheries seem to have done almost nothing to stop damage occurring. And if it cost money to improve, or even maintain the status quo, in my opinion southern fisheries had little hope of things

happening. The NRA started to get their teeth into problems, but were then quickly integrated within the vastness of the EA. With my cynical outlook, I believed that would be the end of real power to Fisheries Divisions within that organization, and to justify that cynicism, grants were soon cut from an original £14,000,000 to £5,500,000. There is hope, though. The River Avon has seen access problems improved, so has the River Itchen, and the River Test now has a *promise* of a new fish pass for easy passage where anglers such as I have complained to the respective

Dave has also had plenty of fish from the Hampshire Avon.

authorities *over many years* that fish had difficulty in passing the obstructions.

It is beyond me why government, even with some opposing councils here in the South, continues to encourage an increasing population by building ever more houses, without considering where the water for these masses will come from, and what increases in capacity will be necessary to sewage treatment plants in order to dispose of the resulting wastes. We must not kid ourselves. Rivers are looked upon by many as waste disposal units, and I do not believe that much consideration is given to the future of our southern rivers in planning, although there is always plenty of *talk* about the environment – but the concept of continually building is political, and without interest in either conservation or ecology. There is little that gives

me any hope for the long-term future of salmon in the lowland rivers and chalk streams of southern England. Perhaps the rivers and streams of the South West will fare better.

As the salmon pass upriver there are areas where they will stay, maybe for a short while, a few hours, or even weeks. I have known salmon stay in my stretch for weeks, even though there have been big lifts of water. In such conditions in past years those fish would be joined by new arrivals from downstream. Some of those would stay, but many would pass through eventually, or quickly. I assume that the fish that stay with us are the progeny of fish that have previously spawned in our stretch, and are reluctant to pass on upriver to stretches they do not have a familiarity with, learned when they were parr. I recall some writer on salmon stating that salmon do not like to pass where they were spawned, so my observations may well point to that being generally the case.

It is considered by many who write about salmon habits that they are more inclined to run at night than during the day. Probably that is normal behaviour on many rivers, but I have seen many salmon passing upstream on the River Test in the day time – and sometimes running downstream, too. On natural rivers where there are few, or not any, man-made obstructions, but rocky natural impoundments of the river and natural barriers to surmount, salmon are known to approach these to maybe 'have a look' before attempting to jump to the upper level. They are usually extremely accurate in the height to which they jump, and never seem to jump higher than necessary. Of course, falls of considerable height and of great difficulty may be less easy to negotiate, and will need a few attempts before succeeding. Salmon stop jumping usually as the sun goes down as they can no longer judge with accuracy the height of the obstruction. These observations do point towards salmon travelling during daylight, or at least negotiating falls during the day.

As salmon are naturally leapers I do not like obstructions where they are expected to find their way through underpasses, such as beneath sluices. Their natural instincts are to find ways *over* obstructions, not to look for a hole to swim through. If there is a big 'head level' above sluices it is impossible for them to swim through, however large the opening.

Salmon do not appear to be monogamous, and when we used to have several redds I have watched cock fish spawn with a female, and have then seen the same cock with a different female on another redd. The female does all the cutting of the redd, and sometimes as early as November I have seen unattached females scraping, cutting redds, even though they do not usually spawn here on the River Test until around Christmas. This preliminary cutting is a common feature of hens here.

For some years before I owned a stretch of this river I used to travel down on Boxing Day to watch salmon spawning. The Test and some of the tributaries used to hold vast numbers of fish, pairing, cutting, spawning and chasing each other, especially aggressive cocks. There were always brown trout hanging around below spawning fish, on the scrounge for loose eggs, and they were continually chased by the cock salmon. The first time I ever saw precocious parr was when a large salmon of about 20lb that was spawning with a hen of some 15lb, turned downstream to chase away a large brown trout. Immediately a little salmon parr was beside this huge (to him) female and induced her to loose a few eggs, which he doubtless fertilized.

Extreme conditions can alter the normal patterns of spawning fish. I think it was during the very cold winter of 1962 when I was fishing the River Test during March for spring salmon, that the extreme cold had held back the salmon and they were spawning while I was fishing. Of course, I was fishing the pools and the salmon were on the shallows, but stale fish were still a nuisance, although I did get a nice 16lb beauty with sea lice, so the cold water had not stopped that fish running up the river.

The problems that spawning salmon have now, as compared to those days back in the 1950s and 1960s, is very poor egg survival, and poor recruitment. Many of our rivers have a silt covering from modern agricultural practices, the proliferation of commercial fish farming and compacted gravels due to the silt. The NRA and now the EA have programmes of silt removal from gravels, but unless the inputs of silt are arrested, the improvement is very short-lived. They have cleaned gravels on the shallows at the top of my stretch where many pairs of salmon used to spawn, but since a fish farm started operating just upstream back in the 1950s, not a single pair has ever spawned there. The gravel cleaning made no difference, and I did not expect it to, because the suspended solids from the farm, although admittedly far, far less than they used to be, are still enough to cover the gravel in a very short while.

A hen salmon generally produces around 700 to 800 eggs per pound weight, and so a good spawning year, with good survival rates over clean gravels, should soon bring a river back into form – but it cannot happen without clean gravels. And as we have said earlier, it is no use cleaning gravels and getting the spawning gravels into good condition unless the input of silt is eliminated. There has always been a certain amount of natural silt entering rivers since time immemorial, but only when it rained, and the flow between the rains was sufficient to keep the fast stretches over gravels clear of silt; but now that the input by man is so great, 365/6 days of the year, as the flows decrease over the gravels the silt settles on them, making them all but useless for the survival of egg and alevin.

Bernard Aldrich, long-time keeper for the famous Broadlands Salmon Fishery on the River Test, told me that he reared salmon eggs in tap water with a 90-plus per cent hatching and survival rate, whereas of those he reared in the river water, less than 10 per cent survived. Eggs naturally deposited within the gravels, according to NRA figures, are under 3 per cent successful.

It is not only effluent from fish farms that alters the salmon's efficiency at reproduction: other insidious pollutions include the influence of pheromones from the thousands of fish within the confines of a farm, which can reduce the biomass of the fish population downstream. In this context, a scientist from the Centre for Environment, Fisheries and Aquaculture Science (CEFAS), which is an agency of the UK government's Department for the Environment, Food and Rural Affairs (DEFRA) and a scientific research and advisory centre, was involved in a study of pheromone emissions from the fish farm just upstream of my fishery. He found that pheromones from female rainbow trout caused male salmon to become ripe long before the females were in similar condition. I have seen cock salmon spawning with brown trout during October/November, and just assumed the cock salmon were merely excited by the activity; but having been given the foregoing information, I now know what was happening.

It was eight years ago that I heard about these results, so among others, I wrote to the Test and Itchen Association, of which I was a member, the Environment Agency, and the lessee of Testwood Fishery, explaining that any interference with the reproduction of salmon was extremely serious, as the salmon of our chalk streams

were not sustainable according to the EA. Given that so many fish farms on our southern rivers are emitting these pheromones, and doubtless creating even further problems for the survival of salmon in our rivers, I was astounded that the only reply I received was an acknowledgement from the EA, but nothing more. This was particularly disappointing in view of the fact that the scientist who carried out the research, twice, considered his findings of national importance.

What a difference in some areas. The River Tyne shows how a river can be returned to glory if the will and the effort is there.

The Journey to the Sea

There are dozens of books written about the spawning of salmon, and the various stages thereafter, egg, alevin, fry, parr and eventually smolt, the stage at which the baby salmon leave the river to go to sea to feed, until returning as adults for the same purpose as their parents. Not a lot is new, other than the study of genetics, and as I know nothing of this I will not write about it. I do find the subject of interest, however, ever since I watched little birds, no larger than a ball of fluff within the hand, demonstrating the capability of nest building. They have never been taught by their parents, yet they can create a structure that will withstand rain and gales, and remain within the violent movement of tree, shrub or bush. They can only accomplish such a feat by having the genetic knowledge to do so.

I see no point in rewriting all that is in other books, so will concentrate on the dangers the little fish face while in freshwater and on the seaward journey – as the reader will have noticed I have concentrated more upon the dangers than the salmon itself during the homing journey.

The Dangers of Siltation

As already described, eggs and alevins have a very poor survival rate on the gravels in southern rivers due to silt within the redds, but those that do survive and wriggle free of the gravel when ready as fry, face many further hazards. The suspended solids that clog redds and kill eggs and alevins can equally cause death to fry by clogging gills. If we look at fish farms, every time they feed the inhabitants, the extra activity causes discoloration of the water, as do cleaning stews and all the other processes. Mature fish can cope, but fry cannot if the suspended solids are too great.

Silt deposition is also caused by agricultural practices since the war, and these in turn have caused an increase in nitrates, phosphates, pesticides, herbicides and sometimes lethal slurry, added to which is an increase in oestrogens, endocrine disrupters and goodness knows what else from sewage farms. We have all read of the changing of the sex of fish due to oestrogens from the contraceptive pill. The tests carried out on roach in our southern rivers have shown that a high percentage of them have both male and female sex organs.

Work has also been done on the chalk streams to improve egg survival by placing eggs in in-stream incubator boxes to minimize the problems associated with silted gravels. A recent practice, according to EA literature, is to move boxes to higher stretches of the rivers to reduce siltation of the boxes. This has apparently worked well, as a figure of 86 per cent survival has been suggested. I imagine that great care must be taken during transportation, as it is known that movement of boxes containing eggs is a reason for poor survival.

Predation by Fish

In the natural course of life in our rivers, coarse fish abound, and they all eat fry, and as the fry grow there is predation by perch, chub, pike and eels, and within our chalk streams, numerous brown and rainbow trout. There is less stocking with rainbows nowadays, and there are far fewer escapees from fish farms than there used to be. Nevertheless, one year we caught over 2,000 rainbows on rod and line – yes – 2,000! How many baby salmon that number of trout took I hate to think, and how many rainbows were left in the river system eating their way through the future of our salmon?

I did not think that eels would be much trouble to spawning salmon, as the salmon spawn in the winter when eels are not very active; however, this last year I saw eel activity all year, due I suppose to the exceptionally mild winter, so they probably would be around any spawning salmon and trout. I have watched eels feeding downstream of spawning coarse fish many times, and doubtless they would eat quantities of salmon fry when conditions were warm enough for the eels to be active.

Salmon parr like a bit of room, and one rarely sees them within two or three feet of another parr – and they are very territorial, causing problems for the less aggressive of their kind. Early hatching salmon would eat their own late arrivals, I don't doubt, but I have not seen or read of it.

Predation by Birds

So there is predation by fish, some insect larvae while the fry are small enough, and then the birds! Kingfishers, dabchicks, herons and grebes are the river's natural predators; a new arrival is the egret, and for a few years now there is also the dreaded cormorant, a natural fish-eating predator in the wrong place. When I was a lad I never saw a cormorant except on the coast – now they are inland by the thousand. I need not write much about them, as all anglers know the great damage they do to freshwater fish stocks in stillwaters, but that damage applies equally to rivers and streams. They are a huge bird with an equally huge appetite, and if the food is available they will often gorge themselves to an extent that makes flight difficult. They then need an exceptionally long take-off, so good tree cover to restrict the ease of landing and take-off for these birds may help to protect a fishery. Unfortunately there is planning restriction on planting trees and shrubs within 26ft (8m) of a river bank, and anglers who chuck bits of fluff about do not like their casting made difficult by trees.

The cormorant problem amply illustrates how pressure is put on government by various organizations, such as the Royal Society for the Protection of Birds (RSPB). In 1995, it was proved by collecting micro-tags from beneath cormorant rookeries, that cormorants ate thousands of salmon parr and smolts, and as far back as 1959 the Avon and Dorset River Board was talking about 'a plague of cormorants' doing tremendous damage to salmon stocks. They paid 5s for the beak of every cormorant shot – that's the equivalent of about £10,

working on the basis of a £12 wage then and a £500 wage today. It shows what a menace cormorants were believed to be – and yet they were still placed upon the Protected Birds List. If only anglers would combine their obvious power with the numbers that go fishing they would be a great force for protecting fisheries, as is the RSPB in protecting birds.

In our rich southern rivers baby salmon mostly reach the smolt stage within 12–18 months of wriggling free of the gravels; they then forsake their solitary habit to form shoals. In years past, during April/May, I used to see shoals of the baby fish hanging around the upstream of our sluices for a couple of days or so, and then I would see them in the pool below, also usually for a couple of days, before they dropped downstream. There were always pike there at that time, and I was reminded of it when I saw a television feature recently that showed the great white shark arriving in certain areas, always at the same time as its prey. Did the pike know when the smolts would arrive and stay in that area for two or three

There is talk these days that grilse do not wish to run up the River Test until late in the year. This is simply not true, and as this picture shows, Dave and his wife have caught many fresh-run grilse through the summer in past seasons – many with sea lice.

days? We also have smolts dropping downstream during autumn, but are they early 2+ smolts, or late 1+ smolts?

Predation by Animals

I have yet to mention mink, released into the wild by the less informed section of the environment movement. They undoubtedly eat smolts and parr when available – and then there is the 'darling' of environmentalists and television, the otter! It is a lovely animal, but otters will damage salmon fisheries, so can we afford to balance the need for otters within our environment against the need for salmon to survive as a species within our river systems? An officer of the EA recently suggested we have an otter holt right beside one of our salmon spawning sites, and I am told otters have been released on the River Test. This I find extremely hard to credit – the River Test has been described as 'the greatest chalk stream trout fishing in the world', and by a past head of the EA as a 'Jewel in the Crown'. It would seem that many environmentalists and politicians have tunnel vision, especially if there is a political advantage. In my old age I have become very cynical of all authority.

Way back in 1977, Bernard Aldrich, the well respected keeper of the famous 'Broadlands' salmon fishery on the River Test, in a speech about the river, stated how, back in 1955, 'Otter trapping was necessary for the positive conservation of salmon stocks.' He also said how pleased he was that by 1977 only one trace of an otter had been found below Stockbridge.

Without doubt otters will eat quantities of salmon parr, and shoaling smolts would be 'manna from heaven'.

The Dangers of Pollution

When I used to complain regularly, over past years, to the authority of the day about fish farm effluent, sewage effluent

and suchlike, I was always told that the river was of excellent quality, and nothing was wrong – and yet recently (at my age, 'recently' is within the last twenty years), 'improvements' to Romsey Sewage Works were to be completed by April 2006 at a cost of £8,600,000, and were described by the EA as a means 'to help clean up the River Test water and improve conditions for salmon and trout'.

It is difficult for a salmon angler such as myself to accept what the authorities say when we are told there is nothing wrong with the river – and then in order to bring this area into line with European standards, they have to spend millions to improve effluents. I mention it here to show how poor the water quality is, due to pollutants from various sources, that baby salmon have to endure during their freshwater life, a state of affairs which is apparently denied by those who should be sorting it.

There are still questions about pollution from industrial estates on the rivers, and at least one of the sewage works on the River Itchen, and probably other southern rivers, too.

On their journey seawards the little fish face yet another danger, due to inefficient screening at the intakes of abstraction units, fish farms and abstraction for agriculture. According to EA sources this is still a major problem, although the 1975 Salmon and Freshwater Fisheries Act said that facilities should be in place to stop entrapment. As there is legislation to ensure this, and the authority knows of it, one wonders why there is still a problem thirty-two years after the 1975 Act.

Other Predators

Once the smolts reach the tidal sections of rivers there are other predators awaiting them. Bass run well up tidal sections and obviously will predate smolts, and rivers will have an influx of various sea fish,

101

Returning a nice fresh fish to the River Test at Abbey Mill Fishery.

especially at high tides. There are also sea-birds, and I am told that goosanders are a particular menace on some tidal stretches. Seals will again spell trouble for baby salmon, as they did for their parents on the homeward migration. Their sea journey out to the feeding grounds won't be much fun, either.

It has been well documented that some sandeel fishing boats catch smolts as a by-product, and those fishing vessels after pelagic species also take smolts if fishing in the areas of the smolts' sea migration.

Before I leave the smolts to their destinies I would mention a theory I had, and published, in 1973, about the way they find their way to the feeding grounds in the North Atlantic.

The Incredible Homing Instinct

Once salmon have been to the feeding grounds we assume various options as to how they find their way back to their river of origin; some of these may have some foundation, such as currents, magnetic field, stars and smell, but I don't think anything as yet is perceived to be factual. But at least they have *been* there, and so have some basis to 'home'. But to find their way on the outward journey is incredible (one of the reasons I described the journeys as 'the *incredible* migrations'), because without previous knowledge of any sort it seems impossible.

The theory I suggested was that they followed kelts, as these had already been to the feeding grounds. What put this in my mind was when I caught well mended kelts in late May, and wondered why they were still in the river so late in the year, instead of getting back to the sea and feeding up. I thought perhaps the smell or pheromones of kelts were enough for smolts to follow when the kelts returned to the North Atlantic to feed. Lack of space precludes any long discussion here, so I leave it to the reader to consider.

Although I have killed hundreds of salmon, on my small salmon fishery we stopped killing them and have returned all captures since 1990, and having just explained to the reader the many, many dangers salmon

A 20lb salmon that has been anaesthetized ready for the insertion of a small radio transmitter.

face during their short lives, I don't think I could ever willingly kill another, even if they became prolific again.

The NRA Tagging and Radio-Tracking Project

I have been involved with the NRA programme to tag and radio-track salmon since its inception in 1991. Because I am so critical of the authorities, past and present, it may be thought that I am against everything they do; however, that is not so, and I will gladly support some of their projects. I have also become quite friendly with a few of the staff going back thirty years, and because we stopped the killing of salmon here in 1990, I think that is why they asked me for fish to help with their tagging and radio-tracking programme.

When they wished to track fish for the purpose of establishing run patterns and spawning-bed sites, the NRA had difficulty obtaining fish for the purpose. Netting fish was not very successful, electro-fishing was

not an option during the fishing season, and the majority of anglers still killed the salmon they caught. Keepers were also of an opinion that rod-caught fish would die if returned to the river. I was quite willing to supply them with fish, although the runs of fish had deteriorated badly and I was not catching so many, which was why I started returning them. The deteriorating runs were another reason why the NRA wanted to gain more information.

The programme started in 1991 and finished by 1994, during which time I caught eighty-two salmon, of which they tagged forty-nine. They also tagged a further thirteen fish from Dead End, which they electro-fished, and also moved many upstream; so altogether I supplied them with sixty-two of the tagged fish. About another forty or fifty were tagged from other sources during that time, I believe. I do have figures for 1993, which were given to me by the NRA: they tagged fifty-seven rod-caught salmon in 1993, of which I caught thirty-two, Nursling Fishery supplied thirteen, and Testwood Fishery gave them twelve.

The small radio transmitter and the tube used to insert it into the salmon's stomach.

Having by this time acquired much more information about electro-netting, I would not allow them to electro-net my fishery any more.

I assume the same procedure happened elsewhere as here, in that fish were first installed with a 2in-long mini transmitter before they were tagged. The tagging was merely to identify the fish that was giving out the signal, especially if it was in a shoal. When I caught a fish I would phone Richard Horsefield, the EA scientist who

was engaged on the project, to come and do the necessary. He had built me a cage to keep the fish in until he was available, as he could not always turn up immediately. Not one fish seemed to suffer any harm by being kept, although Richard might be several hours before arriving here, sometimes at around midnight. Naturally I did not mess about with playing a salmon, and got them in the pen as quickly as possible.

Sometimes Richard would turn up to check on the tagged fish, as some of them

A yellow tag called a 'Floy' tag is inserted near the dorsal fin to identify salmon that have the radio transmitter in their stomach.

104

The salmon, none the worse for the 'intrusion', is ready to be returned to the river, where its migratory pattern can now be 'tracked'.

stayed in my stretch after tagging, so while he was here I would see if I could see a fish and then catch it for him. I can't remember how many, but I know I caught him a few in his presence.

Richard had an elongated box that would be filled with a chemical to anaesthetize the salmon: as soon as it keeled over, the transmitter would be pushed into the stomach by means of a tube, and a yellow tag inserted into the base of the dorsal fin; freshwater was then added to the box, and this soon had the fish back on an even keel and ready to be returned to the river. Several of the fish I caught were good fish, including a couple over 20lb, one of which moved upriver a long way and spawned in a tributary, the River Anton. It was then traced back downstream over a period, but the signal was eventually lost when it re-entered salt water. Apparently it needs a transmitter with a different wavelength to transmit in the denser salt water.

The trouble with the yellow tags was that they were too easily seen and gave poachers an easy target, so they were changed to dark green. But that then made it difficult for the right people to spot them. Such is life! If poachers were given tough sentences and very heavy fines they might be less inclined to thieve salmon and trout.

There were several means by which Richard roamed the river to locate the fish. His H-bar receiver could pick up a signal up to 1,500 yards, so he would walk the river, cycle along some of the banks, and even take to a helicopter to travel the length of a river quickly and, one assumes, very efficiently. The receiver could differentiate between 100 fish by the simple method of the number of blips per minute and the length of the cycle: ten different times between blips, and ten different cycles equals 100.

Richard told me an amusing story about the tagging programme. Salmon in the Itchen were also within the same project and being tagged, and Richard was driving near the river and had inadvertently left his receiver switched on, when suddenly it started indicating a signal. He followed the increase in volume to a pub, and in the rear

Scientist Richard Horsefield checks for signals from salmon transmitters with the 'H Bar' receiver to ascertain migration patterns for the NRA.

garden some internal organs of a salmon were found, within which was a transmitter. The publican had purchased illegally caught salmon; he was, I believe, severely reprimanded.

They did occasionally find transmitters in places where it was obvious fish had been taken illegally. Retrieving the transmitters was a bonus as they cost about £100, and in the early 1990s that was quite expensive.

A 'funnel' system used to trap salmon in a salmon ladder so they can be retained for an EA Broodstock Project.

The Broodstock Programme

I also caught fish for broodstock for the NRA from 1995. The firm Wester Ross Salmon Ltd transported salmon eggs from their salmon farm in Scotland to be grown on in River Test water. Owing to the warmer waters of the Test, the fish would smolt within a year instead of the much longer period in Scottish waters, and they would then be returned to Scotland for growing to maturity in the salmon farm. This operation included facilities on the Test where salmon could be kept until they were ready for spawning, in large circular tanks with good flows of spring water. Unfortunately, by then I was unable to supply many fish, as our fishery was becoming less and less productive due to fish seemingly being unwilling, or unable, to run upriver. However, I did supply them with some fish as, for example, I caught sixteen good fish up to 20.5lb in 1999. I used to take friends who did not fish to have a look at the fish through an inspection panel in the side of the tank, and they were always impressed, never having seen salmon much above 7lb or 8lb in the fishmongers.

Although I didn't catch so many, salmon were electro-netted from my fishery after the season finished to add to my contribution, and we also allowed the EA to place traps in the salmon ladder and one of the streams. By 1999 some anglers who fished the southern rivers were returning salmon to the rivers, so the authority obtained plenty of broodstock. It is difficult to keep salmon to maturity in tanks and there were losses, but many thousands of young salmon were reared until ready for introduction to the river.

Alan Mann, of Wester Ross, with his superior knowledge, also managed to get stripped salmon feeding again by various food introductions, some of which was eaten, and some rejected. A few salmon were kept for a further year for re-stripping, and some were returned to the river. Salmon have now been nurtured to produce over three seasons, and the programme could originate enough knowledge to use fish for four, five or possibly even six seasons.

The 'fish-stop' further along the salmon ladder to stop them passing upstream until they are transferred to the holding pens.

Environment Agency netsmen ready to capture fish turned up by the electrodes when removing salmon trapped at Abbey Mill Fishery in a section aptly named 'Dead End'.

BELOW: A salmon over 20lb caught by Dave Steuart is given to the EA for their Broodstock Project. This was a lucky salmon, because it had doubtless managed to run the gauntlet of the drift netters – net marks are clearly visible on its flank.

The EA operator using the electrode to search for salmon.

A salmon is caught for the Broodstock Project.

In 1976 I went to Ireland at the invitation of the Irish Tourist Board to look around some of the salmon beats. While I was there I saw salmon kelts that had been induced to feed, and I even managed to catch a nice 12.5-pounder from the River Shannon. At the Parteen Weir and Fish Hatchery, Noel Rycroft, the biologist running the hatchery told me a lot about smolts, and surprised me with the information that they could get spawned salmon to feed on pellets.

The Hampshire Salmon Trust Fund, the generosity of the Barker Mills estate, and Wester Ross Salmon Ltd, enabled the

The EA vehicle arrives to transport rod-caught salmon from Abbey Mill Fishery for the Broodstock Project.

Broodstock Programme to carry on until 2003, even though for the previous three years no money was allocated to the programme by the EA, as the government had cut the budget to the Fisheries Division of the EA (originally NRA) by a considerable amount. A pity, as with all the knowledge gained, a well financed and efficient stocking programme would undoubtedly benefit the river until conditions improve and the salmon return to a sustainable level. As the rivers Test and Itchen are under EU conservation directives, I would have thought monies should be budgeted to a well run stocking policy.

Catching Salmon in Southern Rivers on Bait and Spinner

Apart from my love of salmon fishing, as a keen coarse angler I have entitled this section 'catching' salmon as against 'fishing' for them. Much of the fishing for salmon is done without really expecting to catch many, and the rules appertaining to many beats are designed for that purpose only, to make sure not many are caught. Until relatively recently one could fish with quite successful methods on our southern rivers, even in poor conditions such as coloured floodwater, or low or high temperatures; however, the present authority has tried to make it extremely difficult by making byelaws restricting fishing to fly only in the Wessex area until 15 May, and in Hampshire to fly or artificial lure – which I presume means spinner, spoon or plug – until 16 June.

Nor is one allowed to kill any salmon until 16 June in Hampshire. I, for one, do not wish to kill salmon anyway, and almost 100 per cent of salmon anglers at present return them to the river, so one wonders why there must be restrictions on catching fish, for that is the purpose of the bait restriction – particularly as after 16 June salmon can legally be killed, and then you can fish

Kay photographs Dave playing a fresh-run 'springer' in the Hampshire Avon at Ringwood.

The 'springer'. A 16lb beauty.

Dave Steuart's biggest springer – all 39lb of it.

with anything. As fish are being returned to the river, the only restriction I would make is to prohibit worms, as salmon tend to swallow them. Micro-barbs or crushed barbs on the more barbaric hooks on artificials, or changing to smaller hooks, might also help preserve returned fish.

Restricting fishing to fly only for fish that are to be returned to the river is also not a good idea, as fish can be played out more quickly on bait or spinning tackle, and therefore suffer less stress than when being played for a long time on a fly rod.

Spring Fishing

One of the greatest prizes in salmon angling is the capture of springers. These early salmon are superb in every way, usually bright silver with a marvellous steely blue back, and when fresh in the river they have a distinct change of colour between flank and back, a very distinguishable line. This fades in the freshwater habitat, the pure white belly gradually blending into the dark back, and late in the year the belly loses the white coloration, too. They are also big fish here in the south, and as my first serious salmon fishing was during the coarse fish closed season, the springers were the salmon I mostly fished for.

Springers are scarce now, for reasons already discussed at the beginning of my contribution to this book – over-cropping and so on – but I did not mention that probably much of their food supply has also disappeared due to over-fishing, of sprat, herring and sandeel; salmon are therefore not reaching such huge proportions. I only have to mention the Avon, the Frome and the Stour, where back in the 1950s and 1960s in some years a fish or two above 40lb would be caught, and even the Test and Itchen would occasionally produce such a fish. I have seen two fish on the Royalty Fishery, the bottom beat of the Avon, that I would have estimated at

111

over 50lb, and the record for the Avon is a monster of 49lb 12oz. The average weight for the Royalty catch over a season would often top 20–22lb. Unfortunately I didn't make the 40lb mark, although I did manage to get a nice springer in 1977 on the last day of March, a fish of 39lb.

Brian Harris and I both had a beat on the Avon at Ringwood on consecutive days. He had Tuesday and I had Wednesday, and as the beat was for two rods, if we could both make it we would fish together: I would be his guest on his day, and he would be my guest on my day, and if we fished for two days we would sleep in my caravanette. I could only fish it during the coarse fish closed season, because after 16 June I was far too busy in the fishing tackle business, and neither of us could always get the day off. The day I caught the thirty-nine-pounder was Brian's day, and he couldn't get down to fish. He's never let me forget it!

Springers may enter the rivers as early as November/December to spawn a year later; they need a good reserve of fat to sustain them for so long, so they need to be big and well fed. On the Avon and Stour the season starts on 1 February; I remember 1966 particularly because that year I caught my first 30lb salmon from the Stour – but the first ten fish from the Royalty were all over 30lb. I saw Bernard Aldrich (the Broadlands river keeper) soon after I caught mine, and casually mentioned I had taken a fish of 32.5lb; but he had outdone me by having just had his best at 33lb. Unlike today, our spring salmon didn't have net marks. Those were the days!

These large salmon have been very scarce now for more than twenty years, and they were declining in numbers long before that; but apart from man's interference I hope it is just a cycle, and that we will see some return of these wonderful fish. Their numbers have historically fluctuated since the recording of salmon runs began, but

Kay Steuart 'spring fishing' for Avon salmon at Bisteme.

a good stocking programme with selected fish and huge government backing (it would take a great deal of money) could probably help. Referring across the Atlantic shows what can be done with the will and the cash. It would take a while here, as research shows that springers produce more grilse, but selectivity might improve that considerably.

Even with their decline, there is always hope of a big fish. Here on the Test in 1997 I had a fish come adrift that I am sure was over 40lb. I played it for a long time, and after losing it (barbless hooks advised by the EA) I knew where it would be and would watch it for hours. After three days I thought it might have got over the hooking experience, and so I took tackle with me to catch it. It had gone! A friend I showed the fish to had said, 'That's not a salmon, it's a bloody shark!' A fortnight later I had another large fish come adrift (barbless hooks again), but this one had a long healed

Dave's 32.5lb springer from the Dorset Stour at Wimborne.

scar along its back. Something happened to it, for yet later I found the fish trapped in the salmon ladder, dead. It weighed 31lb.

Baits and Tackle

When I first started fishing for salmon in the early 1950s, on the Wessex and Hampshire rivers, we were allowed to fish with any legitimate bait: spoons, spinners, fly or whatever, including prawn, shrimp, plug (I caught my first Stour salmon on a yellow Heddon River Runt) and even worm, but in 1961 (I think) the Avon and Dorset River Board, the authority of the day, introduced a new byelaw to reduce the numbers of spring fish caught.

Similar to the one now operating in Hampshire, no prawn, plug or wobbling bait could be used before 15 May. Shrimp was not mentioned that I recall, so I don't doubt that a few wily anglers fished with them. The byelaw changed the fishing, and

the substitute for the favourite prawn was the Devon until mid-May. In those days metal Devons in blue and silver, and Yellow Bellies, appeared the most popular choice. They got down well and caught a lot of fish (relative to spring fishing) – but a few anglers, including me, wanted a method that would guarantee the depth at which a bait fished, especially early in the season in cold water when fish were lethargic, hugging the bottom, and when dirty water limited the visibility for fish to see the bait at any distance. If one tried to fish very near the bed of the river, metal Devons would sometimes get hung up, and they weren't that cheap for a young angler.

The obvious choice was a paternoster. I have used the paternoster as a coarse angler almost since I was a baby, so I had absolutely no qualms about its use to catch another species. I was interested in salmon as they were a big species, the largest *indigenous* species (I get annoyed when people call them 'silver tourists'), and I did not wish to stop fishing on 14 March, so trout and salmon came within my angling obsession.

The paternoster was perfect for the job when fished with light Devons, wooden originally, but then some very good plastic patterns came on the market under the name of Dibro. They could be purchased as blanks and painted to one's own colour scheme, and they would spin like a top. I still have dozens that I have painted nearly every colour of the rainbow and they all catch salmon, but when the water clears I like black/gold or brown/gold. The plastics were better, in a way, than wooden Devons, as most wooden Devons had plastic fins that would break, and the Dibro had metal fins that added to the flash. My good friend Brian Harris, editor of the famous *Angling* magazine for many years, came up with the idea of replacing the broken fins of wooden Devons with the pull-out bit of aluminium drink cans. They are generally the right size and shape for the larger early season baits.

The tackle is quite simple. A ball-bearing swivel is tied to the end of the line, to which is also attached a weaker length of line, at the end of which is a link swivel to be attached to the lead. From the other ring of the swivel a trace of the preferred length is tied – about a couple of feet will do – and I usually tie a link swivel to this so that I can change baits easily if I wish to change colour or size. If you prefer, and if you don't change baits often, the trace can be taken straight through the Devon and a bead, and then tied to the required size of treble.

Where pike abound it might be wise to have a wire trace, although I have not had too many pike grab Devons, but those that do could easily chop the line and then the angler curses thinking he has lost a salmon through faulty gear. Better to have to unhook a toothy pike than lose baits.

Lead size is important, as it controls the speed at which the Devon fishes across the river; this is because the method of fishing is usually to cast at about 45 degrees downstream across to the other bank, and just let the current slowly bring the bait across to one's own bank. The current in most salmon rivers is generally fast enough to spin the bait effectively and bring it across. The speed of travel across the river can be slowed down or speeded up by simply casting farther downstream to slow it, or squarer to the flow to speed it up. Generally I prefer to change lead size (that's the reason for the link swivel) to change the fishing speed of baits as I work downstream through differing current speeds, as I can then keep my casting angles fairly uniform and know I have not missed any area of water.

In the coloured water of spring in our southern rivers when fish are few (mostly), it is as well to cover every bit of possible holding water, as one must get very close to a salmon to get a take. In fact in all states of the rivers I have found that the nearer I can get a bait of any sort to a fish, the more likely I am to get a take – but be very careful not to touch the fish or frighten it in any way. This paternoster method of fishing has caught me a lot of salmon, and can still be used on the Hampshire rivers from opening day on 17 January, as can a plug. In the Wessex Region fishing in this manner is still valid, but only after 15 May.

A floating plug that has enough action to work within the stream can be fished in exactly the same way as above. I like to remove the middle treble, and I often change the tail treble to a smaller one, but that is merely as a means of minimizing the damage that could be done to a salmon by the large trebles on most plugs. It is as well to check the action of plugs if you follow this procedure, as many plugs do not work so well if the heavy hooks are removed or changed. I also close down barbs.

Where there are still enough springers to warrant taking a crop from the river, there is no need to fiddle about with hooks, apart from making sure they are very sharp. The trouble with salmon is that they don't feed in freshwater so they often only mouth a bait, or nip it, perhaps to warn an intruder to get out of its lie. As the fish is not going to eat the offering, they can be difficult to hook. If a bait is only grabbed by the tip of the mouth, a hookpoint probably often takes a shallow hold in the jawbone, so the angler plays the fish for a while, but then a sudden change of angle and out it pops. Probably a far greater percentage of salmon come adrift than any other fish.

Several times I have watched a salmon knock a bait without opening its mouth, and watched them chase other fish away from where they are at rest. Knowing that salmon often knock a bait without actually taking it, I have amazed friends – who are good anglers – when I have said to them, when I have been fishing in highly coloured water, 'I'm going to catch a fish next cast!' I've then re-cast to bring the bait across the same 'line', over goes the rod – and I'm playing a salmon. What has happened is that I have felt a fish tap at the bait on the previous cast, and then I'm fairly confident that if I cast again to bring the bait across the same place, the salmon is going to take. It has happened several times.

The paternoster is equally useful for fishing with prawn or shrimp, and is very successful. Some traditionalist anglers abhor using these, and they don't like pater-noster either, asserting that the use of such baits through a stretch of river will make it useless for any angler following with fly or spinner. Having proved many times that fish can be caught on spinner, plug and fly (although I have not used fly many times after having had a prawn or shrimp refused) immediately after fishing a prawn or shrimp, I consider their contention to be quite unfounded – maybe they are trying to justify a policy, or maybe it's an excuse because they are failing to catch fish!

There are many times I can recall of fish taking a spinner after refusing prawn; one particular occasion I can clearly remember is a fish lying beneath a bridge, which I cast to and dangled a prawn in front of. As it was a fresh fish I expected an immediate response, but after about half hour with the fish taking no notice at all, I picked up the spinning rod (I nearly always carry two rods on my own water), cast a bar-spoon to pass across the front of the fish – and it charged straight after it, and soon I was playing a nice sea-liced 17lb salmon. I can quote the famous Augustus Grimble, who said the same thing in his book of 1904, that fishing baits through did not stop salmon taking fly. But he also said that prawn and shrimp were far more successful than fly. Who am I to disagree?

Somewhere I read that salmon feed on krill in the Atlantic and that krill are a reddish colour, so it seems logical that a cooked pink prawn must be something they would naturally assume was within their diet. I am a great believer in smell, and once a prawn is cooked the smell is enhanced enormously, and probably the flavour too. A piece of raw meat is difficult to distinguish between one animal and another, but once it is cooked most humans can tell what animal it is by the smell.

Pink may be the normal colour for cooked prawns, but when salmon don't want to know, a change of colour can sometimes do the trick. Ruby red and mauve are the usual changes to make, but I once dropped a black prawn in front of a fish. The fish had refused spinners and plugs and the normal coloured prawns, it had also refused natural brown shrimps and again the colour changes, so I tried the black prawn. I don't remember why I dyed a prawn black, but that fish took with such violence it almost took the rod out of my hand. It is unusual to get a violent take from a salmon, they are usually quite gentle, so I thought, 'I'm on to a winner here!' However, I've never had a salmon take any notice of a black prawn since.

Salmon fishing is very often persistence. As long as you don't frighten a fish you can show it a bait time and time again and eventually it may well take, although with prawn, very often the take comes the minute the fish sees the bait; but I can remember a couple of instances when patience paid off. I was fishing the River Test during a heavy weedcut, and you could almost walk across the stuff, but in the stretch I was fishing with my friend John Denman, a fresh fish was regularly head and tailing. The only way of getting to it was by trotting a prawn or shrimp down. After about an hour with no interest I offered the rod to John. He refused, with the comment 'Why should it take at all, if it hasn't already?' If I recall rightly it was a fish of 15lb, and it took the very next cast.

Another time I was fishing the River Irt in Cumberland, also with John Denman, and overnight rain had made us get up early before breakfast as we were going home that morning; but we considered the rain would have brought up a few fresh ones. We both had fish, and I had caught two and was trying for a third I could see across the river under some trees. I was bouncing a prawn past the fish with just a single swan shot on the line, and started counting the number of times I passed the fish. I had got to thirty-nine when John turned up and said it was time to go to breakfast. 'One more cast, mate!' I said – but as I was talking and not concentrating I made a bad cast with the light weight on the multiplier, and the prawn landed not much more than

a rod's length out. But the salmon came straight across the river and took it. Would it have taken on the fortieth cast if I had put it past its nose again? Your guess is as good as mine!

Prawn anglers and keepers I have known have mostly been so fussy about having a perfect bait. All the legs and whiskers must be intact and correctly proud of the body. I have never bothered, and have caught stacks of salmon on headless, legless and whiskerless prawns; and one fish I remember well continually followed without taking, so I took off the prawn mount, attached a single hook and put a single tail segment on the hook. I got it immediately.

When fishing with prawn on the paternoster, the trace should be shortened to about 12in (30cm). The reason is that a prawn does not float, so it might hang down in slower water, and with a long trace it may

Dave fishing the 'bar-spoon' for spring fish on the Dorset Stour.

well catch bottom. I like to fish it about 12–18in (30–45cm) off the floor, and that is also a good height from the bed of the river to fish paternostered Devons. The dirtier the water, the nearer the bottom the bait should be.

Any reel will do for this sort of fishing – centre-pin if one can cast with the thing, multiplying reel or fixed spool reel. I prefer the multiplier – it just feels right. When the weedcut is on in the chalk streams it is almost impossible to fish by normal methods. I used to like the weedcuts because downstream fisheries had to open hatches to let the weed through, which also let some fish up, and as already explained, weedcuts can be fished with a prawn or shrimp by using float tackle and trotting with the weed. It isn't wise to fish light, as there is often a mass of weed on the line at times, but we landed plenty of fish despite this hazard.

The Dorset Stour

I had a fair amount of success on the Dorset Stour with spring salmon, well up from the sea, whereas the majority of Stour fish came from Throop. The reason I did well was sheer persistence, as by using the methods described I would fish almost every piece of possible holding water, working downstream over two or three miles during a day. It was very hard work, but the only way of finding a fish was to cover a lot of water. Often I caught fish from a stretch or lie that had never previously produced a fish, not to me anyway.

Later in the season as the river cleared and dropped, I often changed to fish with bar-spoons, because the popular contention is that a water temperature of 48 degrees is when salmon will start to rise to fly and become lively. I am not sure I agree, as I have had them chase after spinners when it

Throop Mill on the Dorset Stour, which was renowned as a barrier to ascending salmon until it was 'by-passed' by a new weir. Unfortunately there are still many such barriers in existence in rivers throughout the country.

117

has been much colder than that. However, the lighter spinning rod was less work, and I travelled very light – until I caught a fish, and then it was heavy, because for some years I did not catch a fish below 16lb. A funny thing was that I caught several fish that were 16lb 4oz, all hens, and yet the cocks would vary more. As I recall, all the salmon over 20lb were males.

My very good friend John Goddard – and this is a friendship that has lasted for fifty-six years – asked me to catch him a salmon for his twenty-fifth wedding anniversary: he wanted a silver fish for a silver wedding. So I popped down the Stour and was able to present him with a fresh hen salmon of 16lb 4oz.

What is really disappointing is that the authority has apparently now written off the Stour as a salmon river.

A big spring flood was something I looked forward to, as I always expected it to bring up a fish or two to where I fished upriver on the Stour. The well-known obstructions at Throop were not then able to stop fish getting upstream past the sluices. There was always some difficulty on the Avon, too, with sluice manipulation holding up fish, so a flood there also helped fish get up. I remember an acquaintance, a Mr Palmerino, playing a 26lb salmon in the field behind him when he had found his way to the river's edge when the fields were flooded. I think it was at Ringwood. He hooked the fish, which came to the surface, thrashed, then charged off at the surface into the field. It was often difficult to find the river in the spring – too dangerous for me, I wouldn't even try.

Running Salmon and Obstructions

I do get very angry about obstructions to running salmon. I am certain that salmon can be conditioned *not* to run by continually being thwarted in their attempts to pass obstructions. I feel that electric barriers to guide fish to a certain area can act in the same way. A fish drawn to an attractive flow that gets a shock each time it tries to pass through will give up trying, and

Kay Steuart plays a salmon at Abbey Mill Fishery on the River Test, watched by passers-by on the bridge over the river.

The fish – a cracking 16lb springer.

not try to find an alternative route, as is hoped. I would ban all such electric barriers if I could. It was once assumed that electro-fishing did no harm, but the more enlightened authorities have now changed their minds, with the present-day evidence of the subtle damage that the electric shock can cause.

Spring fish that come into the rivers will run hard and should get past obstructions with ease if temperatures are above about 40°; they will then settle in a lie for a long time. When I first bought my stretch of the River Test at Romsey in 1977, I caught the first salmon from the river during all the following seasons: 1978, 1980, 1981, 1982, 1985 (but this one came adrift), 1986, 1987 1990, 1992 and 1993 – that is, nine times in sixteen years I caught the

first fish. I see in my records that I had caught thirty-one salmon here by the end of May in 1981, all springers, and we ended the season with seventy-seven, of which I caught fifty; but after that things have gone downhill very badly, even though I did have a few firsts.

Salmon are so scarce now in our southern rivers that the EA admits that most of them would fail the criteria that guarantee a sustainable salmon population. It is very sad, as some of the northern rivers in the UK are in top form.

As I have written above, in the Wessex Division waters anglers are limited to fly only until 15 May. The salmon season starts in this area on 1 February, so there is little choice early in the season, unless conditions are exceptionally warm and the water fairly clear, other than to use fast sinking lines and to drag large tube flies over the river bed. I'm afraid I cannot accept that as fly fishing, and feel one might as well be allowed to spin at least.

I leave these methods to be explained by other writers in this book; but it is not without hope that one fishes in this manner, because as I write this in March 2007, I have been told that already three twenty-pounders have been caught at Ibsley, a twenty-eight-pounder has come from the Royalty, and another couple elsewhere.

Summer and Autumn Fishing

There is probably little reason to differentiate between summer and autumn fishing, as the same methods will usually be adequate for both seasons. Of course there is considerable overlap of methods between the seasons, depending on weather and water; therefore summer methods may commence early, or an angler may have to carry on with spring methods later in the year than usual.

One of the main differences in method due to the rising temperature and the clearing of colour from the rivers, is a reduction in size of bait, be it Devon, spoon, plug or whatever, and as current speeds become less, one of my favourite lures comes into its own, the bar-spoon. Of course bar-spoons can be used for spring fishing, but usually the current is far too fierce for the fast-revolving bar-spoon to get down deep enough, and if one casts upstream in coloured water the spoon is whipped downstream past the fish, not giving it a chance to see it properly.

But once the river drops, upstream fishing is such a good way of attracting salmon that I fish that way for much of the summer where the water is too deep to see fish. I very often change the size of trebles on bar-spoons as they are larger, as a rule, than a size I like for fish I am returning to the river, and smaller hooks often take a better

hold: size 6 is plenty large enough for most bar-spoons used in summer.

Although casting upstream is so effective for summer salmon, as from May onwards they seem to chase downstream after a lure in preference to taking it when fished down and across; I have also found that casting upstream just slightly works well. The bait is brought across fast enough to avoid the riverbed, but not too fast, and salmon often follow and then take on the turn, that is, when you have almost run out of water and the bait turns into the current almost under one's feet. Fished in this way the spoon is more broadside to the flow and may well give a bigger impact. It has caught me a lot of fish.

A bar-spoon can also work well during weedcuts when the weed is not too solid. If one can cast upstream into a hole among the floating stuff, it is possible to get enough turns in to hook a fish before

Early summer, and a few fish can be put on the bank. Playing a lively one on the Avon at Bisteme.

The salmon is 'tailed' out by hand.

Another summer fish from the Bisteme beat.

the weed mucks it up. It is better to know exactly where a fish is or where they lie, as the distance the bait travels without weed on it is often very short. I once got a fish my wife Kay had been after when she was fishing prawn. A fish had moved to the prawn, but each time weed had fouled it before the salmon took hold, and the lady was somewhat frustrated. With her permission, I hasten to add, I had a chuck at her fish with a Mepp. I slung between the floating weed about two yards upstream of the fish, but only managed about a yard of travel before I had to lift out before the spoon was engulfed by weed. It was engulfed, but not by weed: that salmon came at the spoon so hard that it shot out of the water through the floating weed – and fought well too.

Kay walked up to me one day carrying a nice fresh 15lb salmon. The water was clear and she had been able to see her Mepp coming across, but suddenly she saw a salmon where the Mepp should be, so she struck. She told me she never felt a thing!

Summer Salmon

The size of summer salmon coming into southern rivers is smaller than springers, and from late June/early July grilse start to predominate. There is an accepted differentiation between grilse and salmon, that most fish below 7lb are grilse, and fish that are heavier are salmon. This is a false premise, however, as many fish in the 5lb class that come into our rivers are '2+ salmon' – that is, they have had two winters at sea, and are therefore not grilse, which are of course '1+' fish. Scales from small salmon that I supplied at the request of a MAAF scientist for a sampling assessment of salmon populations confirmed this. On the other hand, some years ago I had correspondence with the secretary of a club that has fishing on the River Camel and River Fowey in Cornwall, where they have a late run of

Kay Steuart caught these four summer fish spinning a bar-spoon in the River Test.

An extremely good smaller salmon fly on the chalk streams in the summer is the hare's ear, with or without a gold head, but the head gets it down much better, and the gold flash is very attractive. I think the hare's ear relates favourably with the brown shrimp, which is why I have mentioned it here.

Sight Fishing

Sight fishing is not for the fool who stands on the edge of the bank in full view of everything in the river, but it is fishing that I really enjoy when the river clears and I can see fish. Years ago on the River Test, that would sometimes happen by mid-April and one could see into the shallower lies, and into the deeper water, by the end of May at least. Now it does not get really clear enough to see deep until July.

There are still plenty of lies where I search for fish before July, as my favourite form of fishing is when I can see them. There is criticism from some quarters that simply putting a bait to a salmon that can be seen is not very sporting. But if it is all right to cast to a rising trout that you can see, and therefore know exactly where it is, and that it is feeding, then why is doing the same, only with bait or lure, or fly too, when fishing for salmon, much different? It would appear the salmon angler is immediately at a disadvantage as salmon do not feed in fresh water; but in truth, if you know what you are about, and don't frighten the fish, the salmon often takes instantly. If it doesn't, then a different bait, lure or fly can be tried until your patience runs out or the fish takes hold. If fished carefully the fish should still be in the same place as when you started to fish – though beginners at the game often scare the animal.

Good sight, polaroids and experience are advantageous, as is living by the river. I walk my stretch every day when I am home, and I am always searching for fish, all fish, not

spring-like fish into those rivers, continuing into December, and he informed me that they had caught grilse as heavy as 17lb. With a few extra months of sea feeding this is quite possible, as doubtless salmon really pack it on during their months at sea.

Prawn still works in summer and autumn, but shrimp is also a favourite summer bait for the smaller salmon, though I have caught twenty-pounders on shrimp. As with prawn, a change of colour can often get a response from fish that have been around a bit, and have perhaps already seen just about everything that can be thrown at them in other stretches. The same colours as for prawns are fine, but the natural brown colour often works very well.

just salmon, and I am lucky enough to be able to spot fish fairly well. Sometimes it is only a shadow that one sees, but it is the right kind of shadow that attracts the attention until one's focus confirms the fish.

I remember fishing Woodmill Pool on the River Itchen with John Cross. He had a rod there and had talked me into joining him for a season, so I got a half rod which gave me a few days in the season. The pool was a three rod beat, and on one occasion, although John and I could see a salmon deep down, the third rod got rather angry as he could not see the fish and thought we were lying. I dropped a shrimp in front of the fish, hooked it, and when it threw itself about two feet into the air I said, 'Can you see the bloody thing now?'

My friend Tom Saville is always amazed how I spot salmon. I was trying to show him a fish once that he failed to see when he was here trout fishing, and I'm sure he thought I was kidding. 'Give me your rod!' He had a nymph of some sort on, so I dropped it in the salmon's lie, and the fish had it instantly. By the same tactic he did manage to get an 8lb salmon on a trout rod, fishing a gold head – and lost a much bigger fish.

On another occasion I took his wife Pat, a very good trout angler, to fish for a salmon that was lying beneath a hedge. I stood where I could see the fish and told Pat to lower the small plug over the hedge into the river. 'Just a bit more,' I said, and up came the fish. She did not wait unfortunately, felt the fish and lifted too quickly, so I took her to our Mill Pool, cast a Mepp to the place I wanted her to cast to, to show her exactly where it would fish through in the fast currents correctly, turned the reel handle a couple of turns and handed her the rod with an 11lb salmon already hooked. I didn't want to hook that fish, only show Pat where I wanted her to cast, but it's often that quick. All through my record

Spotting salmon on the River Avon.

book there are remarks such as 'Fish seen, instant take.'

I love to watch the way they take a bait. Often they just slowly move up to it and take it in their mouth and I don't feel a thing. If I hadn't seen it the salmon could easily eject the bait without me knowing, but I've already struck by then. I've teased them without having hooks in a bait or lure, and watched them play with prawns, but never seen them swallow one. It would need a whole book to write of all the things I have seen salmon do, like follow a large plug with mouth wide agape and close its jaws shut, but right beside the plug, not over it. I got it later on prawn, 18lb. I threw a paternostered prawn to land in front of a fish across the river under a tree. I usually throw away from a fish and then work the bait to it, but this fish was tight to the bank so I had to cast to land the prawn within its vision. The salmon backed off out of the lie but I left the bait where it was. I watched the fish move downstream some twenty yards, then slowly move back up into the lie, where it took the prawn.

123

Kay Steuart with three nice fish taken from the River Test with the prawn.

Kay Steuart plays a 17lb salmon at Abbey Mill Fishery on the River Test.

Some of the lies salmon occupy only until the sun shines into it; they then move, but are back when the sun has moved round. I've seen salmon lying with bream, and in November a couple of years ago, lying about two feet below the surface, over an 8ft (2.5m) deep lie, were three salmon of about 8–10lb, with a pike of about 8lb in the middle of them. I called a friend to have a look. I can only believe that it was near enough to spawning, about a month away, for the pike to be attracted by some phero-mone emission.

Being able to read a salmon's reaction is a help in catching them. I once watched a salmon imperceptibly, and I do mean imperceptibly, show an interest in a spinner I had cast up and brought down past his lie. Each time the spinner came past there was this slightest of movement that made me keep at it without changing bait. On the eighth cast the salmon took. A few times I have brought a bar-spoon down past a fish from an upstream cast with the fish appar-ently taking absolutely no notice, when suddenly, after the spinner has travelled past by a good couple of yards, the salmon would turn down and chase after it. It is as if they are asleep, or it takes a time to reg-ister. If I had not been able to see into the river there are doubtless many fish I would not have caught.

When using bar-spoons or small lures in southern rivers, none of which are large rivers although the fish may be, I like a fixed spool reel as it is easier to chuck under branches and into small gaps. To make casting even more accurate, if it is necessary to add lead in order to fish deeper, I place the lead, usually a ball lead, on the trace so that it sits on the swivel to which the spinner is attached. It's a bit like the Voblex used to be, which was a headed bar-spoon with the head made of lead. Voblex caught me a lot of other species as well as salmon. As the weight of spinner things that are accepted as 'the norm' that affect our beautiful southern rivers: effluent that discolours rivers is one of them. The bed of the river is my Garden of Eden, and I want to see the weeds waving in the current, clean gravels and fish of many species moving beneath the fronds, and watch the way they all interact – but it takes only the slightest input of effluent to reduce the depth at which one can see all of this.

A typical morning's catch from the Test in the 'old days' taken with the 'Mepps' spinner.

I have caught salmon in nine rivers in the UK, and, I mustn't forget, a loch. I have caught all the Pacific species in Canada and Alaska, big fish, and the clarity of water at some of these places is fantastic. In our little island, and especially here in the South, as the population is continually increasing and being encouraged to increase, I can only see the problems of our rivers get eventually worse, which will not help the salmon. But in the meantime, surely we can improve on the present situation?

Bob asked me to write a sort of 'Then and Now' piece within these chapters. A few decades ago I decided to write a book about a year's fishing, when I was catching all species, but I never seemed to have the time to write the book. However, I did write a few chapters, and the following, about a day spent fishing for salmon, might show the moods of the time, as it was written about forty years ago.

and lead is almost combined it makes for very consistent casting.

Although I am still prepared to have a throw, for some years now my wife Kay, who is an exceptionally good angler, has refused to fish for salmon in the South as she says it is just not worth the effort any more. Until a recent illness she would still fish for salmon abroad where she caught fish to 40lb, and she also fished for other species such as sea fish and sturgeon, and coarse fish in the UK, but not salmon. I suppose it is understandable when she would simply pick up a spinning rod and often get a fish first or second cast, and she would nearly always get a fish if she tried on our water.

As you can tell by much of the foregoing, I get quite worked up about many of the

'First of the Year'

The reader might well assume the commencement of the year to be 1 January, but my year has many beginnings. The 16 June is the beginning of my coarse fishing year – or part year, as the season is but nine months. The 1 February is the beginning of salmon fishing on the Stour or the Avon, but a stretch of the Test I fish has 17 January for its first day, I know not why! Trout fishing mostly comes in on 1 April, although there are other starts to this, too, on different waters, and for rivers and stillwaters.

There are the natural starts of migratory fish; rivers where a salmon or sea trout is never caught before a certain month, or in the sea, where the earliest shark to be caught is always May. Sometimes, someone who doesn't know of these natural phenomena goes out and tries for a species before time – and sometimes succeeds – and then a new start time of the season is born.

The first start of a new season in a new year, for me, comes in March. I have fished through the winter into the New Year for coarse fish, right until it ended on 14 March, and so the first Sunday following this date I start salmon fishing. True, I may have had a throw or two for salmon previous to this date if things had looked favourable for the chance of an early fish, but rarely with success. With the coarse fishing over, however, I start salmon fishing seriously and hard, until that day comes that marks the first fish of the season to my rod, and under the photograph will be a date, and 'Success at last'.

And so my year of angling will begin on 15 March and finish on 14 March. I start the year fishing for game fish, and end it by fishing for coarse fish. Some might say a retrograde step, but in my world of angling the one is equally as enjoyable as the other.

As I go back in mind to relive and relate this year I look forward very much to this new season to fish for salmon, as the coarse-fishing season has just ended badly for me on the Dorset Stour. I had wanted roach, a bag of roach and perhaps a big one among them to bow out with, but it was not to be. Heavy floods had made the river impossible for a whole fortnight, and the flooding had been so severe that fields were under water, and the river's path could only be followed by the eye observing known trees that grew along the bankside, that now

This is the 21lb salmon caught by Dave from the Dorset Stour, the story of which is related herewith.

showed stark, unclothed and shortened in stature from the swirling water's height upon their trunks.

As one looks upon the scene and surveys the incredible width of the water, one wonders the fate of small creatures that may not, could not, escape the awesome power of water as the river burst its banks. Water, which gives life and then takes it away, and to which anglers such as I are ever attracted. It is hard for an angler to cross a bridge without pausing to look at, and into, the waters below, to observe, or imagine, the life within and all around.

Surveying the floodwaters without hope of fishing for those end-of-season roach, my mind wanders back to a similar scene a few years earlier when the floods had stopped me fishing. As the water receded and fishing became possible I had visited the river, fished for salmon, and enjoyed my only early success with salmon and taken the largest salmon of my life. That fish had undoubtedly come up on the flood. Would this flood bring up another early fish?

The following week I rang my farmer friend and was told the river was fishable. It seemed unbelievable that so much water could disappear within a week to put the river once more between banks – but it had! The fields, though soggy, had little water lying upon them and the ditches had drained. Truly remarkable! However, I can recall when the ditches held water all summer, until the River Board (now River Authority) lowered the water table by dredging, rebuilding a weir and widening. The farmers like it; the river, now often a mere trickle in summer, doesn't.

It was carrying plenty of water, as was to be expected, but it was a nice colour, a colour that salmon anglers like in waters where salmon are plentiful. From the Dorset Stour where I fished, salmon rate with four-leaved clovers, so although the colour would make a lucky salmon angler with a good salmon river to fish a happy man, I remained the eternal pessimist.

I shall never understand myself sufficiently to know why I like salmon fishing at all. I like pulling out fish, though one doesn't often do this on the rivers I can afford to frequent. Often the fish just aren't there, and if they are, how do you fish for something that doesn't eat? Without going deeply into arguments as to whether a salmon does eat or not in freshwater, the most argumentative in favour of their feeding would agree that they can only eat very rarely, hence their weight loss

by spawning time, so it doesn't leave the angler much chance. I subscribe to the theory that they don't eat.

Believing that salmon don't eat in freshwater makes the choosing of a bait with which to catch them something of a paradox. One can only use past experience, and such logical reasons as have nothing to do with the fish's willingness to eat. Can it see the bait in this colour of water? With a bit of colour we will therefore use a size that is larger, as we think it is more obvious to the fish. Is it heavy enough to get down to the fish in this deep water, or this fast water, and will we therefore need lead, perhaps a lot of lead? These are questions that tug at our brain, and are little to do with what the salmon would like to eat.

In the sea it must be one of the most voracious of fishes to attain the weight it does in such a short time. Perhaps here is the answer, and those who suggest a salmon's take is a reflex action of feeding are near the mark. Certainly salmon fresh from the sea are more inclined to take than those that have tasted freshwater for a while.

The nice colour of the water that I spoke of earlier, which meant to me, reasonably clear with the bottom showing at a depth of a couple of feet or so, suggested a Devon of 3in in length, but quite brightly coloured to show well.

The most popular colour for Devons on our southern rivers early in the year is the Yellow Belly. This Devon, with its dark green back, contrasts greatly as it spins, with the yellow flashing better than a silver or gold spoon would glitter. In coloured water yellow is a wonderful colour for show, and universally yellow is becoming accepted as the colour for road signs, lorry markings and number plates.

There are many colour combinations that one can try, and doubtless all would catch salmon, but one tends to use that which has brought success. I do like a dark

Another one for Kay, a fourteen-pounder, is 'tailed' by their good friend Denny Paulley, now unfortunately no longer with us.

back to the Devon – black is excellent because of the contrast it gives with the lighter belly colour, and I think this adds to the attraction of the lure, giving life as the pattern changes from dark to light at each revolution. Black, shading to yellow, black/orange, black/pink, blue/orange, all catch salmon within my own experience in nice colour water, and when it becomes really clear, brown and gold is good, or if using the brighter combinations or spoons, taken a size or two smaller.

The Dorset Stour could be called a problem river in many ways when related to other salmon rivers. There are many reasons for drawing a blank. Where I fish the river at Wimborne, it is several miles from the sea with some major obstacles for the salmon to surmount on their way from the salt. They will pass these easily enough when the river is in spate, or possibly even when the river is carrying a good head of water, but this latter situation is rare today owing to the River Authority's desecration

and canalization policy, which drains any extra water away to the sea as fast as possible. There is also heavy abstraction upriver. Those of us who love the river, and have yearly observed its deterioration, consider it has been criminally treated.

The Stour runs into the sea at Christchurch, and is here joined by the Hampshire Avon. I have often read that the Avon estuary is at Christchurch, but it would appear to me that the Avon joins the Stour upstream of Christchurch Harbour and is therefore a tributary of it. Be that as it may, the Avon, of chalk stream character and of far greater flow than the Stour, has good runs of salmon, and I often wonder whether any Stour salmon are drawn to its better waters and stronger currents, or follow the heavier runs of salmon up its course. Salmon are greatly influenced by a strong flow of water, and the Avon has that 90 per cent of the year, whereas the Stour probably has a goodly current only 10 per cent of the year.

Conversely, during freak conditions, when storms or heavy rainfall in Dorset have not reached Hampshire, and the Stour has run full while the Avon has been at a normal level, I have seen a good run of salmon in the Stour. However, this has happened but twice in the twenty odd years I have fished it, and I have wondered whether the pull of water drew Avon salmon to the Stour.

It is sad that nowadays the Stour is often of such a reduced flow. No water – no fish! And you can add to this the fact that it is badly polluted; this increases with low flows, and my pessimism that increases with the years is understandable.

It seems that as soon as one has learned of salmon lies and particular places favoured by the fish, along comes the River Authority and dredges it. Usually the better water – shallows, narrows and the like – are the very places that the authority considers are in need of 'improvement'. It takes years for the river to settle down, and the angler to learn its new characteristics – by which time the authority probably decides it needs 'improving' once more. It seems that authorities hate any shallow water, and remove spawning gravels. This is illegal, but such bodies appear to be a law unto themselves.

Despite this I have caught a good number of salmon from the Stour, mainly by sheer persistence, or dogged stupidity, whichever way you look at it.

This particular day was dull with a steady drizzle. 'Brightening from the west' had been the forecast, and so we looked forward to the latter part of the day being pleasant, or as pleasant as one can expect in March. I worked down the river, and with the current strong I avoided the coarse fish. I do not recall even catching a jack, which at times can be a menace, swimming in strong fast currents where they have no right to be. The deep stretches were worked through with a heavy lead hanging from a nylon link,

A fine brace of spring fish from the Dorset Stour for Dave Steuart.

suspended from the line some 3ft (90cm) above the plastic Devon. Bouncing bottom with the lead ensured that the Devon would be down there too, but working about a foot clear of the riverbed.

I cast to the far side of the river and work it slowly back, walking three paces between casts. With the long, 11ft spinning rod I bring the bait back just within the current on the edge of the slack. If allowed to come back on the slack side I know what will happen – a ruddy pike! With the higher water, eddies and slacks are fewer, and more of the water could hold a fish. This makes for hard work, as so much of it must be searched and little of it can be passed over.

Cast after cast. It can become mechanical, but this is not the way to fish, and one must be aware of anything amiss at the Devon's end. A slight drag may denote a fish or a piece of weed, a hard knock, a hard pull – there are several ways a salmon takes a bait. Concentration is needed to notice the single or double knock that one often gets from a salmon, that is so gentle, so slight as to be almost imperceptible – but there is nonetheless a sharpness about it that spells out a salmon to the hand of the experienced salmon angler. If it were not so it would be far too gentle for any ordinary human hand to detect, but the delicacy yet sharpness of the touch is made by no other fish but a salmon.

Only one reason for this habit of a salmon can I give: it is a warning to the intruder to leave the salmon's lie. It is very important to notice it, as the following cast to the same spot is often greeted with a full-blooded take. If one had not noticed the knock and had taken the usual three steps downstream before casting again, one would have been retrieving the lure below the salmon's position and would not have shown the bait to it again.

One must be forever looking, watching for the roll of a fish that perhaps doesn't break water, its movement shown only by the hump on the surface. The lure must be ever watched as it comes into view in case a fish is following, or turns away, or flashes at it. One then, of course, spends time at the place. I have caught several fish by thinking I saw an underwater movement when my eyes weren't sure.

I must have covered a mile of river, and having come to a long shallow stretch, had changed to a straightforward uptrace lead instead of the paternoster style. Although the Stour carried extra water, these shallows were not really deep enough for the hanging lead, and it would be quicker to fish through them with straightforward terminal spinning tackle. I also changed to a 2.5in bait to fish the shallower water where more light would penetrate.

The current carried the Devon across the shallows for the umpteenth time, and soon they would be passed by. I was thinking that then I would return to the paternoster when I felt the double knock. My stomach turned over and the adrenalin pumped. Strange that this should happen after so many fish of all sorts through the years. I hope it always will! I fished out the cast, my eyes peering into the river hoping to see some huge shape following the Devon, but there was only emptiness.

I had let the current swing the bait across slowly, but so as to fish a little faster past the very spot I had felt the knocks, I made my next cast a couple of yards further downstream and wound back instead of allowing the stream to swing the bait over. The take was not violent, although fishing faster and consequently higher in the water I had expected it to be so, if it came at all. It was just as if I had caught bottom.

I pulled hard, and was answered by a tremendous swirl on the surface, followed by a couple of thumps as the fish shook its head, then rolled and backed downstream a little. My butterflies were now gone and I looked forward with pleasure to the duel to follow, and with fear of the hook-hold failing. One has no wish to lose the first fish of the season, but alas it happens, but not by breakage. Many fish have come unstuck, but if I were to keep statistical information I would probably find that of the thousands of fish I have caught of different species, those that fell off would number far less than 2 or 3 per cent. The agony would be that it would be the important 3 per cent. I prefer happy memories – hang the statistics!

While the pleasurable conflict was in the mind the fish decided to travel upstream close to my bank, and although hugging the bottom, the water was not over deep below me, so I pressured the fish for a look. It lifted and I was pleased to see a big fresh fish and not a kelt, which is a strong possibility early in the season.

The pressure awakened the salmon into activity, and he turned and went downstream very fast aided by the current, straight on down past the rippling, surging gravel shoal, below which he paused to face the flow for a breather. Here I caught up with him, regained all my line, and had a breather too.

Another run downstream, and now when I got level with him there was a spot that I could enter the river. This would be as far as I would need to go, as the salmon was now wallowing and almost ready to be gaffed. Putting the gaff in a springer, which I have done many times, always creates a doubt as one must have some conscience when looking at such beauty and symmetry.

Mine is removed by immediately removing the spark of life and thus any suffering the creature may be experiencing.

Although salmon have fallen to my rod as fresh in appearance as any sea-netted fish, few have carried the corroborating sea lice, and none has come from the Stour. I was thus enormously pleased to note that this first fish was still a host to sea lice, and was therefore proved to be a fresh-run fish; it was also the first I had taken from the Stour carrying sea lice. Inevitably, when the excitement has passed, one views early success with mixed feelings, knowing full well that good starts do not always lead to good seasons.

However, I felt good. Even the sun came out in the afternoon, allowing me to pose with the fish for a better quality picture. By the way, not a monster, but at 21lb a happy start, and a bird in the hand ...

Just to show the man gets around – a salmon from Loch Lomond.

7 Some of my Favourite Salmon Rivers in the British Isles, Europe and Beyond

By Bob Church

Catching that First Salmon on the Fly

In this chapter I would like to acquaint you with some of my favourite salmon rivers in the British Isles, Europe and further afield.

In addition I will discuss my experiences and the techniques involved in fishing for salmon and sea trout from a drifting boat. I conclude the chapter with a brief consideration of the controversial subject of stocked salmon in stillwaters.

Barrie Welham with a 28lb cock salmon from the River Dee.

Bob Church's first salmon on fly: 7lb from the River Itchen.

In my autobiography called *This Fishing Life* (Crowood, 2003) I did mention that catching your first salmon on the fly is an extremely memorable fishing moment. Therefore, if you are a trout fly fisher thinking of trying the fly for the king of fish, the Atlantic salmon – you must remember this. So, find yourself an experienced guide, as I did in Barrie Welham. Here was a man who knew his stuff, and although I had caught a few salmon before, this was always spinning with Tobies or Devon Minnows. Barrie had told me to be good and early at his penthouse flat in

OPPOSITE: Some useful salmon fly patterns include tubes and smaller flies for the River Ness.

Southampton. (By the way, this all happened well over thirty-five years ago, but it is still a clear memory.)

Barrie had taken me to the sparkling River Itchen and I was full of confidence because I knew Barrie to be a perfectionist. 'It will take us about two hours' fishing to fish the whole beat. You get tackled up and put on this Blue Charm number 8, double-hook fly,' he recommended.

We walked across a meadow, and stopped where the river had a fast run along the far bank. Fifty yards downstream the river had a bend on it so sharp it disappeared from view. Barrie said, 'This is the best stretch on the beat. Now fish it down carefully right to the bend, the taking spot is about five yards before you reach the bend.'

I was dropping my fly consistently accurately about one foot from the far bank, casting slightly downstream; this gave it the deadly swing around with the current. Barrie said, 'You have got about six casts left, then you have had it.' Three casts later, and in the exact spot that Barrie had said was crucial, a salmon hit my fly very hard and motored off downstream round the bend.

Barrie pointed out the best landing spot, where the river was only about six yards wide. My Carbon 8-weight trout rod had performed well, and after perhaps ten minutes the fish was in the net. We administered the priest to a nice cock fish grilse of 7lb.

'Only one "first"-caught salmon on the fly, you know, Bob,' said Barrie. As we walked back to the car, I felt really good. If it was now, I would probably have returned such a fish, but it was then and it was normal to keep it. 'Well,' said Barrie, as he drove me back to his home and my car, 'life isn't so bad, after all.' How true that all was at

that particular moment. Also it was clear to me that catching salmon on the fly was far more preferable than with bait or spinning. This lesson has stayed with me in all the years since, when I estimate having around 250 fly-caught salmon on my list.

It does also mean that a good ghillie can give you a quick shortcut to the best taking spots on any new river or beat that you fish. It's all right once you know a water well, but until then take advice from the experienced local man, because salmon 'take' in the same places year in, year out.

Salmon fishing has always been two or three times a year, holidays in Scotland sharing good beats with friends, fishing all day and wining and dining at night. Some often overdo the wining, which means no early start for them! But after breakfast, and fishing by 9am is usually the accepted programme, then a stop from 1pm until 2pm for a light lunch, then pack up at 6pm. This varies on some rivers, but the whole idea of a salmon-fishing holiday week is first,

This is Bob's largest UK salmon on fly, caught on a brass tube with gold body and yellow wing from the River Tweed.

Jeanette shows this 15lb 8oz fresh in, cock salmon from the River Ness Castle Beat. Gordon Armstrong ghillies.

catch a fish on the fly, then you can relax. Our wives usually come along on these trips because they are completely included. They can take off during the day and go sight-seeing or shopping, or even fish, as women do catch quite a lot of the largest salmon caught. (See the picture above of my wife Jeanette, with a 15lb 8oz salmon caught from the River Ness.)

A Really Big Salmon on Fly

Because I have been able to fish so much and for such a long time – I have been around a very long time, really – this has given me the opportunities to try seriously for most species as the years have rolled by. When I hear some anglers go on about the fight of certain fish, I always stand in judgment and say none can fight like the true king of fish, the Atlantic salmon. Having notched up around twenty over 20lb, mostly from the River Tweed, the river draws me back each autumn for a three-day treat, fishing

for the greybacks. These are really large fish that come late in the season. The method is to fly fish using a 15ft double-handed rod and a weighted brass tube, fly fished on a medium sinking fly line.

I was fishing the deep hole at the Bridge Pool at Kelso about twenty years ago, and I had returned two hen fish of good size earlier in the day. I was fishing from a boat with head ghillie Billy Jack. The afternoon was pressing on, and it was very cold, with the bank-side frost not thawed all day (it was mid-November). I put on a yellow and black hair wing with a gold Mylar body, and cast out once more well across the current. The line swung round deep, and I had a terrific take, hooking a monster cock fish. The fight lasted for twenty minutes, and I was giving the fish all I had got with my 15lb breaking strain leader.

The fish gave one spectacular leap towards the end of the fight, then soon he was in the net. At 28lb 2oz he was a big brute of a cock fish, still my best to date in the UK. Salmon are the best fighters, and

135

Billy Jack the ghillie is about to net a salmon with Stephen Church on Kelso Bridge Beat on the Tweed.

I have not changed my views after all these years – except that the policy nowadays is to return virtually all the fish to the water. Nothing changes, you get good years when the fish are plentiful and the water is in perfect order; or the river could possibly be in full flood, and then you watch the price of the day's ticket go sailing down with the flood water because you can't fish – it is a risk you take when booking top beats at the back end on the Tweed.

There is an old saying 'keep your fly in the water', and that is still so true today: when catches are down, persistence means that you get the bonus fish while the others pack up too easily. Salmon are such strange fish, because if they are there and on the take, anyone could catch one. But if things are not quite right, such as low

water for some time, or excessive flooding, it will be the man who puts in that extra effort who will catch. There is always one waif and stray.

Barrie Welham said to me some thirty years ago: 'In May on the Aberdeenshire Dee is the best floating line salmon fishing anywhere.' So I tried it out, and certainly it is a great salmon river with some wonderful beats. I have fished on several of the well-known ones, with a reasonable amount of success. I learnt one important lesson on two very good holding pools called Upper and Lower Roe Pot. Following a drop in high water we were a little frustrated, as all we could catch were a few nice 2lb 8oz sea trout. The river wasn't perfect, but it was good enough. I eventually hooked a grilse for about five seconds, and then it came

Our host Con Wilson caught this one, at just over 30lb: a cock fish, and Stephen Church lifted it for him as he could not lift it himself.

A 23lb 8oz cock fish caught by Bob at Bridge Pool on the Tweed at Kelso. Dr Gardner looks on.

off. Typical of a regular reservoir trout fly fisherman, I had struck far too soon, and I learned that day, once and for all, not to make that mistake again.

In the evening our very experienced ghillie the late Rod Grant showed his expertise, fishing a difficult lie between two large rocks. His deadly method for these middle reaches of the Dee was to use tiny trebles of 14s and 12s, hiding these hooks in the dressing of the tiniest tube fly you could ever imagine. There was a salmon resting in this spot, and Rod caught it: he made it look so easy. The grilse was the first to be caught all week, and that included prime beats upstream and downstream. This incident was in my early salmon fishing days, and the next day the river was up once again in brown flood-water conditions.

I began to understand the frustration of the salmon fisher who usually gets greeted by the ghillie: 'Oh, you should have been here last week, it was perfect!'

Our final session of the week was to be on Saturday morning, and the river had once again settled down to near normality. My fishing mate Peter Dobbs and I made an early start going out of the lodge before breakfast, but I had to wait until midday before I hooked my salmon, after raising three others. I had a classic take, and let the reel run off a yard or so of line on check, just as Rod Grant had told me. The fish was a fresh 7lb 8oz grilse, which was very rewarding after the week we had had.

Aberdeenshire River Dee. A lovely summer floating line river.

Stephen Church plays a good salmon in the Bridge Pool, Kelso, on the River Tweed.

*Peter Dobby doing the netting on
the River Dee.*

While salmon fishing you should always
remember that persistence pays off. The
other lessons I learned on this trip, which
was in my early salmon days, came from
Rod. He made me take my striking hand off
the floating line: cast it out, mend it if needs

Not a monster, but a welcome fish.

*When in Scotland for salmon fishing invariably the
accommodation is good, too.*

139

The famed River Spey near Grantown.

The River Avon is a tributary of the Spey. This 12lb 8oz salmon was caught to order for Reg Righyni.

Reg Righyni follows Bob down. He caught this nice sea trout on the River Avon.

Manager at the Testwood Pool on the River Test with a nice salmon.

be and follow it round, but just hold the cork handle. After a yard or so of line pulls from the reel's ratchet, then you strike. You will find the fly will always be right in the back of the fish's mouth and therefore will not come off. He also gave me the faith to use very small flies in the summer months.

England

One river where I have often been invited to fish for salmon is the Lower River Test. David Train was the fly supplier to Bob Church & Co. He had his own team of very good fly tiers out in Kenya, and we spent many thousands of pounds with him every year. He had a two-day rod on the first major pool as the salmon entered the river from the estuary, called Testwood beat. You have the bank-side house at your disposal, and a big salmon and sea trout holding pool. However, this is a bit of an obstacle for fish wanting to go upstream. (See Dave Steuart's chapter.) David used to bait fish during the morning, then stop for a slow, restful lunch, then fish again with bait until about 5pm; then have another break, finally fishing with the fly for sea trout as dusk approached.

In the plentiful years of the early 1980s, David float fished the shrimp or prawn very skilfully; he became quite an expert at this method, catching records from the Hampshire Avon, twelve in a day from the Royalty fishery. Then he did similar from the Herefordshire Wye, with another twelve in a day from the once-famous Carrots Pool. Of course I can report he returned the majority of them.

At Testwood Pool David Train nets a 20lb salmon for Peter Dobbs.

I remember him hooking a 13lb fresh salmon just before lunch, and it came off. After lunch two hours later he dropped in his shrimp on float over the same run again; as it neared the taking spot, he just held the float back, causing the shrimp bait to lift in the current. This is the magical, induced 'take' situation that fools sea trout

Peter Dobbs and David Train show the catch for the day at Testwood Pool (the good old days).

Bob's catch from Testwood Pool. Today you would keep only one cock fish: times have changed for the good.

On the River Moy, Mount Falcon Castle Beat.

and salmon alike. He landed the fish at 13lb, and it had the tell-tale fresh tear with a spot of blood from where he had hooked it earlier. I was amazed that salmon could be so dumb. David returns all his fish these days, apart from the occasional smoker. He fishes many different rivers, nearly always with the fly.

I and good friend Peter Dobbs from Northampton were David's guests some twenty-five years ago; we were worm fishing, and I had a fish of around 7lb and David had a brace. Suddenly from the weir pool I heard 'Dobbie' shout, and I turned round to see this huge great salmon leap high out of the water; then it tried its level best to get up the weir. David eventually netted

it for him and it weighed just on the 20lb. Needless to say Dobbie soon administered the priest – but I am sure that if the same thing happened today, he would return it.

Ireland

The River Moy in the west of Ireland is a good place where you can catch grilse from the river. These fish are plentiful from June to early September. Most salmon fishers will have heard of the 'Ridge Pool': some days here you can catch salmon almost like catching rainbow trout. The smallest grilse I have ever seen comes from this river – I have seen them as small as 2lb 8oz.

143

A morning's catch on the River Moy, Mount Falcon Castle Beat.

Michael Leonard with a nice 15lb salmon from the Owen Duff river, Galway, on the fly.

In the centre of the little town of Ballina, the river section is known as the 'Cathedral Beats'. I found this very good, and my best method was to use a weight forward number 10 sink tip fly line and a size 12 Yellow Ally Shrimp. But there were lessons learnt on one particular day's fishing: first of all I noticed that everyone was using orange Alli Shrimps, but the fish got so used to them that they completely ignored the orange colour. I, too, started with orange, but I soon changed my fly to yellow, and went down to a size 12 treble. This brought immediate success, with two nice fish as my sink tip line swung the fly round to finish up under the arch of the downstream bridge. I had quite an audience of holidaymakers watching the

salmon's reactions. Not exactly an idyllic situation, but if you want to catch an easy salmon, here is a good place to begin, especially if you are on a budget. Contact the West of Ireland Fishery Board.

Another stretch of the River Moy worth fishing is the day-permit stretch held by Mount Falcon Castle at Foxford. We were a party of six, and between us caught eleven grilse in one afternoon's fishing. A very young Jeremy Herrmann caught his first salmon on this trip, a grilse of about 4lb; when he took the fly out, on a high sloping bank, it promptly jumped back in again – though Jeremy swears he would have returned it anyway. This is to demonstrate to you how effective this river is in summer.

Jeremy Herrmann caught his first grilse here on the River Moy. He turned out to be a world champion.

While holiday-making in this superb fishing area of counties Mayo and Galway, you must spend a day's fishing in the Galway Weir Fishery. This is a massive set of weirs allowing the water to run out of the largest western lough – Corrib; the largest at over 40,000 acres (16ha) it sheds a lot of water. The actual weir is a series of gates that are opened according to the flow, but it is nearly always fishable. Some good springers from teens of pounds to over 20lb are caught each early season. Once again, though, it is the grilse fishing of the summer months that really is quite excellent. Pre-book with Western Region Fisheries Board, Galway Fishery, Nuns Island, Galway. Telephone 00353 91562388.

A return trip to Feeagh (the upper lough of the Burrishule system) was very good, and this time we caught four salmon and some more sea trout. When biologist Chris Mills (*see* page 163) left, the fishing management went to Dr Ken Whelan, a man who had a great understanding of all you needed to know about salmon.

In one brave experiment at the Burrishule Fishery they artificially crossed their

Jeanette with a lovely grilse from the River Moy at Foxford.

145

Fishing the tail of the Galway Weir with the fly.

own Irish wild salmon with the much larger Norwegian strain. From this cross, lots of smolts made their way back to the sea; then after three years some came back, and fish of 22lb and 18lb were caught by anglers – but at the time we all felt that too many salmon were being taken by nets from the sea. The final day on Lough Furness produced another grilse of 6lb.

To fish these two adjacent loughs you can stay in the little town of Westport a couple of miles up the road. Should you wish to do it in real style, making it a marvellous holiday for the wife too, a stay at Newport House Hotel is highly recommended. This is quite excellent, and staying there enables you to fish the Newport river, and a little lough full of small browns up to 1lb 8oz, and higher up, Lough Beltra, which can be very good. Fish a drifting boat for salmon.

Gordon Sim with a 16¾lb Norwegian cross salmon caught in Lough Furnace on a trout rod.

The Cathedral Beat in the centre of Ballina, Ireland.

Iceland

Although some Scottish, Norwegian and Russian rivers can be marvellous for large Atlantic salmon, I think Iceland has to be the most consistent country for sport with a fly rod. A couple of visits to Iceland made me realize what a fantastic, clean and pollution-free country this is, and how perfect everything is – except for the price of drinks. Imagine a country as big as England and Wales, but with only around

Bob was following this man down the beat when he hooked this lively salmon.

147

I followed him in with my sink tip, and caught after two casts on a yellow Alli.

Orri Vigfusson has been a prime mover in getting salmon netting in the estuary in our rivers stopped by raising funds and buying out the netsmen (Orri is on the left).

a third of a million people living there. It is full of rivers and lakes, and doesn't know the words 'pollution' and 'algae'.

My first trip was with Peter Gathercole and John Beer. In fact it was more of a whistle-stop tour of various very plentiful rivers and lakes, which held a few late springers, but lots of grilse, and also the sea trout and sea-run char were just in, too. However, the brown trout were a surprise, as their size and quality were better than any I had seen before. Peter, John and I caught all these species in good numbers. We were guests of the Angling Club of Reykjavík and basically we were on a fact-finding tour to see how good the general game fishing was. The flight from Heathrow was less than three hours, half as much as it takes me to drive up to the Scottish rivers I fish.

Our first two guides, Jon and Freddie, drove us to the River Sog, where they said

we would catch a few. The summer grilse run was just beginning, and we all hooked a fish or two, apart from Freddie. He waded out to the middle of this very wide river with his single-handed 10ft fly rod. Eventually he hooked a big fish, a late-running springer of around 17lb; it took him close on an hour to play it out for Jon to net.

After staying the night in a bank-side hut, we made our way back to Reykjavik. Here we fished a gin-clear River Ellidnar in the city boundary. This river seemed to be full of fish, all grilse from 4lb 8oz to 7lb 8oz. I managed three in an hour on a size 12 gold treble with a Red Shrimp pattern tied on it. This is a Peter Deane pattern, and a big favourite for Iceland's grilse runs. Another very good pattern was a Blue Charm tied on number 12 or number 14 trebles.

After fishing out the first short stretch, we drove round a few houses to another little

Desolate Iceland.

stretch that had a mini weir on it, and here we had a surprise of some beautiful brown trout that the locals don't bother with at all, and almost regard as vermin. After removing the salmon flies that had caught the grilse, we put on the usual Gold Head Hare's Ear, and caught a nice few up to 3lb.

That evening we met up with our new guides, Jimmy and Oli; we made an early start the next day, driving some 200 miles. The journey was hilarious, as we rarely drove on any normal road, just a solid black gravelly sand, which seemed all right for the flat. 'Where are we going?' I asked Freddie. 'Over that mountain,' he replied. 'We will then soon be at Veidivotn Lakes.'

'Hang on a minute, Freddie; is there a proper road to drive on?' 'No,' replied Freddie, adding this rather amusing comment: 'When the last of these volcanic eruptions was dying down, it was blowing tiny black stones high into the air, and when it all landed it was just like tarmacking the whole set of mountains, all the rough bits were underneath.'

There were no trees, very little grass, but plenty of colourful herbaceous alpine plants. I was very pleased to see great beds of wild lupins, pinkie mauve in colour and a very hardy flower. I looked them up, and there are over 200 species of these herbaceous perennials. They certainly brightened up the Black Desert. We made our way through a couple of wild river fords, and soon we were at our destination, a ten-berth fishing hut complete with a lovely hot water bath tub, courtesy of the hot water geyser coming straight out of the rock. I shall never forget the sight of John Beer, stark naked, soaking himself in the tub and sipping a large gin and tonic.

It was decidedly chilly when we dressed the following morning; we went outside with the full chest waders and warmest gear. Peter walked off quickly to a point on the first lake we came to. On the first cast he was into a nice brownie of 2lb – and so it went on for the three of us. The best fish we caught was 4lb 8oz, to a fish-fillet bait:

The Appetiser Lure not only works on reservoirs, but also in Iceland, Canada and Finland.

this was by a young fellow who no doubt would go over to fly fishing very soon. On the way back to yet another new river, the superb Hitera, we stopped to meet Jimmy's son Siggi: he was fishing the Stora Laxa river, which has bright green glacier-fed water and runs at this point through a narrow gorge. Siggi had just netted a 17lb

8oz specimen, about ten minutes before we arrived, another lovely fish.

Then we were off on a long drive to a luxury lodge on the Hitera river. As we sat at the breakfast table overlooking the river, we were watching leaping salmon (grilse) everywhere. The fish were just in and very fresh. It was here that we sampled our best sport.

The first pool I fished I took seven grilse, using my all-time favourite sink tip fly line made especially for me by Mr Dick Tallents senior, thirty-five years ago. It is a weight forward number 10, and has probably caught me over 150 salmon – it is still like a new fly line, and I just could not go on a salmon trip without it. This time it gave me

Fishing the River Hitera.

A fresh grilse caught on the River Hitera.

As well as salmon you can also catch these wonderful char. They run up from the sea just the same as salmon, and are the best-tasting game fish I have eaten.

Oliver Edwards with a brace of char.

Bob and Oliver Edwards sort out tactics.

thirteen grilse from three short sessions on three different rivers. The line just presents the salmon fly at exactly the right speed so the fish has the confidence to take it.

Whilst on the subject of fly lines for salmon, everyone likes first and foremost to use a floater, but if the current is a little bit racy, your fly swings round far too quickly for the salmon to bother with it. If, however, you slow it down and get the fly moving at the right depth, you will get far more action.

The slow sinking can also be good at times of heavier water, and often you need a Wet Cell 2 sinking double taper when casting big tube flies of brass or copper – for example on the Tweed in late autumn.

Sweden

The River Morrum in southern Sweden is the river of giants. I have never seen anything like it for sheer size of both salmon and sea trout. The sea trout average 10lb in weight, and the salmon 20lb in weight.

Sweden's Morrum ghillie Isaac Kristian's favourite fly is an Allsock Fly.

I had two separate weeks fishing the Morrum, Martin Founds of Anglers World Holidays arranging both of them. After booking in at the hotel we had an early dinner, then went to look at the river. As I walked down to the lodge I noticed an angler walking back from the riverside with a very nice fish, which I assumed to be a salmon, of around 20lb plus. He walked into the weighing room and placed it on the scales. The arrow shot round to 22lb 8oz, and I commented, 'Nice fish!' but he didn't look too excited. I looked a little more closely at the fish, and exclaimed, 'But it's a sea trout!' – and it was, too! I asked him if I could take a picture, and he nodded.

I had to get my camera from the car, and when I got back some ten minutes later he said, 'Now for picture, I have cleaned it ready!' And do you know, he had gutted this beautiful fish? He was Danish. I took a photo anyway, as it was as heavy as the UK record. It was hard to believe! After racing through breakfast I was back at the fishery, got my permit from the office, and checked with the others where they were fishing. As we wandered down to the river, we met an angler coming up the pathway towards us with an identical sea trout as the one the night before, another 22lb 8oz – were they *all* that size? I joked.

My best went 8lb 8oz, but I could have had a 16lb had I not been so eager to get what I thought was the best spot on a new beat. At the fishery, which is very well organized, you draw a partner and share a decent-sized stretch, then you change position every hour by moving downstream by one position; this is carried out on a gentleman's basis. My partner, another Dave, agreed that I could take the point. He fished the unlikely spot of an inside bay, with the result that he caught a fish of 16lb.

An example of a salmon of 55lb; it is possible to catch such monsters on the River Morrum Fishery. This was caught on a plug in the estuary.

The River Morrum has safe, good wading.

As you can see, the River Morrum is a beautiful river.

A fabulous spring salmon of 31lb for our guide, Isaac Kristian.

The fishery is state owned and managed expertly by Curt Johansson. I was very impressed with his knowledge, and the way he had restored the River Morrum to its marvellous situation with big salmon and sea trout. Roughly he had done this by getting every spawning area cleared to ensure that the right type of stony gravel was in place in order for the returning salmon to spawn more successfully. Then he selected the biggest of the hen fish, stripped them of eggs, and matched these with appropriate male's milt; this kept the genes of the largest fish intact. After doing this for a few years, the big salmon and sea trout were returning in much larger numbers. Also the

I photographed this angler about to release this fish; a shaft of light makes it a perfect action picture.

A 25lb salmon for Isaac Kristian from the pool above the rapids.

well maintained spawning streams began to do the job naturally again.

Curt did say to me, 'Your famous big springer rivers of yesterday, such as the Hants Avon and definitely the Herefordshire Wye, could still be saved. All it needs is a similar policy, but with someone in charge who will see it through with loving care.'

Before we leave the Morrum story there is one fly used on the river called the 'All Suck': it is a shrimp-style pattern and comes in all sorts of sizes and all sorts of hooks, and is incredibly good. I recommend that you tie up a few, because it really works in the UK rivers as well. This fly was recommended by our guide Isaac Kristian, who is one of the top fishers on this river.

Carol Neal from Leamington Spa was a member of our party and was fishing Beat 4 when she hooked and landed a 25lb salmon; this was quickly returned. Then fifteen minutes later she hooked another of approximately 35lb, which again she returned without ceremony. A German

angler was watching all this, and was amazed at what she was doing: he wanted to know why she was putting such big fish back. He just did not understand that it was because they were red and dark-looking, a far cry from those bright silver springers of April and May.

On one of these days I was partnered with my good fishing companion the late Frank Cutler; he warned me: 'If I hook one of those big ones you'll have to help me out and take the rod!' Frank had suffered from angina for many years, and would often joke, 'Keep taking the pills!' Well, he did hook a big one, and I would *not* take the rod, and he tailed it by hand, then posed for a photo for me, and then let it go. Then got out of the river and took his emergency angina pill. He watched me fish for the rest of the morning.

As I said at the beginning, this is the river of giants, and I was to taste the thrill of hooking one, by far the largest salmon I have ever hooked. I was using a quite powerful 10ft 6in Bob Church boron fly

155

Frank Cutler fishing the River Morrum.

Frank Cutler is into a fish.

Frank Cutler plays his fish.

Frank Cutler tails his fish, then releases it back into the water.

Fishery manager grading fish for spawning.

rod, a wet cell 2 sinking line, and a 20lb breaking strain nylon leader. The river had risen about 12in, which is why I tried the medium sinker – and it worked.

Swinging round suddenly I became connected to a very heavy fish that just didn't move apart from shaking its head a few times. I had waded to maximum depth. My All Suck fly was tied on to a large number 2, very strong wire single hook. The fish finally realized something was wrong, and ran very fast towards me; when it was about three yards from me, it gave an almighty leap: it was massive, at least 40 to 45lb!

It now shot across to the other side of the river, which was quite wide at this point, and began to make its way upstream, keeping to about three yards from the far bank. I held my rod high, as the sinking line began to bounce along the bottom in a big circular movement. Then it happened: I felt the line grinding as it became semi-wedged under a large round rock. Fortunately the fish stayed on, and while I was figuring out what

to do, next thing my guide Isaac turned up, having been checking on the others.

I quickly told him what had happened, and that the line was free enough to take the short, now weaker runs the fish was doing. Isaac then said, 'Keep doing what you are doing, and I will go upstream where I think I can wade across even in this rising water.'

He did this, but as he began to wade out, the line, which was not visible, hit his legs; he then bent down and hand-grasped the leader, but despite 20lb line the salmon broke the nylon just like cotton. Of course, I would have put it back anyhow, but I would at least have liked a quick photo – even though he was a big old cock fish.

The fishery is rated as one of the very best salmon and sea trout centres in the world. This is mainly due to the positive, forward-looking views of the state Forestry Commission, and also of the local anglers, who agreed on a fisheries management and enhancement structure. This all happened back in the 1940s, but the results can be seen today.

The Morrum Fishery is 4.5 miles (7km) of both banks; it produces 200,000 salmon smolts, around 50 per cent by natural means, and around 100,000 sea trout smolts. The unique genetic strain of these fish produces the very fast growth rate, as both species feed in the rich waters of the Baltic Sea. Salmon have grown to 30kg here. Contact the fishery through Anglers World Holidays; at the time of writing the phone number is 01246 221717, and speak to Martin Founds.

Scotland

The River Ness

I have enjoyed fishing several of Scotland's lovely rivers: the wild Findhorn, the Thurso, the Aberdeenshire Dee, the Tweed and its tributaries, the Till, the Ettrick and Teviot; also the North Esk and, as I write, the River Lyon, a tributary of the Tay – this is very much a first-time trip for me. Then of course my current favourite place of all, the Ness Castle beat on the River Ness. This beat has three great two-man pools, with the Black Stream probably the best on the whole river from Loch Ness to the sea.

The new owners built an incredible £1,000,000 fishing lodge for the opening of the 2006 season; it is quite luxurious, which suits the ladies in the party very well. The long-time ghillie there is the very experienced Davey Stewart, and his assistant is none other than the current new World Spey Casting Champion, Gordon Armstrong. Fishing is with floating or sink tip fly line, and size number 10 or 8 flies.

I like to fish the Black Stream first, and then make my way to the upstream head of it. Wading is fine here, but these days I always use a wading stick to be safe, also a special wading angler's automatic life jacket just in case. According to the water's height, it will be a floater or a sink tip.

At the River Ness I usually buy my flies from local John Sinclair, and that expert in the tying of Irish patterns, Del Rodgers,

One minute I was fishing quietly on the River Lyon ...

... then suddenly I was sharing it with a herd of Highland cattle and sheep.

from his fishing tackle shop in Co. Down, Northern Ireland – flies such as the Ness Castle, Cascade, Black Shrimp and various coloured Alli Shrimps. I have the greatest faith in these patterns, along with a few of my own. The River Ness is my new favourite river for fishing for salmon on a floating or a sink tip fly line.

Several rivers run into Loch Ness.

A nice River Ness salmon with sea lice still on it, and several more falling off, leaving a sore spot.

Salmon and Sea Trout from a Drifting Boat

This technique is very similar for both species. It was not until the early 1980s that I experienced boat drift fishing for salmon and sea trout. The beauty of a trip to the West of Ireland is that not only do you

have all that wild brown trout fly fishing to choose from, but also the migratory game fish as well. I have caught lots of sea trout and salmon on all the loughs mentioned, but I recall here my first encounter.

Co. Galway and Co. Mayo both have many loughs that can provide a good day's sport while drifting in the traditional manner. Although I have personally favoured Ireland more than Scotland over the years, some of my friends have done the opposite and had first-class sport in Scotland and its west coast isles. They even had sea trout just into double figures, some going for wet fly fishing on the drift.

This, then, is the ultimate challenge, and covers an early learning session for me. I included the two species together in this chapter for two reasons: firstly, many anglers have that sense of adventure to try new fly-fishing methods, especially when taking a holiday. All the migratory fish loughs I have been to have good family hotels nearby, and they are always set amongst superb scenery, such as the Connemaras.

Bob with a fresh 14lb fish from the Laggan Pool on the River Ness.

Ken Heath congratulates Mike Green on his 18lb salmon from Lady Pool on the River Ness.

A good fish just on dusk for Ken Heath on the Black Stream on the River Ness.

Our ghillies Davey Stewart and Gordon Armstrong take the morning's catch as we return for lunch.

161

A grilse for Rodney Barley on the Black Stream, River Ness.

Secondly, it's all about that extra challenge: you know you are fishing for a completely wild species, a far cry from your normal small fishery stockie rainbow back home. This thought alone is enough to motivate you into feeling that you are doing something special. If you are successful and have good sport, you will be so elated. This will be unforgettable, and your main talking point whilst in fly fishermen's company until your next holiday comes round.

Irish loughs I have fished in recent years are Innagh, Costello, Kylemore Abbey, Ballynahinch, and where it all started for me, the Burrishule Fishery, which is Lower Lough Furnace and Upper Lough Feeagh. As Paul Harris and I made the short journey from the lovely sporting Westport Hotel, we were driving through Mayo's wild countryside and were admiring the simple things others could miss, such as fuchsia hedgerows, honeysuckle, foxgloves and a host of lovely wild flowers that adorned the hedgerows and verges. The sweet smell of summer filled the air.

Fish on in the twilight.

The catch and release of salmon.

Bob returning a salmon.

Bob returning a salmon from the net.

Going back to that time, biologist Chris Mills managed the Burrishule Fishery and was carrying out a detailed study of the salmon and sea trout that moved into Furnace and on to Upper Lough Feeagh. He was a most interesting man to talk to, and I could have listened to him all day – except there was some fishing to be done.

Chris had designated the top local ghillie at this time for Paul and me; called Pat Hughes, he was now fishery manager there. He had followed in the footsteps of his father as a ghillie at this exciting venue. We were advised by Pat to fish for the sea trout on Feeagh, where there would be a possible chance of a salmon.

The set-up as regards tackle is the same as for normal drift fishing for trout, as learned on the English reservoirs. The leader cast should be 8lb breaking strain. We were advised that our top dropper should be a well greased Daddy Long Legs, with the centre and point flies whatever we fancied. Apparently the Daddy had been catching

The 'Pot' on the River Ness is between the Laggan and Black Stream. The river runs through a narrow channel very fast, but this spot often holds a fish or two.

sea trout well for other anglers earlier that week. We didn't need telling twice, so we both put one on. Feeling in an experimental mood, I took from my fly box a Black Hair Wing pattern which had some pearl flashabou mixed in the wing. Ghillie Pat smiled and gave an approving nod, so on the point it went.

Incredibly we were both into sea trout right from the start, nice fish in the 1lb 8oz to 2lb 8oz class. And within ten minutes I was into a salmon, which took the Daddy; but after two good runs and a flurry of spray, it came off. Paul was getting good action on a Stoats Tail fly from the sea trout, but he raised two salmon that shied away.

When fishing short line wet fly tactics, it is worth remembering that the method that kills the more plentiful sea trout needs a very fast retrieve, but misses out on the

A huge fish, which would have broken the UK record for salmon had it been kept: 2in longer than Miss Balintine's fish and with a 20in girth, it was caught slightly upstream of our beats on the River Ness.

The million-pound lodge we stay in with our own chef. When booking the Ness Castle beats, this comes with it.

Paul Harris with a nice grilse from Upper Feeagh.

salmon. On the other hand the very slow salmon-style of retrieve, dropping the rod on the take and so on, misses out on the sea trout. We lost five salmon on this day because all were taking on the fast retrieve, but of course they were not being hooked properly. All were summer grilse of around 6lb to 7lb mark.

Trout anglers are well known for losing salmon because they always strike too quickly. You must allow the salmon to turn down on the fly, pausing long enough for him to be pulling off line before you strike. This is something that is far easier to do

Top ghillie and caster Gordon Armstrong doing the perfect Spey cast.

Going out on Lough Furnace.

when you are fishing a river and are after salmon only.

We had become so involved with the sea trout that it was only at the end of the session that we realized things could have been very different. Instead of catching lots of sea trout on single hook flies and fast stripping, we could have used small doubles or treble hair wing flies and fished slowly, and boated five or six salmon. Not that it

Three grilse for Paul Harris and Dave Whitrum off Lough Furnace.

Lady angler with a nice Lough Furnace fish.

Mel Parrott and Jeanette Church drifting for salmon on Lough Belta in Ireland.

mattered, because we had experienced a lovely day's sport with plenty of sea trout (most of which we returned).

The next day we decided to try the Lower Lough Furnace for salmon only, even though we were advised by Chris that few fresh fish were in. Even so, during the

The lovely Kylemore Abbey. When on form, it is brilliant.

167

Fishing the stream that divides Feeagh from Furnace. This is the result of persistence – a big salmon that was an Irish Norwegian cross breed.

Then ghillie, now manager Pat Hughes at Burrishule Fishery, searches for a good sea trout fly.

morning period there were a number of salmon rising and slashing here and there, but once again they proved elusive. When they are not taking and rather stale it is difficult to tempt them with a fly rod. Rain, of course, was badly needed to liven them up. I raised the only fish of the day, which refused my fly at the last second.

Stillwater salmon fishing is no different from river salmon fishing, inasmuch as you do need things to be just right to get these magnificent fish in a bold taking mood. You also need a certain element of luck, but I will say one thing: having blank days salmon fishing can still finish up being very good indeed. The sheer anticipation alone keeps you going, cast after cast, because you always feel it will be the next one that puts you in contact with the king of fish. I feel you need a few blank days to make you appreciate the real worth of catching a salmon on the fly: wait until it happens to you, and you will know what I mean. This, then, is just a brief example of what you can expect, and there are many waters like this to select from in the west of Ireland.

Alan Pearson, who now lives in Ireland, Lough Conn. Here he shows a nice trout. He was the first man to promote smaller fisheries, such as Avington, Dever.

A trip to Ireland need not be expensive, since the fishing is so cheap. You can enjoy a day's salmon and sea trout fishing for the same price as a boat on Rutland or Grafham. I have introduced the west of Ireland to a number of friends over the years, and each one has enjoyed the fishing and the good company so much that they return as often as possible. Dr Ken Whelan runs the Burrishule Fishery these days, and he is very good. Booklets on the fishing can be obtained from the Irish Tourist Board, Baggot Street Bridge, Dublin, Ireland.

Perfect conditions for lough-style drifting: overcast with a lovely wave.

Stocked Salmon in Stillwater

Salmon in stillwater was not a concept that was well received by most true salmon fishers. However, because I write articles for the press, I was always looking for something new so I had to try it out. To my knowledge the first person to do so was Tony Chattaway. He stocked two lakes in Gloucestershire with grilse-sized salmon from a Scottish sea loch: it was known as the Ross Salmon Fishery. Dr Robin Bradley, one of the pioneers of salmon breeding, arranged a special transporter for fortnightly stockings.

This was a bold new venture for Tony, who had quite controversially stocked a rainbow into Packington Trout Fishery, which broke the long-standing 8lb 8oz record from Blagdon. The fish was caught at this popular Midlands fishery by day-ticket angler Brian Jones; it weighed over 9lb.

My son Stephen and I were invited to try out this new stillwater salmon fishing; it was a sort of press day, with many well-

Cock fish (upper), hen fish (lower).

known trout fly fishers in attendance and fishing. Steve Windsor hooked the first salmon: it jumped quite high three times and was gone, and he also rose another, which refused to take.

Meanwhile Stephen raised two, hooking one of them; he was obviously enjoying the experience, as he played it with a big grin

Bob with a 10lb salmon that was stocked eighteen months earlier into Earith Lakes' deep trout lake. Still in perfect condition. It took a nymph.

Bob returns a salmon.

on his face. But it fell off at the net, provoking a torrent of invectives. We all flogged the pool to a standstill for an hour or more, and I was as much at fault as anyone, I was so eager to see how these fish would perform.

Eventually we took a break to allow the water to settle down, and went away and talked it over. The plan was to forget our normal fly fishing approach as per reservoir rainbows, and think more like a river salmon would do. It seemed to me the fish were behaving just like river fish. They were taking up resting positions in little weedy bays and any feature they could find. From their reaction to our flies it was obvious they would only come to the fly if it passed their chosen territory. The rise was classic, a fast swim to the surface where the fly would be either taken or rejected at an inch or two's inspection.

The take will give problems to any trout fisher, as your strike when rainbow fishing is no good for salmon. So I changed up to a size 12 treble Silver Stoats Tail, dressed a little heavier than normal. I had been

Bob and son Stephen with a brace of salmon apiece from Tony Chattaway's Gloucestershire lakes.

wasting my time for the first couple of hours, because now first cast in front of a weed pocket a salmon shot out and took the fly. I waited for a few seconds as the fish dived back down to its lie, and then I struck – and of course this one never got off. This proves beyond any doubt that the key to the proper hooking of a salmon, whether it be a stocked fish in stillwater or a wild river fish, is that you simply must allow it to take two or three metres of slack line. This allows it to turn down, before you simply lift; then the fly will be well into the mouth and a good hook hold guaranteed.

It was all a novel idea, and many trout fly fishers seemed to try and catch a stillwater salmon. Many of the small fishery or gravel pit fisheries began to stock a few salmon in with their normal trout stock: Ringstead, Elinor, Earith, and even the reservoirs at Toft Newton put them in, and results were fairly good in farming terms, as most were caught during the course of the year.

My best stillwater-stocked salmon came from Earith Trout Fishery. Owner Ray Bermeister stocked about twenty into his deep gravel pit fishery. One and a half years later I was fishing in a competition there with a sink tip fly line and a number 10 Gold Head Montana nymph. I had come to the end of my retrieve, but I always fish the last length of line out merely by lifting the rod to the vertical position, then pause with the fly about five feet down. As soon as I got to the stationary 'hold' position I had an almighty take and all hell let loose as the salmon, a bright silver bar, jumped three feet from the water, then dived for the bottom about fifteen feet down.

I prayed that it stayed on, as I had caught no trout in the first hour of a very difficult day. And it did, a magnificent fish of exactly 10lb when at the scales; along with a nice brown of 2lb 8oz and a stockie rainbow of 1lb 8ozs, it helped me to win the competition.

I mention the detail of this to point out that I thought the experiment to be a success, but I think in the end it was the cost that slowed the salmon stocking down. Several fisheries still stock them as a sort of extra treat to their customers. But this fish was in fine condition after one and a half years in the deep pit, full of nymphs and shrimps.

The Conservation Policy for 2007, shown on page 174, was sent to me for publication in this book by Bob Lawton of the Spey Fishery board.

Everyone is making the conservation effort now. Orri Vig's fine work on buying off estuary netting stations is all for the good in the future. Salmon are quite incredible, they have been almost written off many times. But despite dubious foreign ships netting them in their feeding grounds while at sea, they are a survivor.

Salmon and Sea Trout Loughs in the West of Ireland

- Lough Costello
- Lough Furnace
- Lough Feeagh
- Lough Kylemore Abbey
- Lough Innagh
- Lough Beltra
- Lough Cullin
- Lough Conn
- Lough Corrib

Bob Church's Atlantic Salmon and Sea Trout River List

I have only listed rivers and loughs from which I have actually caught a salmon or two – and of course sea trout.

- River Itchen: river of my first salmon on the fly
- River Test: I caught some good fish here, salmon and sea trout
- River Tweed: scene of my most successful big salmon on the fly – five 20lb-plus in a day. Also my largest salmon on the fly, 28lb 2oz
- River Teviot, River Till, River Ettrick – all tributaries of the River Tweed
- Aberdeenshire Dee
- North Wales Dee
- River Spey, and its tributary the Avon
- The Hampshire Avon
- The remote River Thurso
- River Findhorn: I had a 20lb salmon here, and Dick Shrive had one of 39lb 8oz
- In Ireland, the River Moy, River Owen Duff
- The River Morrum in southern Sweden is something else; see my further notes below on the results from this unique river
- River Hitera: Iceland offers the top salmon fishing. My first entry into the River Hitera fishing down about 75m I caught seven grilse within an hour
- River Sog: also in Iceland, the River Sog produced a 17lb 8oz salmon for our guide. The river actually runs through the outskirts of Reykvavik and was good; I even caught three here in the middle of the day
- River Big Laxa: the northern Iceland lower River Big Laxa holds some fine salmon; then on its upper reaches it is the best brown trout river I have ever known – average size 2lb to 8lb

Of the salmon I have caught from these rivers, 95 per cent were on the fly, and over the years attitudes have changed. In my early days not many were returned, and our party would keep perhaps a brace each – whereas now, nearly everything goes back unless you get a decent cock fish for smoking. My wife Jeanette achieved this in 2006 whilst fishing the River Ness in September. A fine, fresh, sea-liced cock fish of 15lb 4oz: we had him smoked.

- Finally the River Conway, River Dovey, and River Towey in Wales

Remarkable Records of the River Morrum

- Salmon, fly caught, 1992: 26.72kilos
- Salmon, spinner caught, 1991: 24.98kilos
- Sea trout, fly caught, 1946: 12.2kilos
- Sea trout, spinner caught, 1974: 14.7kilos
- Pike, spinner caught, 1923: 22.5kilos

SEA TROUT CONSERVATION POLICY 2007

Photo: Ian Neale

1. FINNOCK: Release all fish of 10 oz. / 25 cm / 10 " *or less.*

2. SEA TROUT: Release all fish of 3 lb. / 50 cm / 20 " *or more.*

3. BAG LIMIT: 2 sea trout or finnock of takeable size per calendar day.

4. UNSEASONABLE FISH: Release all unseasonable fish (smolts, stale fish, kelts, over-wintered finnock).

SALMON CONSERVATION POLICY 2007

Photo: Ian Neale

1. CATCH & RELEASE

- Until 30th June each angler must release the 1st, 3rd, 5th etc. salmon and grilse caught.

- After 30th June all hen salmon and hen grilse must be released.

- Throughout the season all stale or gravid fish must be released.

- Escaped farm salmon must be retained.

2. METHOD

- Where possible anglers should be encouraged to fish with a fly.

- All hooks should be pinched or barbless.

- Where spinning is allowed only one set of barbless hooks may be used on a lure.

3. FISHING EFFORT

- Where possible the numbers of hours and rods fished should be limited.

8 Salmon Fishing with Mike Green

By Mike Green

Early Days

Fly fishing for salmon is widely regarded as the pinnacle of sport fishing, and without doubt there is little to compare with that heart-jolting moment when there is a swirl, the line tightens, and you are connected with the king of fish!

As a lifelong angler and a keen trout fisher I had my first chance on a salmon river when I was about thirty years old. The location was the famous and exclusive River Helmsdale in Sutherland, and the reason I received my invitation was that the water was 'on its bones', having had no rain during the previous eight weeks, and no prospect of any!

Nevertheless Lesley, my first wife, and I were pleased to accept the opportunity to deputize for the tenant of that week (in May, I think), and to go and see what it was all about. We had a great time with our ghillie Andrew Sutherland, a terrific guy (now sadly long deceased), and caught a great number of modest brown trout, but the only salmon we saw during the week was in the Little Rock Pool on Beat 6 – and which I naively thought I was going to catch! Little did I realize that it had probably been lying there for two months, had seen every fly in the book and consequently wasn't even slightly interested!

However, as the result of that trip, some two months later Andrew phoned up excitedly and said that the tenants were unable to fish the following week, and that heavy rain was at last expected at the weekend. I'm afraid a few appointments were hurriedly rearranged, and Monday noon saw Lesley and I up at Helmsdale again, in a hired car from Inverness airport. Andrew was hopping from one foot to the other as we frantically changed into our fishing gear and took off for Beat 5. As we drove up the Strath road, which runs alongside the river, the scene was totally unforgettable: the salmon, having waited in the river mouth for almost three months, were streaming up in a frenzy, and I clearly recall the spray showering off their backs and tails as they negotiated the shallows. I have never seen such an amazing spectacle in all the years since. I played and caught my first salmon within thirty minutes on a 10ft trout rod and a fly called Hairy Mary (size 10), and gaffed it myself (gaffs were commonplace in those days); and Les caught her first one from that same pool, later in the day. We had five fish that day and never looked back!

Subsequently we were offered the first week of April on a regular basis, and in those days the spring fishing was superb. At this time of the year the salmon are breathtakingly beautiful, bright silver with a lilac sheen on their flanks that never appears to be quite the same once summer arrives. One particular catch is worthy of special mention, in the spring of 1972. I mentioned the Little Rock Pool on Beat 6 earlier, and when it was our day to fish there I broke my pattern of fish-losing (I seem to recall losing five in a row!) with a

First wife Lesley proudly holds the 30lb salmon she caught on fly from the River Helmsdale, Sutherland, in April 1972. I believe it is one of the largest spring fish ever taken from the river, and possibly the best to be landed by a lady fisher?

The morning's catch from Beat 6! In those days it was accepted to retain all fresh springers for the table. More recently, spring salmon numbers are sadly depleted, and 'catch and release' has become routine.

bright and most welcome eight-pounder. I left Lesley fishing this area whilst I went two hundred yards further downstream to a pool known as the Manse. I covered the water as best I could for an hour, but caught, and saw, nothing. I was then aware of Lesley making her way hurriedly down the bank and looking rather flustered. My first reaction was that the ghillie must have fallen in or been taken ill, until she blurted 'I've had three, and one's 30lb!'

'You're joking!' I said, but she again insisted, 'No, I really have – just look!'

I gazed up the river and could clearly see the great silver beast lying on the bank.

That magnificent sea-liced fish weighed 29lb 8oz at Helmsdale station the following morning when we despatched it home by rail, so I think we can safely say it weighed 30lb when caught – some achievement on a fly rod, and one I feel sure I shall never equal. I did, however, get my consolation prize on the final day of our trip when we were on Beat 3.

In the prevailing conditions the spots to concentrate on were the tail of the bay, and the upper and lower Torrish pools, and we basically rotated on these three places throughout the day. At this time of year the fish are (hopefully) running the river,

The 23lb spring fish that brought back my sanity after a string of losses, and don't I just look pleased?

And so it was on this occasion. I had been given a home-tied blue and yellow tube fly by a canny and kindly old fisherman called Arthur Chamberlain (again now sadly long departed). I had fished this fly all day long on a slow sinking line, and was making my way down the Upper Torrish Pool for the umpteenth time when, with the light starting to fade, miraculously the fly was taken with a solid bump and line screamed off the reel. What a feeling! This one thankfully stayed on, and some twenty minutes later I was able to tail out a cracking 23lb springer. No doubt there was some substantial celebrating that evening, but my recollections are a little vague!

Basic Tactics: Spring

The early season technique is to fish the fly – usually a 1in to 3in tube fly – as you would fish a Devon minnow or Toby-type spoon: sub-surface, steadily and slowly across the stream, hopefully at right angles to the flow, and in front of the fishes' noses. Depending on the river, most anglers use a 15ft double-handed rod to achieve a good distance,

and the idea is to effect a 'collision course' between your fly and the arrival of the salmon. It sounds very chancy, and indeed it can be, but there is always the hope that even if you have fished down many times, when you repeat the process they could have just arrived, or maybe changed their position into a 'taking spot'.

Accompanied as ever by my faithful Labrador 'Jake' (who lived to the age of seventeen!), here I am again on the Helmsdale, playing my only fish of the week, a ten-pounder, hooked, played and landed in the Manse Pool. The Little Rock Pool, where Lesley caught the big one, can be seen in the background above a long shallow run.

My good friend (and dentist!) Malcolm Patrick, with his spaniel and a handsome brace of Helmsdale springers.

preferably to the far bank if this is possible. A ten-weight line is perhaps the most commonly used, but certainly between nine- and twelve-weight, and the type of line is determined by the depth of the pools and the flow of the stream. A wide, shallow and steady current may require a floating, slow-sink or sink tip line, whereas a narrower, deeper and faster flow would suggest some form of sinker to get the fly down to where the fish are lying. As a rule, if they are interested they will come up for it, and you certainly don't want to present the fly *below* them, as this is more likely to frighten them, rather than induce a positive response.

In general, a cast of about 45 degrees to the direction of flow would be considered ideal. A more square delivery will fish the fly faster across the lies, whereas a more downstream cast will have the opposite effect. It follows, therefore, that the slower the current (or 'carry', as they refer to it north of the border), the more square the cast should be, and vice versa. I see many fishermen casting what, to my mind, is much too acutely downstream: by the time the cast has straightened out and the fly has started to 'swim' across the current, it seems to traverse only two or three metres before it arrives directly downstream of the rod tip and 'on the dangle'. Though it is now 'maintaining station' to a following fish, it has effectively *stopped*, giving the salmon the chance to scrutinize your offering. This situation is usually disastrous, and as a standard technique, personally when I feel that the fly is approaching 'the dangle', I always give two or three slow pulls to keep it moving upstream and away from a possible following fish before retrieving for the next cast. A positive take often comes at this time, and I suggest it is a good habit to adopt.

Speaking of fly movement, it is *imperative* to achieve a nice straight delivery, with the fly landing at the end of an extended cast. In situations where the actual fly can be observed, you would be amazed and dismayed at just how far it drifts lifelessly downstream on anything less than a perfect straight cast, before the slack is taken up by the current, and it starts to 'swim'. In my view it is far better to sacrifice a few yards of distance in favour of a straight delivery, ensuring that the fly 'fishes' almost from the moment it alights on the surface, and this will surely put more fish on the bank in the long run.

Projecting out these big spring flies, which may be tied on brass tubes of up to 3in long in some instances, is rarely pretty, and usually necessitates a standard over-head cast. The best bet is to slow things down and wait for the 'clonk' as the heavy fly reaches the end of the back cast, before smoothly pushing the rod forwards again and sending the line and fly out to where the fish are hopefully lying. I must confess that, particularly in the early days, more than once I have had the rather unpleasant experience of hitting myself on the back of the head or shoulder with a spring tube fly. It is rather like being hit by a small hammer, and definitely not to be recommended! However, it does tend to sharpen up your casting technique in the hope of avoiding a repeat performance!

As for covering the pools, the normal plan is to take a good step or two downstream between each cast. Some anglers seem to make endless casts from the same position,

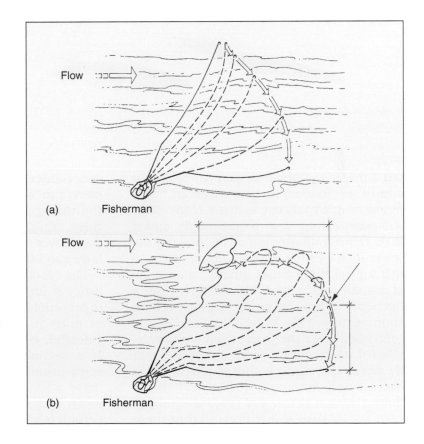

(a) A good straight cast. The fly 'fishes' from the moment it alights on the surface. Takes can be expected at any time during the swing.

(b) A poor crooked cast (wasted fishing time). The fly drifts passively downstream to the point marked with a solid arrow. The fish is unlikely to be attracted. The fly only 'fishes' correctly in the area below the arrow. Fisherman (a) is certain to catch many more fish than fisherman (b) over the long term. The unfilled arrows show the path taken by the fly.

(a) Flow Fisherman

(b) Flow Fisherman

Spring tube flies and 'Waddingtons': top row – Gordon's Fancy variants; second row – prawn fly and the Belgian flag; third and fourth rows – Willie Gunns; and bottom row – collie dogs.

but I prefer to 'move on' unless I have had a 'pull' or 'follow', or have made an indifferent cast. My theory is that a ready taker will come a long way to take the fly, and it is therefore rather pointless in covering the water inch by inch. I would much prefer to fish a pool three times quickly, than once at a snail's pace, and feel this gives me a far better chance of presenting my fly to a running fish. This strategy has served me pretty well over the years. Even with 'stale' fish (of which more later), if they see that fly again and again before it crosses their noses, surely they are more likely to become 'bored' with it before you reach the 'taking' cast, rather than if it is presented to them as a sudden surprise. I have witnessed this many times when observing lying fish from the vantage point of a rock or cliff above them whilst a colleague has been fishing (the River Shin in Sutherland is particularly good for this).

The 'inch-by-inch' approach produces little, if any response, whereas if the fly is presented to them 'out of the blue', one or more fish will race up and either take (ideally), or refuse it at the last second. If a second cast is made in the same spot, usually a salmon will come up and 'have a look', but from two feet or more away, and subsequent efforts are ignored completely!

Tying the Belgian flag: the fashioning of this tube fly needs very little explanation. (a) Trap a slightly bent, short length of 18swg wire in the vice on which to mount the tube ready to start. (b) Slide the tube on to the wire. (c) There is no 'body' to worry about, so simply tie in the tail of yellow buck tail with the fibres extending approximately a centimetre beyond the tube. (d) In similar fashion, tie in the red buck tail about half way along the tube. (e) Finish the fly with black buck tail as the main 'wing' tied in at the head, and the job is done. (f) Slide a short length of silicone tubing on to the tail of the fly, leaving enough trailing at the rear to slide the treble hook into. So there you have it, a fly that takes just a few minutes to create, but a pattern that would be hard to beat, in early and late season.

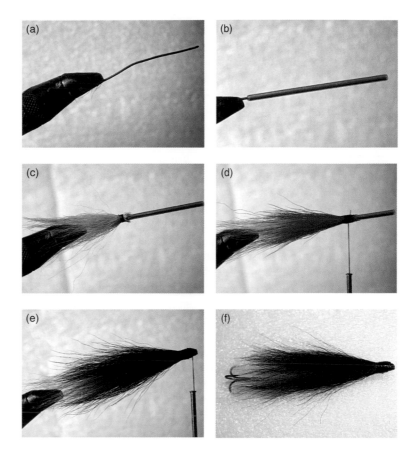

However, I am jumping ahead rather, as all this is not really applicable to spring salmon, which will usually 'have a go' if you are lucky enough to be in the right place at the right time !

Years ago when I was with some friends fishing the Tweed at Kelso, we were having a great time and catching plenty of fish, as indeed was everyone else in the perfect conditions. (One has to be a bit lucky on the Tweed, as it can be fining down nicely and fish pouring through, and then a rainstorm in the hills will put the water up three feet and turn it the colour of Ovaltine! As it can take five days or more to recover from a spate, it is then a case of packing your bags and going back home, licking your wounds! I have had many frustrating visits to the Tweed, as well as some memorable ones, it has to be said.) Anyway, to get back to this particular week, one gentleman, whose name I can't recall, though well into his eighties, was doing exceptionally well. He asked me if we were 'working' the fly, and I wasn't sure what he meant, so he demonstrated.

Basically it involved moving his rod tip up and down as the fly swung round in the stream, which gave it a sort of 'stop/go' action. He was convinced it made the fly look more attractive to the fish, and I must admit to being a dedicated 'waggler' ever since! Just holding the rod tip still, as probably the majority of anglers do, produces plenty of fish of course, but I do believe that 'waggling' can make that vital difference.

As to the flies themselves, the construction could hardly be simpler. There is no absolute necessity for a body as such, though some people would dress a black wool or silk body with a silver or gold tinsel spiral, or alternatively a gold, silver or pearl mylar tube. The wing fibres, which can be bucktail or one of the many synthetic materials (slinky fibre is especially good) are tied in 'streamer' style (*see* photos on page 181), either just at the head, or perhaps at a further one or two positions down the tube. This latter technique can produce an attractive tricoloured effect, as in the case of the highly successful 'Belgian Flag' tube fly, which has been a great fish catcher for my friends and I over the years. The combination of red, black and yellow used in this particular fly is quite popular and effective, and used in many other successful flies, such as the famous 'Willie Gunn'.

I remember on our very first trip to the Tweed the ghillies *insisted* that we used black and yellow flies, or as an alternative *yellow* and *black*! They seemed deadly serious, but we found it most comical! I would be pretty happy to fish a spring fly of almost any colour you could name, and will never forget one afternoon at Kelso when the late great Sam Allitt caught several 20lb salmon on a fly I would not have had in my box!

The dressing had been completely stripped away from the head end, and at the tail all that remained was a sort of 'grass skirt' of shredded mylar tubing (*see* diagram below). However, those fish weren't as fussy as I am, and Sam had a truly memorable catch – and even had the nerve to suggest the fly as a good pattern to reproduce (my pride would not allow me to do that, however!)

As an alternative to tube flies, the Waddington-type flies are both popular and effective, and getting back to the Helmsdale, I recall we used to fashion flies on suitably bent paperclips. They worked well too, and as I have indicated earlier, with spring salmon fishing it is really more a question of being there when the conditions are favourable and, most importantly, when the fish are there too!

Backing Up

Before I finish the spring fishing section, I must mention the technique of 'backing up': perhaps not popular on many rivers, this method has produced many a salmon for me when the accepted policy of moving down the pool steadily has proved ineffective. As the name implies, the idea is to make long square casts at the tail of the pool, then take two or three steps upstream and strip the line back, slowly or fast as

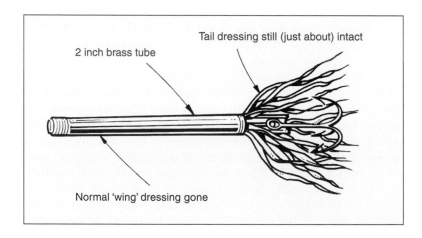

2 inch brass tube

Tail dressing still (just about) intact

Normal 'wing' dressing gone

Sam Allitt's successful Tweed fly. Basically a naked brass tube with a 'skirt' of shredded mylar tubing after a good mauling by several big salmon! It just goes to show how unfussy they can be when they are 'in the mood'!

conditions dictate, before making the next cast. This fishes the fly faster and more squarely across the noses of any resident fish, and can sometimes provoke a positive and aggressive response.

Though not to everyone's liking as it is quite hard work, backing up is widely practised on the Helmsdale in the spring, and really suits the long, deep and steadily flowing stretches that typify the middle beats of that river. Unfortunately many kelts tend to be taken this way, but at the same time fresh springers sometimes hang about with kelts, and it doesn't take too long to realize which you have hooked. If you have not fished this way before, it is definitely well worth a try, and can sometimes produce the only fish of the day!

Setting the Hook

Salmon fishers argue endlessly about what to do when a fish takes the fly, and will probably always disagree about this topic. The 'hit them immediately' brigade will argue that if the line has tightened, the fish has the fly in its mouth, so why wait? Also when using a spinning rod you don't feed line to the fish, but tighten up instantly. Having said that, I am *convinced* that, in my early days of salmon fishing, being a keen trout fisherman, I could not stop myself striking and lost so many fish as the result of this. It was some time until I was able to discipline myself to do *nothing* until the fish roared off with the line, but those Helmsdale ghillies kept at me, and eventually it became my conditioned routine! I now fish with my hand on the rod, but not holding the line, thus allowing the reel to give line when a fish takes. But an old fisherman who had caught several thousand salmon was quoted as saying 'It doesn't matter a damn *what* you do, he's either got it or he hasn't!'

I will therefore leave it to readers to make up their own minds regarding this matter.

Basic Tactics: Summer Fishing

As the weather warms up the line is almost always a floater, and the flies that prove to be effective tend to be smaller and tied on singles, doubles and trebles. Personally I prefer singles or trebles as I seem to have, over the duration, lost countless fish on doubles, but that's just me. I am sure thousands of good fish have been landed on doubles. You must form your own opinions! Size 8 is perhaps the most widely used, but at times anything from a size 14 to a 4 can be usefully employed, again depending on river height and flow. As a very general rule a larger fly should be used for bigger, faster, deeper rivers, and smaller ones for slower, shallower stretches. Of course there are always exceptions, and it can often pay to 'ring the changes'.

I recall a particularly hard week on the River Shin in Sutherland when the beats were full of fish, but they were not in the slightest bit interested in our offerings. Having gone down to the tiniest flies in my bag, for devilment I tied on a big yellow spring tube fly, and swung it over a deep dark gulley between two rock 'cliffs'. On the first cast a coloured cock fish of about 8lb flew up from the darkness of the channel and swallowed the fly as if its life depended on it! The ploy failed to work again, however, and that was the only fish I caught for the whole week. It just goes to show that strange things can always happen!

Speaking of fish being stale and indifferent, which they often can be if they have been in the river for some time, a good idea is to try at first and last light. At these times they can be 'off their guard' and make a mistake. As I get older I seem less inclined to keep that dawn appointment (which can be 4am in June!), and have been known to let others deputize for the evening stint, while I enjoy a glass of whisky! Nevertheless, as with many forms of fishing, the

A selection of my summer patterns: 1 – Muddler; 2 and 4 – M.G. black palmered shrimp; 3 – Elver fly; 5 – Hairy Mary; 6 –Silver Stoat; 7 – Logie; 8 – Blackie; 9 and 10 – M.G. 'specials'; 11 – Silver Stoat; 13 – Tosh; 14 – Black Shrimp; 12, 15, 16 and 17 – all Ally's shrimp variants.

early and late approach will often produce the best results.

Dibbling

Trout fishers will be familiar with 'bouncing' their dropper flies across the waves, and how deadly the technique can be in the right conditions, as opposed to just pulling the flies subsurface. That same action can be equally successful, and indeed is rather easier to perform, in the broken water rushing into the head of the pool, and also in streams and runs where there is speedy, choppy, wavy water. Naturally a dropper must be employed, often a bushy or palmered pattern, and this is then 'dibbled' across the wavelets using the tail fly as an 'anchor'. Either fly is likely to be taken, and if it is the dropper, the salmon must of necessity break the surface to secure its prize – always a spectacular sight.

Dibbling is invariably a summer and autumn method, and can be devastatingly successful with 'stale' fish on the right day. Whilst on the subject, salmon can, of course, be caught in lochs when fishing in traditional trout style. At Grimersta on the Isle of Lewis the accepted approach was to use a Blue Elver fly (made from the feathers from a vulturine guineafowl) on the many little lochs that punctuate the river course, and also in the head of the pools. When Lesley and I had the opportunity to fish there for a week we had success with

Brotherly teamwork! A somewhat faded photo of my twin boys – ghillie and fisher – with a fine summer ten-pounder from the River Ness.

giant rainbows! This was very exciting in a wild, remote place, and proved that it often pays to try different ideas.

During that same week, by the way, fishing the river where it joins the sea we caught, and lost, several salmon on sea trout flies in the short spell of total darkness, the only time it has ever happened to me.

Foreign Salmon

I have fished in Alaska four times, and on two occasions have personally caught a hundred sockeye/red salmon in a single session. Why I did it the second time I can't imagine, as once should be enough for anyone! On the second occasion I had my twelve-year-old twin boys with me, and even they became a bit complacent with catching a fish on almost every cast. But it's not so difficult to catch salmon when you have an estimated four *million* occupying the pool in front of you, all gathered up below a huge and treacherous gorge (*see* photo on page 188).

Nevertheless it is interesting to note that these fish, though packed like sardines, tend not to respond very well to the normal 'down and across' technique recommended

this pattern, but found that stripping a large Muddler through and across the waves was even more effective – those lovely fresh Atlantic salmon charged after them like

A young, but very accomplished, James plays a salmon on the west coast Little Gruinard river in Sutherland.

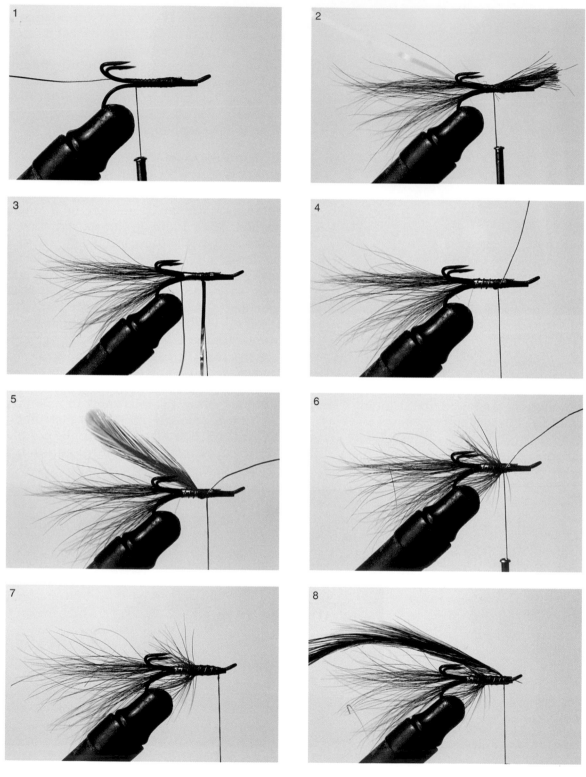

Tying the Black Shrimp. 1. Having secured the hook (which can be size 10 to 6, single, double or treble, as illustrated) in the vice, the first task is to wind on the black tying thread. As the thread is wound towards the tail of the hook, a length of silver flat tinsel is trapped and tied in together with some medium silver wire, and both left trailing to the rear. 2. The tail fibres of black squirrel are then tied in using two or three sparse bunches, ensuring that they are held tightly in position, and the thread is then wound forwards about one third the length of the hook. 3. Trim off the unwanted squirrel fibres, and wind the tinsel forwards in tight touching spirals, as shown. Secure the tinsel with three turns of tying thread, and trim off any excess. 4. The wire is then wound forwards over the tinsel, reinforcing it, but this time it is not trimmed, merely bent backwards temporarily out of the way. 5 Next a Hot Orange or Red Cock hackle is tied in, given three turns using hackle pliers, making sure to train the fibres back during the process, and then trimmed off. 6 The front section of the body is now formed, either with black silk or, if you prefer, by winding and tying the thread up and down the shank until an appropriate thickness is achieved. 7 The silver wire is then retrieved and wound forwards in tight spirals over the black body. It can now be trimmed off. 8 The front hackle of black cock is now secured as shown, the flu fibres being slightly longer than the length of the hook. 9 Give the black hackle three or four turns, depending on which 'looks' right to you, and tie off. Our fly is now almost completed. 10 The finishing touch is now to tie in a small jungle cock hackle feather at both sides of the head, and then to tie off with a whip finish. Apply a clear varnish to the head, and if you are fussy like me, a further coat of black varnish which seems to add a touch of class. (No doubt the salmon couldn't care less, but it looks better to me, and as you know, confidence is all important.). So, there you have it, the Black Shrimp on which I have caught a large number of salmon, and should I be restricted to using just this one pattern, I would not feel at any great disadvantage. Do give it a try, and I would be very surprised if it lets you down.

for Atlantic salmon. The method we were introduced to (and which worked like a dream), was to fish the fly like a falling leaf, by allowing it to drift through, then with, the current, and without retrieving. With such gin-clear water, I was fascinated to observe the fishes' response. They don't seem very interested in a fly travelling across their noses, but one dropped literally *at* them is often engulfed and rejected in the blink of an eye. In circumstances where it is not possible to see the fish itself this amounts to a 'lightning' lift of the fly line, followed by an immediate slackening as the fish ejects

the fly – and when they are packed tightly, this can result in ten to fifteen 'takes' every single cast! At any stage, if you strike when you see the 'lift', the result is one sockeye salmon cleanly hooked in the scissors – and don't they just go! The phenomenon really has to be seen to be appreciated.

Should you choose, just for an experiment, to fish in the conventional 'down and across' style you would still catch fish, but only one every half an hour or so, whereas with the 'freefall' technique it is practically every cast. It has been wonderful to experience these things, but at the same time it

A more grown-up James Green enjoying the battle with a good salmon on the Laggan Pool of the River Ness, a beautiful river to fish at any time of the year!

My twentieth fish of a wonderful (and record-breaking) week on the Ness Castle Beat of the River Ness. This was about three years ago, when six fishers landed eighty-six salmon, fifty-six of which were safely returned. This one weighed in at 18lb, and took a self-tied, size 10 Palmered Black Shrimp. A lovely fish like this, straight from the sea, can put up a tremendous struggle on fly tackle.

The almost unreal photo of sockeye salmon massing up prior to running the gorge of the Newhalen River in Alaska. The guides told us there were more than four million fish in this one enormous pool! Six of us landed 500 fish in the day here with barbs and points cut off our hooks! We fished one side of the water, whilst six large grizzly bears filled their bellies on the other. One of these repeatedly leapt in from a flat rock about six feet above the surface, causing a noise and splash as though a Tiger Moth had just crashed! An unforgettable experience!

makes you realize that this is *not* what you need. A fish every cast, even if it is an acrobatic and hard-fighting one, is in fact something of a nightmare for an angler, requiring relatively little skill and technique; and a non-stop session of playing fish becomes rather dull in a fairly short time. I have come to regard the *perfect* salmon fishing day as a fish in the morning, another one in the afternoon, and a couple of follows or pulls. Things tend not to work out this way, but it would be ideal if they did!

Incidentally, regarding the sockeye fishing, because they were so tightly packed, we clipped off not only the barbs, but also the points of our single hooks to avoid the possibility of foul hooking, and I recall how very few we lost despite their amazing antics during the fight: I would say it was no more than one in ten, and naturally it made catch and release quite simple.

I also fished for chinook (king) salmon in the Nushagak river in Alaska with Roy Thomas, who is married to my ex-wife, and we caught twenty kings to 30lb on fly in one day. This was completely different fishing, being traditional long casting with a 15ft fly

M.G. playing a sockeye on the first occasion of taking 100 fish in the day! It is rather like fishing to a conveyer belt of fish, five yards out – too easy really, but for all that they are fantastic fighters, as you can see from this photo!

A young-looking M.G. with a fly-caught 25lb chinook or 'king' salmon from the Nushagak River, Alaska. This was my first trip there with Roy Thomas (who was dating my then wife at the time, which caused some amusing incidents at the fishing lodge).

rod and good-sized shrimp fly or lure. King salmon never jump clear of the surface, but roar off like trains, and you must be careful to keep your fingers well away from the reel handles when attempting to brake the spool, or you will risk injury. They are a wonderfully strong fish, and fight to the end – a truly worthy adversary.

I have also caught chum salmon, which again respond to traditional 'down and across' casting and come in a multitude of colours. They sport unusual teeth, and for this reason are also sometimes referred to as 'dog' salmon. All Pacific salmon enter the rivers as bright silver fish but very quickly colour up, and of course they all perish after spawning.

Catching so many fish in the Alaskan rivers inevitably tends to devalue the worth of salmon in general, but having said that, there is something so special about a fresh-run Atlantic salmon. A few years ago some friends and I had the opportunity to fish the 'Big Hole' camp in New Brunswick, Canada, where the Miromishee and Sevogle rivers come together. It was the very first week it had ever been let commercially, and we were not sure what to expect. As it turned out, the accommodation and catering were quite superb, as was the fishing. Using single barbless hooks and single-handed rods, six of us landed a hundred grilse and sixty-two salmon during the week, a score that as yet has not been equalled, and perhaps never will be. Without doubt it was the very best week's salmon fishing of my entire life, and I recall my personal tally was forty-four fish, many of which took a lightly dressed size 10 Silver Stoat, dibbled as a dropper fly. Furthermore the Junction Pool, where the two rivers met, was a mere forty yards from the comfortable cabin I shared with my father.

Speaking of him, I remember hooking a fish on the far bank of the above-mentioned Junction Pool, while dad was fishing

This is a chum salmon: these enter the freshwater bright silver, but quickly become multicoloured, as you see here. They take a fly readily, and are splendid fighters. They are sometimes referred to as 'dog' salmon in view of their large and unusual teeth.

opposite on the 'camp' side. Seeing I was into a salmon, he gave me the 'thumbs up'.

'If I get this one out it'll make me thirty,' I shouted across.

'Well, you shouldn't have eaten all that bacon at breakfast!' he replied. I smiled and said nothing!

Two Extraordinary Experiences

I would like to relate two incidents that I will never forget.

The first occurred many years ago on the Laggan Beat of the River Ness, one of my most favourite stretches of water. Indeed I was waist deep in my much loved tail of the beat, and the conditions were idyllic, being warm, calm, overcast and the water gin clear, as it always is on the Ness. My casting was going well and I felt totally content – almost part of the scenery, as the floating line snaked out and the fly (I don't recall the pattern) landed gently on the surface of that smooth flow. As the fly alighted on one particular cast, which to me was identical to all the others, I felt the heart-pounding thrill as if I had already had a take. There was no swirl or sign of a fish, yet I *knew* there was one coming! As the line began to swing round I felt that excitement more and more strongly for three or four seconds before the rod dipped and the line screamed from the reel. Incredible as it may sound, I *felt* that fish coming to the fly before it actually took it. Make of it what you will, but much as I would like it to, it has never happened to me again in all the many years since.

Lesley's view was that I was so 'in tune' with the ambience of the situation that I telepathically picked up the excitement of the fish, and I can't think of a better explanation. I am quite sure that it was definitely *not* my imagination.

The second event is indelibly etched in my memory for ever. I was fishing the Stanley Beat of the River Tay in August as a guest of the Thomas brothers. My fishing partner for the week was Phil Thomas, and our location for the morning was known as the Corner Pool. There was no scope for wading, or indeed moving much at all at this spot, the 'crack' being to make your way out on to a flat ledge, in front of which was a vertical drop into a glide approximately fifteen to eighteen feet in depth. It was a bit like fishing off the edge of a cliff! Below this ledge was an attractive pool, at the end of which the river swept round a right-hand corner (hence the name), and down two hundred yards of white water. Fishing the shrimp had finished a couple of days previously, though the pool was perfect for this method. We therefore fished a bunch of worms on a link-ledger, gauging the amount of lead to enable the worms to trundle gently along the riverbed before it became time to retrieve and recast. (This pool did not really lend itself to fly fishing.)

We fished for an hour, side by side, without any result.

'Pity we can't fish the shrimp,' I said to Phil, 'I'm sure it would work today.' Then I had an idea, and added, 'I wonder if a huge Ally Shrimp Fly would do the trick on a shrimp-type rig?' We decided it would be worth a try, so I went to the bank and rigged up a size 2 Purple Ally Shrimp on a simple link-ledger. (I'm not sure why I tied some so large, but it looked good, regardless.) I was using a strong spinning rod and a brand new spool of 20lb Maxima nylon, which is very reliable. Out and down went the massive fly, half a dozen 'bounces' along the bottom, and everything locked up with a solid thump.

'Well I'm damned,' I exclaimed to Phil. 'I'm in, first cast!' Nothing moved an inch and the hefty rod was bent double.

'It's the bottom,' said Phil, 'You've hooked that nasty snag!'

'No, it's definitely a fish, and a bloody big one, too!' I replied. After three or four minutes 'the bottom' slowly moved ten yards upstream, sulked for a while, and then swung around and returned steadily and unstoppably to its original 'taking' position. It was like being attached to a submarine!

By now our terrific ghillie Jimmy Barratt had joined us on the ledge, and was urging me to stay calm as this was a very big fish. I didn't need telling! I just kept the rod double and put as much pressure on the fish as I dared, but it made precious little impression. The great beast cruised about in slow motion doing exactly what it pleased, and I knew full well that I was hooked up to the biggest salmon of my life. After about half an hour I was starting to gain some line, but the fish had moved out further into the pool and the flow. Jimmy's friend Jordie appeared on the cliff path behind us, taking in the scene.

'Do you see it, Jordie?' asked Jimmy.

'Aye, I see it!'

'Is it a big one?'

'Mon, it's a *monster*!' came the reply, which did little to calm my nerves, because, although tiring now, the considerable current was taking the fish slowly but surely downstream. I tightened the clutch, put my fingers on the spool and did my level best to ease it back towards our position. But I was losing the battle. The rod was simply pulled down, and the reel grudgingly gave line in a series of sudden shrieks! Looking back I should have clamped my hand on the spool and held on for dear life. If I could have got back just fifteen yards of line and manoeuvred the giant fish into the quieter water I feel sure we would eventually have landed it – but it was not to be! Round the

corner it went, and two hundred yards of line howled off the reel in a continuous scream!

We later retrieved nearly all the line, which was frayed in many places, and thankfully the fly, which the fish had managed to get rid of. Needless to say the disappointment was immense, but that massive fish had won its life back, and I believe that is the way we should look at things in such circumstances.

As an afternote I sat down, put on a new spool of nylon, made up a similar rig, and walked out to the ledge once more. In the meantime Phil had still not had a touch on the worms, but almost unbelievably, on my very first cast I was into another fish! It was nothing like the first one, and in five or six minutes I had bullied it to the net, all the time being cautioned by Jimmy to take it easy as it was also a good fish. The scales showed a remarkable 26lb! I have never caught a bigger Atlantic salmon, though at the time I remember having a job to be thrilled. How big was the proverbial 'one that got away'? We shall never know!

Mike Green 'dibbling' with a single-handed rod on Sutherland's Little Gruinard river.

9 The Small Fisheries

By Bob Church

In this chapter I shall relate how the small fisheries came about, and how they fall into the system we have today. Alex Behrendt opened his Two Lake Fishery in Hampshire in the early 1960s; this was a season-ticket water stocked with good-sized rainbows and browns. Then in the early 1970s Tony Chattaway was employed to manage the newly opened Packington Estate Fishery, and in 1975 he stocked it with some big rainbows. One of these was caught by Brian Jones: at 9lb 3oz it beat the UK record of 8lb 8oz, caught in 1924 by Colonel Creagh-Scott; this was a Blagdon reservoir-caught fish,

and had held the record for many years, since the 1930s.

The fact that a stock fish could beat a long-standing grown-on specimen caused a great deal of controversy. However, a special fishery, to be known as Avington, again in Hampshire, was set up by the late Sam Holland. He built various hatchery systems, and then growing-on ponds, and started a very selective breeding programme, taking eggs from the biggest and best female rainbows, and also a good conditioned and well shaped male fish for the artificially stimulated fertilization.

Bob lands one of Sam Holland's giant rainbows of that period, at 16lb 12oz. It was a big fish. Sam seemed pleased, but it was too dark-looking for me.

Growing Record Rainbows

Then the race was on as to who could grow the largest rainbow, and small fisheries popped up here and there all over the country, spreading to Wales, Scotland and Northern Ireland, and I have fished two in the south of Ireland. For the next decade Avington led the way with big rainbows, until Alan Pearson took the new rainbow record on to the list with an 18½lb specimen.

Then came Nigel Jackson, who built his Dever Springs Fishery single-handed (now owned by Con Wilson); he grew on some massive rainbows with what he called his 'ranching style'. Using a nearby shallow lake, he was able to give the rainbows a much larger area than in the stew ponds, with regular feeding in the clear water. So they grew fast, and the extra space meant they were fit and with no fin or tail erosion. Nigel actually grew a rainbow of 36lb 14oz, but it died in Dever Springs shortly after being stocked.

Nigel now runs another very small fishery called Sutton Springs. He stocks this with double-figure fish only, and provides you with a wheelbarrow when you purchase a £110 (at the time of writing) day permit – you are allowed four fish, and the barrow is to wheel the four fish, which could be around 50lb to 60lb in weight, back to your car boot. Nigel is a genius at rearing these big fish on; when at Dever he grew browns to 23lb. Usually experienced fly fishers go after these, even though the fishing has been described as 'shooting tigers in a cage'.

Small fisheries can be anything from a half-acre puddle to gravel pits of fifty or more acres. Now I must refer to Elinor Trout Fishery, one of the lasting catch-

Nigel Jackson stocks a 23lb brown trout into his Dever Springs Trout Fishery.

This happy fly fisher was extremely pleased with himself. This fish was caught at the very consistent Elinor Trout Fishery.

Sutton Springs, Nigel Jackson's new fishery, is quite small and is stocked with double-figure trout only. Bob's four limit rainbows were 18.12, 16.12, 14.00, and 13.4: total 62lb 12oz.

Jeanette Church wins the first-ever Small Fisheries Trout Competition held at Dever Springs between England and Wales. She easily won the event with nine rainbows, and was the only woman chosen.

and-release waters. You can keep your limit of six if you want to, but most regular supporters buy a season ticket and put them all back. This is a terrific water for buzzer nymph fishing and for those who like to fish the 'bung' method: it can mean fish after fish using 'Skinny Nymphs' tied on barbless hooks (usually this means de-barbing a normal barbed hook nymph with some mini pliers).

I have explained the 'bung' method in detail in the next chapter; it can be controversial in some fly fishers' eyes, but I say live and let live, and see no harm done. Check the way to set up and fish the method (*see* page 216), and use it on waters such as Elinor, where it is favoured by many who fish there.

The Big Rainbows at Dever

First I must tell you a quite funny story. It was during the Christmas holiday break in about the mid-nineties. The weather was quite mild, and my old fishing friend the late Frank Cutler asked if I would take him to '… that Dever place where they catch the big rainbows?' Like me, Frank was used to catching reservoir trout, where 'a big one' was 3lb to 4lb grown on. It must have been the day after Boxing Day, my birthday, and I drove the two-hour journey to Dever; Frank was very excited, and had specially tied a few favourite weighted nymphs for the occasion. I think at the time the day permit price was £50, which made Frank splutter a bit.

Frank Cutler had caught a quick limit at Dever and decided to help this lady fisher out: his advice looked to be spot on.

Frank Cutler enjoyed his trip to Dever Springs; this 7lb 8oz rainbow was his heaviest of a quick eight fish.

He tackled up quickly, and was away fishing here and there around the two lakes. After an hour he appeared beside me as I tried for a big fish I had spotted in the small lake. 'How many have you got?' he said. 'None,' I replied. 'You're having me on!' Frank said. 'They're as easy as shelling peas!' he added. I told him I was fishing for a double-figure rainbow I had spotted, and which appeared from time to time right in front of me. I was trying it out on different coloured nymph and mini tadpole patterns.

'Well, I've finished, I've got my four fish, what do I do now?' said Frank. 'I told you to be selective and go for the bigger fish,' I said. Frank quickly replied, 'Five- and six-pounders *are* bigger fish to me, and that's what I have, four of them, so what do I do now because they are too big to hide?' Frank's dry wit was always so funny. I told him you have to either pack up and watch the others fishing, or buy another ticket. Straight off the top of his head he said, 'But that's another week's pension!' I just could not fish seriously after that, and we went for a pint in the village pub. But he came back with me, purchased another permit, and caught another limit on the day, when most anglers had ones and twos. On his first visit he had found Dever quite easy.

Artificials for Stillwater Fishing

I look on the small fisheries as a good day out with fishing mates. If you go more casual than normal, enjoy the social side and have a laugh or two, it's good for your health. Frank died at eighty years old, some ten years ago, but his close fishing friends still miss him even now, and he is often mentioned in conversation.

The other big trout water in Hampshire is Avington, where there are three pools to wander round and fish. I like it here, and it is also where I first met Alan Pearson, one of the greatest drinkers you are ever likely to meet – and he could fish a bit, too, as I found out. With his 'x-ray vision', as I called it, he could spot fish lying deep down far better than most. This is one of the main secrets of catching big trout in the clear waters of the small fisheries, and it helps to have a decent pair of Polaroid glasses and a wide-brimmed hat – you can get by with a baseball-style hat that shades the eyes. The method is not to stand in one place, as many do, hoping the fish will come to them, but to walk slowly round the lake or lakes – called 'stalking' – to spot your fish, which should be larger than the standard stockie. Check its depth; this could be right on the bottom, or two feet or so above it.

If it is on the bottom, a heavy-weighted nymph or tin head-style tadpole is best – in fact the tin head sinks at the right enticing speed, and you very often get takes on the drop. My wife invented this range of mini nymphy lures with painted-on eyes, yellow with black pupils; they come in all colours, but she will always be known for her Olive

Jeremy Herrmann, the ex-World Individual Champion, won everything possible and then retired at thirty years old.

Damsel Nymph version on a size 10 hook: this one is deadly on all clear-water small fisheries. In fact it is so successful that expert fly fisherman Jeremy Herrmann, who won everything before retiring from the competition world, said: 'If I could use only one fly, fishing anywhere in the game fishing world, it would be Genies Olive Tin Head' – praise indeed!

The Mayfly Nymph is another very good artificial to use on the many stillwater fishing lakes and pools that later have a natural mayfly hatch. Dick Walker designed an excellent pattern, which he came up with after studying behaviour patterns. The two species of mayfly are both bottom burrowers (*Ephemera Danica* and *E. Vulgata*): they live in the sandy silt bottom where

Jeremy Herrmann quoted: 'If I had to use only one fly anywhere I fish throughout the world it would have to be Genies Olive Tin Head on a size 10 hook.'

Another great summer fly for the southern waters of England is Richard Walker's Mayfly nymph.

they make a little tunnel. They like a good current, and will not tolerate a slow current and muddy bottom. In lakes close to mayfly rivers – in the Cotswolds, and Hampshire and Dorset – these lakes are usually old gravel pits restored to the wild and producing a handsome lake as nature begins to work on it again.

It has been observed that sometimes mayfly nymphs will swim up to the surface, have a look round, then dive back to their burrows, almost like a Corixa would. Of course, mayfly time is widely known as 'duffer's fortnight', but this is not always the case. Sometimes in a massive hatch there are just too many flies on the surface

Bob plays a 2lb brown trout in at Lechlade in the Cotswolds.

These flies are all suitable for any stillwaters, including all the trout reservoirs and small fisheries.

for your measly artificial to be picked out. The best conditions are for a regular but moderate hatch – then they will be coming to your artificial time and time again. I have fished to good mayfly hatches on Lechlade, Milestone, Church Hill Farm, Lower Moor plus Dever and a few others, and it is good fun – and you can always fish barbless and put them back if they are plentiful.

The Dick Walker pattern was of course underbody weighted, and enabled you to fish along the bottom as the natural does. I shall never forget Dick Shrives' words. The maximum of trout you ever get up feeding is about 10 per cent, leaving 90 per cent feeding down below. Our instinct on seeing rising fish is to quickly put a dry fly on. I am the same as anyone in this,

199

Bob's Spent Mayfly pattern fishes well in the evenings.

Bob with a fine brace of small fishery stocked rainbows; they came from Dever, both from the top lake. The largest was 16lb 8oz and fell to the Mayfly Nymph during the morning, and the fish of 12lb 8oz fell to long-range dry fly fishing in the afternoon sun.

but don't forget the bulk of the trout will still be on the bottom – so if it is a lot of fish you are after, stick to the weighted nymph, but if it is visual pleasure you like best, keep a dry on. I once caught at Dever a 16lb 8oz rainbow on nymph in the morning, and then made it a great brace by hooking a 12lb 8oz fish on a dry Mayfly in the afternoon. That was a massive brace at that time – they are both in one glass case looking down on me. If it

Bob's best brown trout was 13lb 12oz and came from Chalk Springs, a fabulous clear-water trout fishery.

Bob's best blue rainbow trout is this immaculate fish of 7lb 2oz; I really love fishing here at Chalk Springs.

was today, of course, you would not have done it, and would just have taken them to a good smoker (which currently I have in Judy Stockdale of Mears Ashby near Northampton).

To be honest, mayfly times should be reserved for dry fly fishing only. I had three such sessions this past season when I disciplined myself to dry fly fish only. Although it can become difficult at times, the sheer pleasure of seeing a trout rise up and take your artificial off the top cannot be bettered.

When the mayfly hatches, the nymph moves quite quickly to the surface, pauses for a few seconds, then the skin splits and the dun emerges. The dun is also known as the 'Green Drake' by some schools of fly fishing tradition. The fly itself is now a yellowish olive colour.

The dun quickly takes flight to the cover of the bank side, where it will find a suitable leafy hedgerow to perch on out of the wind. It then sheds a layer of skin from its whole body, including even the very delicate wings – and we now have the sexually mature adult. The males are slightly darker than the females, and they begin their famous 'mayfly dance'. A swarm of males gathers together and they begin

Milestone Trout Fishery produced this well conditioned golden rainbow weighing 6lb 12oz; the angler is Con Wilson.

Another set of flies; at the top of the photo are various dry Mayflies. Some smaller dry flies are suitable for small fisheries – but also rivers.

their dance, usually doing this in harmony: they fly upwards, then stop, shred their wings and, in parachute fashion, descend. Soon the females will join in, and mating occurs in mid-air. Now the fertile females return to the water to lay their eggs, and once this is over, the fly is completely exhausted and dies. We call this stage the 'spent mayfly'.

It is at this 'spent' stage, with wings outstretched, that the trout gorge on the easy pickings and rise freely, usually in the early evening. They will be seen slowly moving around just sipping in the spent mayflies – and when this happens, they are yours: but I emphasize the spent pattern, and it needs to be static.

You will need a few good mayfly patterns in your fly box, because although the peak mayfly time is known as 'duffer's fortnight', the trout can still be very selective. Make sure your pattern is the right size: mine are tied on a lightweight number 10, long-shanked hooks down eyed.

Another angler stands by to net.

Chalk Springs Trout Fishery

Chalk Springs Trout Fishery consists of three serious, good-sized pools and one small beginner pool. To say that I enjoy a day's fishing here would be an understatement: it is so exciting to be able to look into each of the pools, and even in the deepest,

RIGHT: John Emerson unhooked this barbless fly whilst the fish was still in the fine mesh net, and with camera at the ready, had a quick photo.

My best catch ever rainbow, which went 27lb 2oz and came from Earith. I kept the huge trout submerged in the net until weighing scales and camera were ready. The large fish took a Ginola mini lure of my own design.

I kept him in the net to recover a little before carefully returning him.

Tying the Dick Walker Mayfly Nymph

Let me give you the tying construction of the Dick Walker Mayfly Nymph. It has been around a long time, but I have not seen one to beat it.

- **Abdomen and thorax:** six or seven ivory-coloured ostrich herl feather strands wound over four layers of copper wire. Then tie two bands of medium-brown ostrich herl near the tail end.
- **Wing cases:** buff hen feather fibre with the tips turned back and under to imitate legs; tie these in two separate stages, throat style, one is at the head, the other half way along the thorax.
- **Tails:** four or five spent brown hen hackle fibres.
- **Tying silk:** medium brown, also used to rib the abdomen.

This pattern should be fished singly during the pre-hatch period; it will pick up a few trout before the rise begins, and again after it has ended.

Elinor Fishery is a large, mature gravel pit of fifty acres. It has fly hatches throughout the year, and is an ideal small nymph water. They practise catch and release, and it works very well. Fine rainbows are caught at Elinor.

Genial Sam Holland grew some very large super rainbows that were triploids: mine went 15lb 8oz and Peter Dobbs' fish was 11lb 8oz. Avington was the place to go for a specimen trout in the 1980s.

Andy Keenan can fish all three Avington lakes from his wheelchair; here he caught a 12lb 4oz without any help.

This young man was so pleased to catch this big rainbow at Ringstead Grange: it went 7lb 8oz.

This tying of a Suspender Buzzer was a Peter Pike invention, but it is still excellent on all these small fisheries.

This Olive CDC dry fly is equally good when olives are hatching or olive buzzers.

about fifteen feet, I can still see the bottom and any trout swimming over it. These are the perfect conditions to try the 'stalking method'.

When casting at fish it can be very interesting observing their reactions. Some follow, and have the fly in and out of their mouth in a flash without you even feeling the slightest pull on your retrieving hand.

Bob with Nigel Jackson, creator of Dever Springs and now Sutton Springs. Bob had this 15lb on a Genies Olive Tin Head.

A perfect rainbow of 13lb 8oz, from Earith's top lake known as the Sporting Lake. It took the fly as the sun set.

Famous nymph fly fisherman Arthur Cove with a 7lb rainbow from Ringstead Grange, caught on a Pheasant Tail Nymph.

Expert fisherman, Peter Cockrill, nets a nice rainbow for Lord Mason of Barnsley. This was a charity fund-raising day at Dever Springs.

The insect known as the 'buzzer', correct name Chironomidae and with nearly 400 varieties, is a trout's main food from late March until May.

Bob and Chris Ogborne had a good session at Dever Springs where we made an hour's film in a day. When the damsel fly starts hatching from June onwards, get the Genies Olive Tin Head on, and make sure it has the painted-on eyes.

The fast-swimming damsel nymph crawls to the bank in thousands from June until September.

An artificial crane fly, alias daddy long legs

Graham Smith with a 7lb brown trout, which overwintered in Ravensthorpe Reservoir. He returned it.

The trout's reaction to different colours is also remarkable. If you keep casting the same coloured Black Tin-Head fly time and time again, at first the trout show interest, perhaps following or tapping the lure, then you can see they ignore it. But change the colour, and you will see the difference in their actions – many times I have had the same trout take it immediately. This happens quite a lot, and for salmon, too.

Chalk Springs can boast the very best brown trout fishing for top conditioned full tail and finned trout in the country. They are also excellent for providing the exotic, such as blue and gold rainbows – in particular the blue are lovely fish, but just like the golds, they give their position away because they are very visible, even at long range.

Because of the long distance involved (Arundel) I only go to Chalk Springs once or twice a year. My best fish there are brown trout 13lb 14oz; golden rainbow 8lb 6oz; blue rainbow 7lb 2oz: each of these fish had been fished for extensively for two-thirds of

the day before I showed them something completely different and they fell for it.

I most definitely recommend a trip to this top class fishery. It may not hold the very largest trout in the land, but it does have stock fish so good you would think they were wild. At the time of writing contact Jonathan and Darren, tel: 01903 88 37 42.

Avington Fishery

The breakthrough to producing regular specimen-sized rainbows really took off under Sam Holland's work, which he conducted whilst he owned the Avington set-up. He created the term 'jumbo trout', much used at the time, and with my weekly column in *Angling Times* I had to find out more about it. Then top Avington rod Alan Pearson and I had a difference of opinion in our respective columns – he had a trout column in *Anglers' Mail*. It was the mid-1970s and a peak time for angling, especially stillwater trout fly fishing.

Catch and Release

I first started to mention the benefits of catch-and-release trout fishing after I had fished to these rules in the World Championships in Tasmania, where it worked very well with the hardy, wild fish. The rules dictated that barbless fly hooks were used, and a controller quickly measured your fish in a special tray before releasing it back into the river. It was a win–win situation for both competitors and fish.

Some fisheries in Britain operate catch and release and say it works, and last year's experiment at Ravensthorpe is a prime example of how successful it can be. However, the whole subject is as emotive as ever among anglers and fishery owners. Many anglers think that if they pay a high price for their day ticket, they are entitled to their pound of flesh, so limit bags are always on their mind – I know this is so because I have been down that road myself. But times change, and now there are certainly many fly fishers who are supporting the catch-and-release policies of an ever-growing number of fisheries. However, I would stress that it is not being forced on any angler; I just think it is a step forwards to have the choice.

Some river and loch fly fishers must be thinking: 'What is he on about? There's nothing new in catch and release – we've been doing it for years with wild brownies. We think nothing of slipping these back all day, and we know the trout are none the worse for it.' Yet they still reserve the right to keep an occasional brace for the table.

Reservoir fly fishers showed signs of being conservation minded when they began to put all the easily caught, early season browns back. This has been a voluntary practice for quite a few seasons now.

On the increasing popular competition front, reservoir boats are regularly fully booked. Legally you are allowed two tickets equalling sixteen trout, but times are changing here as well. Some clubs fish to a limit of eight fish and add a time bonus, but this can sometimes lead to a false result.

I think the idea we have adopted for the Bob Church Classic is much fairer. Competitors will fish the catch-and-kill quota of six fish, and from then on use de-barbed flies to fish catch and release, with the boat partner acting as witness and scorer. At the end of the competition, each released fish will add 2lb in weight to the competitor's final score.

Score cards are issued at the pre-match briefing, to be used by those fortunate enough to take a limit. They must net and unhook any bonus fish outside the boat once their partner has agreed the fish is caught. At the end of the session, partners will check one another's cards and sign them.

Although some fishery managers embrace catch and release, others – usually at the smaller waters – claim the practice results in a lake full of fish that nobody can catch. In my experience, catch and release does not seem to work at places such as Dever Springs, where the fish are stocked big into small pools. But it does work at the larger gravel pit fisheries such as Elinor and Earith, in Cambridgeshire, where I have caught rainbows to 23lb 8oz, and my best of 27lb 2oz, which have later been re-caught. The debate will doubtless continue to rage.

Bob playing a fish in the World Championships at Avington in 1987.

Alan eventually invited me down to Avington to find out for myself what it was all about. Of course I met Sam Holland and got on well with him from the word go: we had a similar sense of humour. For my first meeting with Alan we both finished with an 8lb rainbow each. We settled our differences over a pint, and along with Sam, arranged a day when we could try and break the UK rainbow record.

Sam wanted a team of good fly fishermen to go to Avington in a bid to catch one, and this team was Dick Walker, Alan Pearson, Peter Dobbs, Dick Shrive and me. Also reporting the day was John Wilshaw, who also fished. Sam had complained he had introduced a couple of rainbows over the current record, but the anglers who hooked them had reported their casts broken all ends up, i.e. the nylon cast had broken leaving a fly hook in the trout's mouth. Naturally this was not good.

Our team was confident that with our sensible tackle, should we hook some of the big ones, we would land them – and we did just that. Peter Dobbs started with an 11lb 4oz fish from the top corner of the middle lake. Fishing in the central area of the same middle lake, I was using a new line for the day, a floating long belly fly line. When my take came it ripped off line at such a speed that a full fly line was out to the backing; gradually I coaxed the fish back, and eventually netted a superb 15lb 8oz beauty, at the time my personal best and about 2lb under the record.

Then Dick Walker landed fishes of 11lb 14oz and 12lb, plus also a tiddler of 4lb, while Dick Shrive caught a 13lb 8oz fish. But the honours of that memorable day went to Alan Pearson who *did* break the UK rainbow record, with a fine fish of 18lb 7oz, and two other doubles of 13lb 7oz and 11lb 14oz. Sam was very pleased, of course, but had the last word: 'You have done OK, but you missed the biggest fish, which is still in there!' Showmanship or salesmanship, I don't know, but it was an amazingly exciting day's sport!

The events of the day were covered by *Angling Times* in dramatic style, and caused quite a stir – the letter pages were full for a couple of weeks afterwards, with such comments as: 'Pheasant shooting with an atom bomb.' At the end of the day we all have our choices, be it big fish like this to catch – and it's quite expensive for the day ticket price.

Perhaps, like me, you favour the extra challenge of the big reservoirs where the skill comes in locating and catching fish by finding out the depth they are in. And maybe you are only switched on by catching wild brown trout from just one particular Scottish or Irish lough. Either way, always enjoy your sport, and you can enjoy all three categories. I like a change of scenery throughout the season, and so cover all three styles.

Gravel Pit Trout Waters

I would add here that there is another type of trout fishing that comes under the banner of small fishery. This consists of the many gravel-pit trout waters, some of which are quite large, and which are rich with life. These waters suit trout stocking and produce good grown-on fish similar to the reservoirs. Waters I have fished are Elinor at 50 acres (20ha), Ringstead at 33 acres (13ha), Lechlade, Milestone and Packington, and of course Earith Trout Fishery, where I have had some quite excellent results.

I have fished at Earith for around twelve years and caught my heaviest rainbow at 27lb 2oz, and my best six fish limit bag at 62lb 10oz. It was a real red letter day, as other fishers that day caught ones and twos. In the catch was obviously the 27lb 2oz fish, but also an 11lb perfect over-wintered rainbow.

For this day's fishing my boat partner at Earith was John Emerson; I started the day by showing him one of my lightly weighted lures – it was new, and I had named it 'Ginola'. I tackled up with a clear Bob Church number 8 Slyme fly line, which is a slow sinker. I was to fish a single number 8 lure with this new Ginola – and what a tremendous day's sport this set-up gave me: everything went right. The six trout I caught during the day were weighed and witnessed as I landed them, and immediately returned.

By the way, my leader that day was a long length (5m) of 6lb green Maxima. I had always found it very reliable, and despite all the fluorocarbon line, I still think Maxima nylon in green takes some beating. This leader landed all those big fish for me without any real bother; I just took my time with the largest trout, but the over-wintered 11lb fought the hardest, and it surged a long first run of forty metres straight to

a near bank-side bed of dead rushes from the previous year's growth. Such days live in your memory forever.

As I write, it is the first week in October, and Mike Green and I have just had by far our best session for trout for the whole 2007 season. We had an invitation to fish a certain gravel pit fishery, which I have to say is very good. Mike and I had ten fish each, all catch and release; my best two went 11lb and 9lb, and the rest were all over 4lb. Mike's fish were from 4lb to 7lb: what an afternoon's sport! He caught on a Damsel Nymph, and I caught on a Black Tadpole Tin Head with a bright painted red head.

It had poured with rain all morning, so we didn't start fishing until 4pm, packing up at 6.45pm as it got dark. The fish were mad on taking our single flies on a 12ft leader of straight 8lb fluorocarbon. A floating line and long casting was the order of the day. We both had a very satisfying glow on the journey home: as we said, 'Very simple tactics are often the best.'

At this autumn time the larger gravel pits such as Elinor and Ringstead have shoals of perch fry gathering round certain bits of feature, places such as boat jetties, and thick weedbeds close to fairly deep, clear water. If you want to catch some of these larger resident fish as opposed to recent stockies, make an early start. Fishing for trout in the early morning has two big advantages: firstly, because few anglers are prepared to get up that early, you will have plenty of space to fish in; it will be almost like your own private trout fishery, and you will probably have the water all to yourself.

Secondly, trout come into the margins during the night to feed and are likely to be still there when you arrive. So you could be in the position of 'stalking' fish without having to wade. If you can get a fly to them they will usually take confidently, because they will have been feeding there for many hours without any interruption.

Catching Big Trout

I can remember one or two interesting early morning trips when I found a few really big trout close in, chasing and feeding on coarse fish fry. These trout often lie in ambush in a weedbed, and charge out when the shoal of fry passes by. This causes a great bow wave, followed by fry leaping from the water in a bid to escape. Altogether, it is very similar to the way pike feed.

To catch these fish, first study their feeding pattern and try to pinpoint the spot at which they ambush their victims; once you have done this, you will be ready for action. Use a floating fly line, a 13ft (4m) leader of 8lb or 7lb breaking strain, and tie on a buoyant floating fry pattern. Modern ones are made from either clipped deer hair or synthetic materials such as white plasterzote or ethafoam.

You will see the big trout bull dozing the shoal of fry and stunning some of them as they tear amongst them. Then, when the shoal has eventually dispersed, the trout stop, turn round, and mop up the casualties floating on the surface in the breeze. So you cast your buoyant lure slightly upwind of the ambush point, and allow it to drift towards the spot where the trout are waiting in the weeds. Most likely you will see a huge swirl as your lure disappears from the surface. Wait a second, then strike hard – and the chances are you will be connected to a fish over 3lb, and possibly a five-pounder. During July, when the shoals consist of thousands of pin-head fry, a small lure is best; by the end of August and into September those fry are two or three inches (5 to 8cm) long, so alter the size of your lure accordingly.

Some of the high class small fisheries such as Avington don't allow for an early start, and open their gates at 9am. However, it is important to be ready to fish at this time, for the best sport will still come in that first hour before the fish have been disturbed. You will find that the recently stocked fish patrol the margins until they find a place they like to rest in. To catch these, equip yourself with a floating or intermediate line, a leader no more than 4m long of at least 6lb, and a selection of leaded nymphs, bugs or lures. I have found the Westward Bug very good at Avington, where it has caught me plenty of big rainbows to 16lb 12oz; Dick Walker's Mayfly Nymph, Alan Pearson's Green Beast, and Shrimp, Black Leech, Damsel Fly, Brer Rabbit, Partridge and Orange and Wonder Bugs are all good alternatives.

Most of the time big rainbows hug the bottom, and in gin-clear water it is easy to misjudge the depth. A good method is to cast your nymph and let it drift down on to the bottom in a spot where you can clearly see it; a clear gravel patch is the obvious choice. When a trout cruises by anywhere in the vicinity, begin a figure-of-eight retrieve. With the fly starting off on the bottom you can be sure it will pass through his line of vision, because rainbows will rarely rise right up from the deep spot and 'take' on the surface. Of course, the extra thrill of seeing the trout's reaction as he follows the nymph, then attacks it, is one of the most satisfying moments in fly fishing.

As I have mentioned, the behaviour of the fish in some gravel pits is very similar to that of reservoir trout. Certainly this is true of 50-acre Elinor, which is half the size of Ravensthorpe. My last visit there was on 26 September 2007, when I was hosting a corporate day of fourteen fly fishers, ten of whom were complete novices – but something happened which switched the trout on. It was a very windy day, and I think a few of these businessmen wondered what they had let themselves in for! To cut a long story short, owner Edward Foster, Paul Haskey, my wife Jeanette and I got them all casting quite well – anyway enough to catch a trout at this top class water, which encourages catch and release.

Edward gave me the nod that they had been on Daddies for a couple of days; so now it was up to me to put in the 'finishing touches' and show them how to catch a trout – and there was a bit of pressure on this! They were all ready to cast out, and were equipped with floating fly lines and a single well greased up Daddy Long Legs on the point.

So I make my first cast, dropping my Daddy right on the edge of the ripple, no more than ten yards out from the bank. Like magic, up came a 2lb 8oz rainbow and engulfed it, a satisfying moment – but it also demonstrated very well what they needed to do, and they did! The total catch for the session was fifty-two trout caught, and all the novices caught ones, twos, threes and one got four. The four experienced fly fishers all caught well, one taking sixteen trout, all to the Daddy.

So watch out when September comes around, because you too can join in on the best time of year for surface fish – and don't forget to leave the fly static, then re-cast: you only need a short line. A little trick if they are not rising is to kick all the rushes and high grass, as this releases more daddies that will be blown on to the lake's surface, where they drift out to the waiting trout.

> ### Bob Church's List of Small Fisheries
>
> These are the main small fisheries I have fished the most; they are listed here in no particular order, but I can recommend them.
>
> - Chalk Springs in Sussex
> - Avington in Hampshire
> - Dever Springs in Hampshire
> - Lechlade in the Cotswolds
> - Milestone in the Cotswolds
> - Elinor in Northamptonshire
> - Ringstead Grange in Northamptonshire
> - Patshull Park in Shropshire
> - Packington Estate in Warwickshire
> - Earith Trout Lakes in Cambridgeshire

Cyril Inwood was not only a good river fisher, he could fish small waters too.

10 The Loughs of Ireland

By Bob Church

There are a great many beautiful wild loughs all over Ireland, and many of them will produce good trout fishing. Some have salmon and sea trout for the angler as well. I have always concentrated on the four western loughs in Conn and Galway: the smallest is Lough Carra, with only brown trout; Lough Conn, with brown trout, salmon and a few sea trout; Lough Mask with brown trout and its varieties, ferox and gillaroo; and finally, the massive Lough Corrib, with lovely brown trout fishing and salmon in summer, and as I also found out, the incredible ferox. They are all such lovely scenic loughs to fish; just being out in a boat on a good day, there is nowhere I can think of that I would rather be.

'Buzzer' Fishing

The buzzer is the trout's most common food in March, April and May. This section on buzzer fishing is aimed at the Irish lough fishers for early season, and of course the high numbers of fly fishing visitors from all over the UK who come to fish at this time. I was aware of the feeling of unease from some Irish fly fishers when the subject got round to modern 'buzzer' fishing. The buzzer is really a *Chironomidae*, an insect with around 400 different species; over in Ireland it is called the 'duck fly', or the non-biting midge.

These insects in one form or another are the trout's most common occurrence food.

Lough Corrib.

Lough Feeagh. Jeanette Church plays a very big salmon on a size 14 Bibio, but alas, it came off after twenty minutes or so.

The larvae are bottom dwelling and known as the bloodworm; the ascending pupae are known over here as the buzzer nymph; and finally there is the emerger, which you can see on the surface when there has been a good hatch. From March until May, hatches of this fly are very good at all our reservoirs, and we have developed several

Bob with a Lough Carra wild brown trout, which took an artificial daddy.

A hatching buzzer pattern; a good one from Peter Gathercole. It can be fished dry.

different fishing methods to catch the trout that are feeding on them. The same thing seems to be happening on most of the Irish loughs, but only in more recent years has it come to light that the English reservoir tactics can give quite amazing catches on such massive waters as Lough Corrib.

First of all, buzzer fishing should not take place in the normal high wave drifts over the rocks: this remains the best place for the wet fly fisherman. What you should look for is more sheltered water such as a shallow bay with a soft bottom, where last year's weed has rotted down, and where the new weed growth will not have begun properly. A nice light ripple is just perfect, as you don't want the boat to move too fast. So you go to the top of the wind: in England we would drift slowly with a drogue out, and if we found a real hot-spot hatch we would anchor up for a while. The late Dick Shrive used to say:

> *The buzzer evening rise starts at about 10am, because when the pupae first hatch from the bloodworm into a free-swimming nymph, they are at first very feeble. Their movements are laboured, and there are swarms of them on the lake bed, all active but which cannot as yet swim properly.*

The main reason Dick always fished deep was because on the lake bed the larvae are very vulnerable, and the trout would be feeding freely on them. Eventually they pick up enough strength to ascend to the surface, but this can be a slow process, so again they are very vulnerable. The situation then often gets even worse because they get trapped in the sticky surface film just as they are about to emerge. When this happens in a light ripple, the trout can be seen to 'bulge' rise, knocking off the insects that are struggling to break open their wing cases. Of course many hatch successfully before the trout have time to eat them – and so the whole process of mating in the nearest sheltered hedgerow begins again, followed by egg laying, and so on … At this latter time you can use a black dry emerger to good effect.

Now although this can be lovely fishing, it is nowhere near as prolific as fishing static with the ascending pupa artificials. Let's now look at the 'Bung' method, because once you have tried it for yourself, you will be amazed at the quality of the brown trout you will catch from all the loughs you fish.

The 'Bung' Method

The so-called 'Bung' method was evolved in the south of England at Bewl Water. It was the brainchild of Billy Rankin and perfected by all Bewl good nymph fishermen, and of course it soon spread up to my local Midlands waters, such as Grafham, Pitsford, Draycote and Rutland. It was the new way to present a *Chironomidae* pupa completely static at three depths, around 4ft (1m), 8ft (2m) and 12ft (3m), and is quite deadly for catching big trout, stocked rainbows or wild browns as they take static pupae so confidently. You can go longer from your floating fly line to get deeper should the need arise.

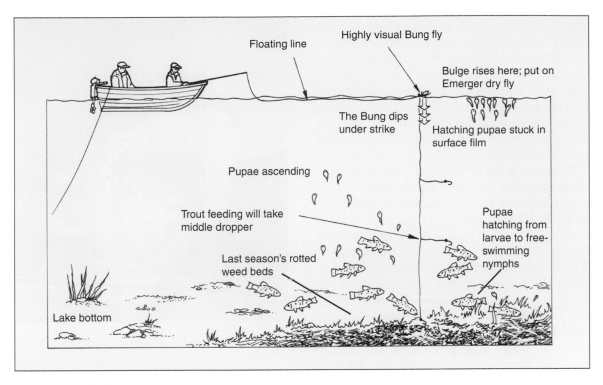

Floating line

Highly visual Bung fly

Bulge rises here; put on Emerger dry fly

The Bung dips under strike

Hatching pupae stuck in surface film

Pupae ascending

Trout feeding will take middle dropper

Pupae hatching from larvae to free-swimming nymphs

Last season's rotted weed beds

Lake bottom

The 'Bung' method.

Always remember you need to use a 'sight bob' to fish this method. So if you are using a big buoyant 'Booby' for the sight bob, the hook would stop at the rod's top eye – therefore 12ft (3.5m) would really be a maximum, otherwise you wouldn't have arms long enough to net a trout hooked on the point fly. Some fly fishers have got round this by using well greased tow wool as the sight bob; it can be done in such a way that it will pass through the large diameter rings. It comes in various fluorescent colours to suit visibility in varying light conditions.

The Flies and Set-Up

So how do you fish this method? I use 8lb fluorocarbon for my leader, tied at the distances I mentioned earlier. We call them 'Skinny Buzzers' because they have the minimum of dressing on them. With a medium action 10ft rod taking a six-, seven- or eight-weight floating line, right at the beginning of the fly line I tie my cast on the leader loop, making sure to leave a long end, to which I will tie my 'Bung' fly. This is usually a size 10, wide gape hook, with two extra large booby eyes and a very over-dressed tow-wool wing. I grease it up well with Mucilin to give it maximum floatability, because it needs to hold up 12ft (3.5m) of fast-sinking fluorocarbon clear line with three Skinny Buzzers on them.

Tie up a few different sizes to suit the weather conditions, and use very bright colours such as fluorescent yellow, lime green or hot orange – though sometimes in certain light conditions black is best.

Now put on your Buzzers, size 10s or 12s, though I put a heavy size 10 on the point because we want the leader to sink very quickly, which it will. Then on the dropper next to the point tie on a black or green Skinny Nymph. Now this leaves the top dropper fishing – or should I say hovering – only four foot (1m) down. I can easily put on another Skinny Buzzer, but I prefer to put here a Diawl Bach size 10 nymph using red fluorescent tying silk to show a bright red head.

I cast out a fairly long line – about twenty to twenty-five yards is about right – at a slight angle to the drifting boat. As the big floating 'Bung' settles, I am now almost float fishing, and I get strikes as the sight fly is pulled under very slowly and sedately. These are quietly confident takes that would never give you a pull on the hand, so you must strike the hook home in a way similar to dry fly fishing. The way to do it is just to take up the slack fly line as the boat drifts forward. You don't want the ghillie moving the boat while you are fishing, because the nymphs need to be static for the best effect.

Remember, the best hatches are in shallow water six to twelve feet deep (2 to 3m), so if I can reach the bottom with my point fly I would try a red bloodworm-type Buzzer. One London fly fisher called Micky Bewick has been a fishing friend for many years, and like me, loves coming over to the west of Ireland where he usually tackles Lough Corrib. In the last few seasons he has had wonderful catches on Skinny Buzzers and Bung tactics (he puts back all the trout he catches); one day in spring he had four browns over 4lb to his rod.

From my observations since coming over to Ireland in 1967 – forty years ago – I would conclude that you have many very good fly fishers. What I suggest is that you give the 'Bung' method a try in spring, then judge for yourselves.

If you really want to fish the Skinny Nymphs but don't like the Bung style, use a floater or sink tip fly line and a very long

As you can see, brown trout love the buzzer.

Buzzer and nymphs.

Fly Patterns

These are fly patterns that I would suggest you try. First, the bottom-dwelling larvae which are the bloodworms fished on the point:

Bloodworms
Hook: size 10 or 12 medium-shanked
Tying silk: red
Body: metallic red Lurex
Rib: the finest silver wire you can find
Thorax: build up with your tying silk
Shell back: pearlescent Mylar
Varnish: clear; varnish the whole nymph twice

Ascending Pupae (known as the
Buzzer Nymph)
Hook: sizes 10 or 12, medium-shanked, curved if possible
Tying silk: fine black
Body: thinly once up with tying silk
Rib: one strand of clear or pearl Lurex with the narrowest width
Thorax: black tying silk
Wing cases: cut from a Walkers crisp packet
Breather: tiny speck of white marabou
Varnish: clear; varnish whole of nymph twice but not the breather

Diawl Bach (Variation) top dropper
Hook: sizes 10, 12 or 14, medium-shanked
Tying silk: fluorescent red
Tail: ginger hen hackle fibres
Body: bronze peacock herl
Rib: thin red metallic Lurex
Throat hackle: ginger hen hackle fibres
Varnish: clear; varnish red silk head only

If the trout are seen to be rising freely to hatching 'buzzers', change up quickly to take advantage of this. At such times I have done well with these two dry fly patterns – just fish the two flies well spaced out on a 5lb breaking strain sub-surface nylon (*not* fluorocarbon which sinks too quickly: save that for the nymphs).

Emerson's Hanging Emerger
Hook: size 12, fine wire, long-shanked
Tying silk: black
Body: very, very thinly dubbed on claret red seal's fur substitute
Rib: the finest possible gold wire
Wing: tied parachute style, a very generous bunch of brown Cul de Canard feathers
Varnish: clear

Kevin Garn's Emerging Buzzer
Hook: size 12 or 14
Tying silk: black
Tail: black Cul de Canard fibres
Body: black seal fur
Rib: finest pearlescent Lurex
Thorax: black seal's fur
Hackle: one turn only of black cock hackle, but cut off fibres on the underside of the fly
Varnish: clear

The 'Bung' as a Sight Bob
Hook: size 10
Eyes: a pair of booby eyes, in this case orange, but could be any good colour
Wing: over-exaggerated big blob of tow wool or similar.

---

leader, as long as you can handle, about 18 to 21ft (5 to 6m) will do. After casting out, allow the nymphs to sink well down, and retrieve very, very slowly – we call it 'twiddling' – in a slow figure-of-eight will do.

Buzzer Action on Lough Corrib

The following anecdote relates how Micky Bewick experienced the buzzer action on Lough Corrib.

In the year 2000, the very experienced fly fisher and fly tyer Micky Bewick visited Lough Corrib at mayfly time – obviously he had timed his visit to be at the mayfly peak, during the week known as 'duffer's fortnight', when normally all the trout are rising regularly, taking this natural large fly. Usually it is possible to catch plenty on dry artificial patterns. However, when Micky went out in the boat on Corrib, he was greeted with sunny, flat calm conditions. He cast out three dry Mayflies, then soon realized how ridiculous they looked; as he observed, 'As there were a few buzzers hatching off, I put up a twenty-foot leader and three buzzers to fish static at varying depths.'

In four successive sessions Micky took at least four browns averaging 3lb, and the locals are still talking about his 'revolutionary' new tactics today. It just proves that methods developed on English stocked reservoirs can be made to work on the wild Irish loughs. Micky returned to Corrib this

Robbie O'Grady with a standard size brown trout on Lough Mask.

BELOW: Lough Mask.

season, and on his first session he took four trout of 3lb 14oz, 3lb 5oz, 3lb 4oz and 3lb within three and a half hours. He used olive or black lightly dressed seal's fur Buzzer patterns, ribbed with plastic nymph glass.

Not to let a new method pass him by, Basil Shields took the idea one stage further by trying the skinny, varnished buzzers. He was rewarded with spectacular sport, with fish of well over the average stamp for Corrib. At the time of writing, Basil has a boatyard and a superb 'B&B' on Corrib. Basil has concentrated on the weedy bays (some are as big as Grafham) where there is an abundance of natural fly life, attracting the bigger specimens looking for an easy meal. My fishing companions Carol Neal and Kevin Garn had already been out with Basil for a few days before I arrived, and had caught on a mixture of tactics. The Buzzer was still working, as were traditional wet fly methods, but another English technique was working even better: static Hoppers were accounting for more than their fair share of fish, with Carol and Kevin taking eleven trout to 3lb in one session.

Basil is a great boatman and fisherman; he will take you out, but book up now. At the time of writing he can be contacted on telephone 00 353 945 52550, and his address is Ardnasillagh Lodge, Oughterard, Co. Galway.

Lough Mask, My Favourite Water

Lough Corrib is a great water, with 365 islands, one for every day of the year. Conn and Carra are lovely places to spend a day's boat fishing for the wild browns. On to them soon, but I must give first mention to my favourite Irish water, Lough Mask, at 21,000 acres (8,450ha). For many years we have stayed with Nan and Robbie O'Grady at their little guest house on the Castlebar road, Ballinrobe; Robbie has always been

Basil Shields shows a lovely brown trout while practising with Bob on Lough Mask.

The boats leave Cushlough Bay on Lough Mask for the World Cup match. Robbie O'Grady has won this event twice.

221

Bob with a superb brown of 3lb 10oz, caught on Lough Mask in the World Cup.

Two big browns from Lough Mask in the World Cup, giving Bob 2nd place out of 700 entries.

A Mayfly.

a great ghillie and entertainer, and we had some exciting times on the unpredictable Mask.

When we first went over there were usually four of us, and we would go in spring for the first olive hatches. Some thirty years ago we were catching them on buzzer patterns, but these were nowhere near as sophisticated as today's approach. The late Frank Cutler used to make those trips, as did Alan Pearson, Paul Harris, Peter Thomas, Peter Gathercole, Kevin Garn, Jeremy Herrmann, Dave Allen and Stephen Church. My wife Jeanette came over towards the end of the more wild occasions.

For the last twenty-five years I have been attracted to the week's fly fishing festival held at Mask called The World Cup. This event, which has 600 plus entries every

Kevin Garn won a boat for the biggest fish caught in the World Cup on Lough Mask.

year, takes place over the week of the last few days of July and into August, taking in the Irish Bank Holiday. The competition is run by Ballinrobe Fly Fishers, and there are four heat days with around 140 anglers out each day. The top 20 per cent qualify for the final which is fished at the end of the week followed by dinner and presentations.

The best our party has done was Peter Thomas and Kevin Garn, who both won the best overseas angler. Kevin had the biggest fish (one year) of the week in a heatwave, and for this he won a 19ft Burke boat. In 1986 I finished second overall, losing out by 1¼oz to a German angler called Kurt Menrad. That day was difficult and I caught two lovely fish on a Mayfly, the best over 3lb; another took a Claret and Mallard, but I also dropped two other fish of around 1lb 4oz right at the net. I thought I was unlucky, *but* I won a 6hp outboard engine!

Lough Carra

We used to fish Lough Carra quite a lot because it was so attractive. There was always a good fly hatch, and the dry fly worked well here, with marvellous results. I have done best with a very delicate dry Mayfly pattern, often taking twelve to fifteen fish like this. Daddy Long Legs are also very good, and often tempt the bigger fish.

I was out one day with Peter Thomas when we noticed the strong breeze was blowing a lot of mating damsel flies off a big bed of onion-top rushes. This phenomenon stretched for about 500ft (150m). The joined-together blue male and olive female were blown on to the water in high numbers, and the trout were rising in fair numbers taking them. We tried everything and caught one or two, but we hadn't got it right.

Adult olive, which are abundant in Irish loughs. Trout love them, and eagerly rise to them.

I studied my four fly boxes carefully and there, tucked in a corner of one, was a fly called the Goats Toe size 10 pattern. This is tied with the metallic blue feather from the male peacock's breast. I tied it on, greased it up so it floated – and never looked back, taking at least a dozen browns on it up to 3lb.

If you do fish on Carra or Mask, call at Nan and Robbie's guest house: he has now retired, but his capable son Kenneth is following in Dad's footsteps and he has his own boats on both loughs.

Choosing the Right Fly

For some time now the English reservoirs have been less productive to the wet fly drift fisherman. This is mainly because there is less fly life and lots more daphnia blooms. As we know, the daphnia goes deep on bright sunny days, then there are few opportunities. However, on dark, heavy cloud days with a good westerly wind, the daphnia is up in the top two to three feet of water. When this occurs it all gets washed to the downwind areas of the reservoirs,

where you may just get a team of wet flies working again.

On the four mentioned loughs, the three-fly wet-fly cast still works very well because there is good fly life throughout the trout season: duck flies or buzzers in March, April, May; olives in April, May and again in September; mayfly in May, June, July and August; sedges in May, June, July, August and September; damsels in June and July; and crane-fly – or daddies – in August and September, as they all hatch in good numbers. You can see why it is a good idea to fish imitatively in Ireland, because it still has the fly life – unfortunately we don't.

A marvellous method on Lough Mask was to use a sink tip fly line and set my cast up with three flies. The fly that really worked for me was a Green Peter Muddler, tied rather scruffily; the larger brown trout were taking it on my top dropper some five to six feet down when drifting on to the top end of islands where you get a bit of back-wash. Last time there I had a nice 3lb 8oz – and was outdone by a 5lb to 6lb fish that I saw clearly before it dived unstoppably on to the submerged sharp rocks.

Dry fly fishing works very well too, but you need to choose the right day of a warm, light, westerly wind with grey rolling clouds. I can vouch for the effectiveness of the dry Mayfly both on Mask and especially Carra, where I have had marvellous sport, fishing two well spaced out delicate Mayflies as late as August.

Let me recall some of my memories of trips to the west. But first, a rather funny story of when the four home countries international was held on Lough Arrow. On this occasion I was England team manager, and we had a good team out who had practised very well on the two official days prior to the match. It had been virtually a flat calm, but very light breezes sometimes created a very slight ripple. The olives were about and hatching, but fish were not taking them off the top

Adult olive freshly hatched; Peter Gathercole's pattern.

Spent fly returns to the water in the evening to lay its eggs; it is known as the Apricot Spinner. Peter Gathercole's pattern.

with any confidence. So the English team fished with size 12 Olive Nymphs, with the very slowest of slow-sinking slyme fly lines. This was coupled with an equally very slow figure-of-eight continuous retrieve.

Talking in the bar during the evenings, it seemed we had worked out the best line of approach: we were getting much better results than the other countries, and they were all making us favourites. But come the next day, competition day, and it was blowing a force 5/6 wind with two- to three-foot high waves all over the lough. We cursed our luck and the Irish were just smiling confidently as they entered the boats – prior to this they had not caught very much at all.

Suffice it to say, Ireland won the match by a couple of trout more than England, who came second. My friend Basil Shields fished for Ireland that day, taking three good browns. The method England had perfected in the calm should be remembered by any Irish fly fisher faced with those near flat conditions at olive time. The England team did help the Irish to celebrate their

victory that evening – and it was, of course, a very late night.

I was out on Corrib with Jeremy Herrmann about three seasons ago during olive time and just prior to the mayfly. Again it was light breezes. Jeremy had arrived a day before me and he related at supper, 'Bob, I can't believe it, I have blanked today but it will probably do me good. I look forward to fishing with you tomorrow when we can work out how to catch them.'

Suffice to say he did work it out very soon the following day. He put up a very slow sinking intermediate fly line and three size 14 sparsely dressed nymphs. He used 4lb sub-surface nylon and made up his leader, a very long 21ft so he could fish his nymphs well spaced out. It was still very difficult fishing, but he caught seven nice, bigger-than-average browns, and I had three. It was interesting that there was a heat for the big spring competition being fished that day, and the winner from over 100 competitors had only three fish. Jeremy reckoned he was retrieving his nymphs on a figure-of-eight at no more than 12 to 18in (30 to

45cm) below the surface – so some good proof there for this method.

Now what about the larger mayflies? Well, I have had some great sessions when they have been hatching. Let's forget the so-called 'duffer's fortnight' when hatches are at their heaviest, because often any reasonable dry fly Mayfly variant will catch you a lot of trout. By the way, as a kindness to your fish, be sure to press the barb down on your fly, so you can return them easily, without damage. Also, on Corrib and Conn watch out for the mayfly peak in June, because salmon (grilse) will be moving through these two loughs in reasonable numbers and it is a good time to catch them. The classic head-and-tail rise over your dropper from a salmon is one of the most thrilling moments any fly fisher can experience.

Some Personal Experiences with Mayfly

I want to end by telling you of some experiences I have had by fishing the Mayfly on loughs Conn, Mask and Carra during August, long after the main mayfly hatches have disappeared. First Conn: it was 12 August and I was out with Paul Harris and we were amazed to witness the heaviest hatch of mayfly we had ever seen on Conn. Between us we landed twenty-three trout on dry Mayfly, all caught between 10.30am and 6pm.

Although the right flies are very important, so too is a good ghillie, and on this day we had Kieran Connolly, one of the best on Conn. Although he now lives in England, he always has six weeks back home near Pontoon, spending his time being a ghillie on either Conn or the smaller, adjacent Lough Cullin.

Kieran uses the back oar only to manoeuvre the boat's drift, always keeping us about ten yards away from the rocks, and it was in the narrow zone that we hooked most of our

Sometimes it is a good idea to collect live daddies, and dap with the natural insect.

twenty-three trout. At first we fished just on Mayfly on the dropper of the cast, and as all fish were falling to that, we changed to three Mayflies on our casts.

We didn't cover the same drift twice, and it was all action from start to finish: altogether we think we raised over a hundred fish. It is now just a memory of a lovely day afloat, but the message is, remember to keep a Mayfly on the cast here in August. A good set-up is a size 14 Black Spider on the point, a size 10 Green Peter in the middle and a Mayfly on the top dropper. The fish were up to 2lb 8oz, not big, but lovely fish. On a later day I had a lovely brown of 3lb 12oz, and my wife Jeanette went one better, tempting one of 4lb, all on the dry fly. The American pattern Yellow Humpy, a size 10, caught two big ones for Jeanette and I. It

Lough Carra is a good water for dapping.

floats high on top of the wave, and Conn's brownies pick it out well.

Finally, what about the lovely little Lough Carra? At 3.3 acres (1.3ha) it is about the same size as our largest reservoir Rutland or Lake Windermere. Here I used a very delicate little Mayfly pattern, and this, too, is in early August. I suppose my favourite dry fly for Carra is the yellow-bodied Daddy Long Legs in size 10 long shank.

There are so many good drifts on this very safe lough, you cannot help but catch a lot of fish – but don't motor back up the drift or you will catch nothing. So my tip is, keep a mayfly on your cast all season from June to September.

Of course the olives, the big sedges Green Peter and Murrough, and the Daddies, will all bring trout up to the surface, and then the dry will be first choice. Cast out and just figure-of-eight, keeping up with the slack line as the boat drifts forwards. It really works best if these dry flies are fished static and with some finesse. I also take off my fluorocarbon line, which sinks, and go back to shaded green Maxima or Drennan Sub-surface of 6lb breaking strain.

Dapping

While on the subject of surface fishing, I must explain the dapping method, which is so fascinating to try. You can do it with live mayflies, daddy long legs or the all-time favourite in the height of summer, the grasshopper. I have seen crickets used, too; these extra large hoppers are purchased from pet shops, and they do attract the larger trout.

I must admit, very few English fly fishers ever try dapping. Tackle is simple. The rod need not be special – I use a 15ft old soft salmon rod or a 14ft match rod, and a wide arbour reel with 100yd 10lb nylon on; to this I tie on about 4 to 5yd of special blow line, which, when the long rod is raised, will fly out like a kite. So first tie on a leader of about 10ft (3m), and put your hook on a lightweight size 12 or 10, then hook up either a grasshopper in midsummer, or two live daddies in September. I don't even bother with mayflies, as fish are easy to catch on artificials.

So the bait is on the hook; now lift your rod up vertical and play out some line from the reel, then lower your rod so just the hook and bait touch the water. It doesn't matter

Ken Whelan overseeing the rainbow project on Ballin Lough.

A beauty from Lough Owel.

if it lands with a bit of a plop, because this seems to attract the trout towards your baited fly hook. I remember pulling into Cushlough Bay one evening with Robbie, alongside another boat and its occupants. 'How many did you get?' asked Robbie. 'Twelve,' was the reply. Robbie answers, 'Good heavens, what on?' Then he looked to see their long dapping rods – his immediate comment was that our six on wet fly was better than their twelve on the dap, but the point he was *really* making was how effective dapping was at catching brown trout.

The technique is to keep working the rod up and down so as to lift up your artificial Daddy and keep dropping him on the water with a plop. This is actually how the natural hits the water, and it induces the reaction take. You can use either the natural, or the artificial tied Daddy; I like the pattern with the detached hollow tube of deer hair for a body – this certainly makes them unsinkable. However, if there are plenty of natural daddies about (correct name crane fly), then why not collect twenty-five or so naturals. I shall never forget crawling around on my knees looking for, and catching grasshoppers. Use these insects on a size 10 fine wire hook, and dap them in exactly the same way as I explained for the artificials. Takes vary from a little sip to an explosive up, over and down on the fly. Unmissable, or so you would think.

The late Jimmy Murphy, a fine Lough Mask boatman, had a fine brown trout of 13lb set up in a glass case in his house; I noticed this when I called to organize a day's fishing with him. Then he told me the tale as only Jimmy could, reliving the epic battle so vividly it was as if I had been there myself. Related Jimmy: 'Your Englishman was dapping with three live daddies, and he was overjoyed at catching the huge fish.' Jimmy netted it aboard after fifteen minutes or more. The man was so grateful he returned to fish with Jimmy again the following year, and presented the set-up fish for all Jimmy's clients to see.

About Rainbows

When in the west of Ireland, there are so many good places to fish, if you don't fancy your first choice of water because it's off for some reason, you can always find somewhere just as good. But I must tell you the fishing is seldom easy, except for one lough we found: Ballin Lough, a shallow, rich limestone lough managed by Ken Whelan. He was experimenting with rainbows, and as we found, they were obviously doing very well. Ken's comment was: 'I want you English fly fishers to fish for the rainbows – you are used to catching them on your prolific reservoirs, and I will come along and watch how you do it!' Well, it was a marvellous day's sport for Jeanette and me, and for Frank Cutler and Kevin Garn, in another boat.

The English tactics worked a treat: fast stripping hot orange lures, Buzzer Nymphs fished slowly in a team of three, and even heart-stopping Muddlers stripped fast on the surface. It was a great day, and Ken needed a few fish to carry out his growth studies and eating quality, and also to check on the general health of these rainbows, which for some unknown reason have mostly not been wanted by many Irish authorities.

I have often thought that Lough Owel would be a good experimental lough to try

Jeanette on Ballin Lough. Fish were retained for study.

RIGHT: *Ballin Lough's young ghillie gets a near-4lb.*

out the rainbows. They already stock with brown trout there, and it is close to the bigger populated areas of Ireland, which would help give consistent sport despite high fishing pressure. Rainbows are a fantastic fighting fish when introduced to big sheets of water; you only have to look at the two big English reservoirs, Grafham and Rutland. Once in the water for about three months, these fish continue growing and take on a grilse-like appearance.

I always remember fishing in the World Fly Fishing Championships on Grafham, where I was drawn to fish with Dick Willis of Ireland. Being my home water, I arrived on my boat jetty ten minutes before the off. Dick was already in the boat and in the bow, and said: 'I'll leave the engine to you, Bob. I have never fished or seen this lovely water before; take me where you want to fish all day!'

First I told him to take off the floating line he had put on, and to put on a fast sinker, if he had one. Remember, I didn't know Dick at all – in fact we had only just met

for the first time. Dick promptly wound in his floater, took it off, and produced a reel with a brand new line on. He said, 'I did my homework and purchased your Canadian lead-impregnated, fast-sink line!' – to which I replied 'Snap!' as I fitted the same line on mine.

We went out to Church Bay, where Dick had three takes, and three stockies were in the boat, while I had one take which I missed. The fish were taking a bit of a hammering in the shallowest water of about fifteen feet, with several boats now working the same drift. Two drifts later Dick had five and I had boated at least two, of which one was a much better fish. This was in the days of stocking with 1lb rainbows and a few browns, by comparison with today's larger stockie trout of 2lb.

We left the stockies, and I took him over to the left-hand point of Sludge Bay, a big shallow area about the size of two football pitches. A northerly wind was blowing us along perfectly, with a drogue slowing down the speed of the drift. The fish on this

On Lough Corrib you need flat calm conditions to fish properly for ferox.

downwind side were feeding on daphnia, and I knew the recipe for these; suffice to say I finished the session at 5pm with twelve rainbows and came second, and Dick had eight rainbows topped by a 4lb 12oz fish, the most handsome rainbow you have ever seen. He came third, a successful day.

Dick hooked this big fish with about ten minutes left in the competition, and this is how the story goes. Dick said, 'Bob, I am into a fine grilse here!' I replied, 'Dick, there are no salmon in here, it's a reservoir. A flooded valley with a little feeder stream to top it up, and also water is pumped in from the Great Ouse river, which has no salmon.' But Dick insisted, 'But I tell you this fish is bright silver, I have seen it flash, and it's so fast and powerful!' I explained this is what rainbows are like if they have been in a big water for a while. This fish had almost certainly been stocked a year earlier at 1lb, and had grown on to nearly 5lb in two years. Dick boated it in the end, after lots of runs and several scary moments. He was so pleased, and said, 'I will never hear a bad word spoken about rainbows again; the fish was just a bar of silver!' Dick and I formed a friendship that day which has lasted.

My point I am making is, what's wrong with stocking with rainbows? A water such as Lough Owel would be a good test, and browns and rainbows get on fine together. If they don't suit your fly fishers after a year – although I would bet good money they will – they can do no damage, just don't stock them again, as they very rarely spawn successfully on these UK and Irish waters.

Trolling

Only very occasionally does a really big ferox trout get caught on a fly. Usually you need either to troll the big loughs of Mask and Corrib, or Scottish waters such as

Stephen Greaney is a superb ghillie and puts Bob on to the fish. It was a very welcome 5–6lb ferox that Stephen quickly releases.

A 10lb 8oz ferox followed; after a quick picture, that was also returned.

231

Finally the jackpot, a perfect ferox of 17lb 3oz.

Loch Awe; we have even got them in England's Lake Windermere. Anything that is rare and beautiful attracts, and you could say this about the handsome ferox.

Flat, calm days with not much happening for the wet fly fisherman are just perfect for trolling for ferox. This huge member of the brown trout family is a really exciting one to catch – and, I must add, also to return alive and well. One calm day on Corrib this happened to me. I was staying with Basil Shields at Ardnasillagh Lodge with my other three fly-fishing friends. They wouldn't come with me on that day, so I went alone with one of Basil's ghillies, the experienced but young Stephen Greaney.

He told me we would do some specialized trolling with a dead wobbled 9in roach as bait, a multiplying reel with 15lb breaking strain line, then the special three swivels' trace with two barbless trebles on. The trace was then threaded though the vent and out of the fish's mouth, the first treble shank going right into the vent where it acted as a harness, with the second treble 2in (5cm) behind the hooker. The roach bait is bent so it wobbles perfectly at the slow trolling speed, which is kept constant so that the roach runs at a depth of 25ft (7.5m). With the numbers of arctic char dwindling in Lough Corrib, the roach has taken its place in the food chain for both ferox and pike.

The kit we took out in the boat to make sure that any hooked and boated ferox did not get damaged in any way was a pair of long-nosed pliers for unhooking, a specimen-sized landing net with soft mesh, an unhooking mat which can double as a weigh sling, and finally an accurate dial scales and a camera to record the catch, making for a good memory.

Stephen was certainly very knowledgeable, and I told him as we motored out that a 10lb fish would be a dream fish for me – and he confidently replied, 'No problem!' He was right, too, because on the first

Gordon Burton proves there are still big ferox in England, with a lovely 12lb fish from Lake Windermere.

strike I had a 10lb 8oz ferox: what a beautiful fish! I photographed it and returned it, and it swam off none the worse for its ordeal. I then had another of 5 to 6lb, which we quickly unhooked; we then went in for lunch on an island where we had arranged to meet friends at 1pm.

They, of course, had blanked all morning wet fly fishing, and didn't look particularly happy. Soon we were off again, back to the trolling, and our friends back to the wet fly. My anticipation for another take was immense, and with half an hour to go before we packed up, my rod arched over and the water exploded after I had about six tap-tap-tap nods on the rod tip. I am positive the fish follow the bait and head-butt it with the object of knocking it off its swimming course. When they feel it is safe, they grab it and are hooked.

Some anglers say trolling is boring, which I suppose it is if the boatman doesn't know the hot spots where ferox regularly turn up,

the right depth in which to run your bait, or the right bait – in this case, dead roach. When you have actually caught a big ferox, you will appreciate it is never boring, and the anticipation is there every moment you are expecting a big fish to take. My ferox went 17lb 3oz, and swam away all right after being photographed. But it wasn't that easy, and it took me twenty minutes of careful playing with just one hook-up – the barbless treble. The worst moment came after about five minutes when the fish was deep and fighting hard. It turned and ran straight at me so fast it slack-lined me, giving me the feeling that it had come off; but luckily I managed to regain the fight after gathering in the slack line.

The adrenalin then hit me and I was on a real high, and couldn't wait to get back to Basil's and tell the boys what a fantastic day I had had. John Emerson in particular had said, 'You won't catch me trolling if it were the last fishing left to me.' Now he

John Emerson with his ferox of 9lb 2oz.

had suddenly changed his mind, and asked if he could come out in the boat with me the next day. I said no, because he was wet fly fishing in another near-flat calm. But I am such a soft touch, he did come out with me, *and* I gave him first strike at both rods. The only fish of the day caught was an 8lb 8oz ferox. But now he had tasted it, he wanted to go again the following day, even though the weather had changed and it was a perfect wind for the drift and wet fly fishing.

This time he took our other friend with him, while I went off fly fishing. He had one fish of 9lb 2oz, and Dave Neal at the first attempt had an 8lb; Stephen was the boatman all three days, and did really well for us. All fish were returned unharmed.

As far as the Scottish lochs are concerned, Loch Awe seems to be the one to go for; and in England Lake Windermere still produces the occasional big ferox. For some very good reading look up a book called *Ferox Trout and Arctic Char* by Ron Greer, published by the Swan Hill Press

of Shrewsbury. Of course, on many waters where there is fishing for ferox the anglers use some kind of artificial such as diving plugs, for instance the Depth Raider or big spoons; and another essential in your equipment is a depth sounder-cum-fish finder.

My favourite loughs and lochs for ferox or brown trout are the following:

Brown trout	Ferox
Lough Corrib	Lough Corrib
Lough Mask	Lough Mask
Lough Carra	Loch Awe
Lough Owel	Loch Garry
Loch Watton	
The many Thurso little lochs	
Loch Tay, Killen end	
Loch Lintrathin and Loch Leven	

11 Fishing for Trout and Grayling in Rivers

By Bob Church

No matter how much excellent stillwater or lough fishing I do, I still always enjoy some trips on our best trout and grayling rivers. I would go so far as to say that if you have become an accomplished stillwater fly fisher, and very successful at catching trout, then you should look at river fishing as a new challenge. The tactics discussed here will work on most rivers.

For a start your tackle will be much lighter, with rods between 7ft and a no. 4 fly line, to 9ft with a no. 6 fly line. For upstream dry fly fishing I always have a line made up with a Bob Church special tapered hollow braided cast, which tapers down to the thickness of 5lb breaking strain nylon. Then I use no more than 3ft of 4lb nylon, or less if the fish are spooky. With this set-up, my selected fly for upstream dry fly fishing will turn over completely straight even when casting into a strong wind: it gives you the edge, with far more rises because you present the fly so perfectly and quietly. Of course it goes without saying that you will need a flick up landing net, polarized glasses, chest waders, a wading waistcoat and jacket, and if you are an older person, like me, an automatic life jacket.

ABOVE: *These days they all go back.*

LEFT: *Trevor Housby with a big catch of grayling.*

LEFT: *Mayfly was on, but only sparsely; however, Bob still manages to get one.*
BELOW LEFT: *Bob netted it.*
BELOW RIGHT: *It was a 3lb 8oz brown trout.*

Grayling are a perfectly wild fish, and very good to fish for once autumn has come, when other species such as brown trout and salmon are out of season. Some of our prime rivers are now stocked with rainbows, including the famous River Test in Hampshire. I have been fortunate enough to be able to fish on many of the famous beats on this still very lovely river; some say it has been spoiled by the stocking of rainbows, but I like them, they give good sport and fight better than browns.

Selecting the Right Fly

Waiting for a hatch to begin and a rise develop was taught to me after a day's

Bob lands a rainbow in the Newport river.

When mayfly is on, wade to the centre of the river if you can, then face upstream and cast for rising fish.

Soon you will cover a rising fish and hook it.

Net and release it using barbless hooks. This is the River Test at Long Parish, Hampshire.

fishing on the River Test with Barry Welham in my early days. Then I was mostly a big reservoir fly fisher, a style of fishing at its peak during the seventies. Barry had wandered off looking for fish with his Polaroids on; while he was gone I couldn't wait, there were no trout rising so I thought I would put up a standard Black Gnat size 14 dry fly pattern. That would surely bring up a fish or two. I think I caught one on the Black Gnat and one on a dry olive. Barry came back and I asked him what he had caught.

He said, 'Bob, come up here and sit on the bench with me. When you fish a place like this you give yourself a gentleman's handicap: I haven't even cast out yet! This handicap is, wait for the hatch to begin, then determine what the fly is that the fish are taking – then match the hatch and catch a few fish!' Then it all happened just as he said it would. On my two or three times a year to fish the Test I still cannot reach the sporting respectable style of Barry because I am too impatient. I think if I can see a fish in its chosen lie I can catch it,

Sometimes it is too deep to wade, so take care with your back casting; it is better to roll cast.

Geoff nets it for Jeanette.

Jeanette plays a fish back for Geoff Clarkson to net.

Geoff Clarkson shows it, and returns it to the water.

but something black or olive usually sorts a few fish out.

Back in the eighties when the England World team was practising prior to the Championships, we had some high number catches from the Test. This fishing was arranged for us on the condition we kept the grayling, which Rags Locke would distribute to local village people who liked eating them. We used to catch very well with our weighted nymphs, shrimp patterns, Sawyers Killer bugs, and caddis and hare ear variants with gold ball heads.

Grayling were introduced into the River Test in 1834 when fifty fish were given to the stretch of the Test by Lord Malmesbury. The small grayling were only 4oz apiece, but they thrived so well that the river holds good wild stocks today. When we practised we realized there did seem to be a large head of grayling present. In a short day Brian Leadbetter and I caught over fifty grayling, and although Rags said the fish were not wasted, that was the last time I would take part in the culling of such lovely fish, except the odd one for eating.

Other stretches of the River Test are stocked with rainbows, such as this 7lb fish for Ron Randall.

Brian and I have travelled the world together in our efforts to do well for England in the World and Commonwealth Championships. I recall a day's practice one summer day on the upper Welsh Dee, from where it runs out of Lake Bala downstream to the road layby. We chose to fish wet fly olives, and a size 14 traditional Greenwell's Glory did the business for me. Brian used similar tactics, slowly allowing our flies to come round with the current. It was a case of cast and walk a couple of steps respectively, and stop a little longer at an obviously deeper, pool-holding spot.

Fishing the Corwen stretch of the same River Dee, Brian found that as he went down in hook and fly size with dry fly, the better his results were. We all followed suit and started catching grayling well on a difficult stretch. The best pattern was an Adams upright wing.

The Rolled Nymph

I had been talking to a Polish international fly fisher when we returned to the hotel

Until recently you had to kill all grayling because they ate the salmon eggs. Here Brian Leadbetter and Bob shared about thirty grayling in half a day's fishing. These fish were taken by Rags Locke to pensioners in the village. It was the last time I killed any grayling.

A 2lb grayling from the River Test returned.

A recent 2lb grayling quickly returned.

after the first heat day. I gave him a Cat's Whisker for the lake session on Brenig, and in return he gave me a very simple weighted nymph on a size 10 hook. It was so simple I thought he was kidding me, but this nymph was what he was doing the damage on. It had an under wire-weighted hook shank, then ordinary brown wool tied on with white thread, picked out and dubbed on to form a nice shape, then ribbed with thick copper wire and finished with a quite large, pure white head; it was varnished to finish off.

He had told me the truth, because I caught six grayling from a difficult peg the next day, and I came second behind Chris Ogborne on Brenig with five fish to the Cat's Whisker. So it pays to watch other anglers' styles and the flies they use. The UK fly fishers had one big learning curve during this competition: we were by far the best fishers when using stillwater techniques, but it was the Eastern Europeans who led the way on the rivers, in particular Poland and what was then Czechoslovakia.

LEFT: *Brian Leadbetter fishing the Welsh Dee, where all the World England team were practising for fishing in Tasmania.*

Fishing for wild rainbows on New Zealand's North Island.

The Rolled Nymph: Brian Leadbetter caught this beautiful trout of 6lb.

During that Championship, held in Wales on the Dee, the style 'Czech nymphing' won the team event for them, but a Polish fisher came first individual. Czech nymph fishing is now an accepted style used by any UK fly fisher since that day, and it is a 'must' to learn it for yourself.

According to the power of the river, you set up your leader cast. For a normal, steady current I like a Hare's Ear Gold Head on the point, and a black or olive Spider Nymph on a dropper. For faster, more powerful rivers I have seen a Polish fly fisher fishing a river in spate with three gold heads 'Czech Nymph style'. It was the flooded River Norse and, needless to say, he won the competition comfortably ('Rolled Nymph' is now called 'Czech nymphing' by the British).

The method is to short cast upstream, then allow the current to bring the nymphs back to you and then past you. All the time you hold your rod high, showing the curve,

A good grayling on the Rolled Nymph.

241

which you concentrate on intently. As soon as the loop begins to go straight you give a firm strike and you will either have a fish on, grayling or trout, or you will have caught the bottom. The idea is to get your weighted nymphs just right for the speed of the flow.

Fishing like this you can wade and fish steadily across the river, then turn round and come back after taking a couple of steps downstream. Sometimes a little trick of shuffling your feet in the bottom silt and gravel releases enough natural feed to get the fish going, although in some circles this is frowned upon – but it is effective.

After a few practices I got rather good at this, and was doing well. On a practice day in a morning session I managed twelve nice grayling from the Dee. Packing up for lunch I wandered downstream to find Svoboda, the Czech international, fishing in mid-river wading up to the maximum of his chest waders; in the same morning he caught twenty-four grayling. He is a great river grayling fisher, and helped Czechoslovakia win the World Championship on the Dee.

Many of these grayling have been caught and released before, so they are shy, and for that reason you very rarely get a 'thump' take on your hand. This is why it is so important to study the curve and hit the bite early, before the grayling has time to eject it. I have watched trout in the clearest fishery in the country, Chalk Springs at Arundel, which provides excellent fishing this way: the trout can follow your nymph fly, mouth it completely, and then eject it without you even knowing; certainly you don't even feel a pluck on your retrieving hand. The same thing is happening with these grayling, which are dropping the nymph after mouthing it; however, by watching the slack, curved line begin to straighten, you are in charge again – try it, and see for yourselves.

Rainbows on the Itchen and the Wye

Another Hampshire river I must mention is the River Itchen. When I first fished this river it was supposed to be brown trout only and a few grayling, as well as salmon. I was fishing there as a guest of Tony Pawson, who said I would not catch rainbows there that day. But my first fish after covering a confident rise was an immaculate 3lb 8oz rainbow! I remember spooning the fish's stomach and it was full of fresh green lily leaves, so it must have been a vegetarian – they get everywhere! Since then I have fished the Itchen a bit more, and its grayling average is quite high, with a 2lb possible on most visits.

I used to fish the Derbyshire Wye quite a lot, and it is unique because it is the only river where rainbows can breed successfully. I was introduced to this lovely stretch

We travelled north to Lapland, where three rivers run over into Russian borders; one of these is the lovely River Kuusinki.

After two weeks in Lapland I lost a stone in weight because we had to eat reindeer at every meal, and I hated it.

The Norwegian angler shows us the way and catches this fine brace of brown trout; so we went for them ourselves the next day, with success.

by John Neville, a local angling journalist. He booked me into the local pub and B&B at Rowsley, and was there waiting for me as I was having breakfast. 'There should be some mayfly about,' he mentioned casually, 'but you needn't bother with those, just tie on my parachute hackled Coachman – that's the only fly you'll need.' John is also an excellent fly tyer, and he gave me a couple of his size 14 special dries, which I was happy to use despite having boxes full of all sorts and sizes of dry fly.

Suffice it to say, I caught about thirty fish, mostly all wild, self-bred rainbows – but this was nearly forty years ago! But I have never forgotten that trip to that lovely Derbyshire river. Of course I have fished there many times since, and there is a much greater number of stocked rainbows now; also the grayling population is up a lot. So when you are given expert local advice, take it, and you will be on the way to a good catch.

Fishing in Lapland

Some of the best river fishing I have had can be found in Lapland, and here the grayling are present in high numbers. I concentrated on the two rivers Kuusinki and Kitka; the England team members had practised on the River Wharfe and River Ure, where the grayling and browns were all right to catch. I enjoyed those away weekends with the camaraderie of fellow team members.

Based in the Kuusamo district of Finland, we were so far north that we were in Father Christmas country, Lapland. To get there you need to fly to Helsinki, then take an internal prop plane to Kuusamo; this allows you to get a good look at the Finnish countryside, which alters very little all the way. It consists of thousands of lakes and barren silver birch and fir forests. I checked the records, and amazingly there are 187,888 lakes in all, and some are very large.

Lapland is the 'land of the midnight sun'.

England was going for a hat trick of World Championship wins. The food at the hotel was based on reindeer meat, and for the whole two weeks it was reindeer steaks, stews, pies, soup, you name it and reindeer was in it. A lot of these animals were

Bob caught his best ever wild trout on the River Kuusinki, at 7lb 6oz; it is caught on a Hare's Ear with a short olive marabou tail.

moulting, and they looked scruffy and mangy, and the thought of eating their meat put me right off. There was never bread with their cheese, just biscuit bread like Ryvita – so I lost one stone in a fortnight as we were walking a lot in chest waders in temperatures of 80° to 85° Fahrenheit.

But the fishing is really fantastic, provided you fish for grayling and the very large brown trout, which are unique. The Kitka was a nice river with plenty of flow in my beat, and here I managed fifty-one grayling: these had to be more than 28cm (11in), but my grayling were mostly in between 24 to 25cm (9.5 to 10in). I also caught five trout, of which only one counted as the size limit was 35cm (14in). The Finnish organisers had stocked about six to eight pools with brown trout, and it made a lottery out of the World event, because if you drew one of those pegs you were in the top catches; however, we never did.

The Kuusinki river was my favourite because it held the big brown trout that were quite difficult to catch. We saw the Norwegian team bring two large brown trout into the hotel, so we asked our local

A haul of grayling up to 5lb, from the river where it runs into Russia. Certainly they are big. The slide was given to me by Peter Piskerov.

The River Kuusinki is excellent, with good wading and plenty of fish.

guide to take us there the next day. These were the trout most wanted by anglers who live in the Kuusamo area. Lake Paanajarvi across the Soviet border is where the trout come from, to spawn in these three suitable Finnish rivers: Kitka, Kuusinki and the Oulanka. The story goes that these trout were a special challenge because they don't eat anything while in the rivers; therefore fishing differs from ordinary trout fishing, and you should be tackled up as for big sea trout or salmon.

We had excellent results on our minibus travels to various stretches of the Kuusinki river. This came to a climax on the final practice session when we landed four huge Russian browns: Chris Ogborne with one of 6lb, Brian Leadbetter one of 6lb 8oz, and myself with a beauty of 7lb 6oz; mine took a Hare's Ear size 12 weighted nymph with a short olive marabou tail. (It was one I liked when looking into Charles Jardine's fly box, and he gave it to me.) Our guide John Vainio had the best fish at 8lb 8oz, and it was his best fish ever. My 7lb 6oz

fish remains my best ever wild river brown trout. I had ignored the local advice about big flies and strong tackle, opting for a 5lb breaking strain leader with a Zulu wet fly on the dropper.

I did try the heaviest tackle first, but caught nothing on it, and no sooner had I changed to the lighter outfit than I hooked the big fish and was into it, a Russian brown. I was fishing a fast rapid that was quite shallow, and I had chest waders on; one third of the way across the River Kuusinki I cast my nymph into a flat mini pool no bigger than an average living room, and all hell was let loose! The first leap was four feet in the air, and in my heart I knew I would never land this fish because I was half a mile from the rest of the lads and without a net, as we were returning everything.

But my luck was in, because after several dazzling runs I was still hanging on, trying to keep a steady even pressure and keeping my rod high. The reason for this was that I had the single size 12 Zulu dropper on, and this could foul any rock as the big trout

245

zigzagged through them looking for an escape route – but the hook held. Nearly fifteen minutes had passed, and the fish was getting closer and closer: I had slowly backed up, and now I was close to the bank. The fish made another huge leap as it charged into no more than a foot of water, but on falling back it somewhat stunned itself, and without ceremony I leapt on it and pushed it on to the bank as you would a tired salmon. Naturally I was thrilled, and this was the only fish I kept during the whole two weeks' fishing. It was a magnificent specimen. It ate very well, too, making a welcome change from reindeer – and I was very hungry!

Russian trout actually begin their lives in any of the three Finnish rivers; they then migrate downstream to a giant lake in Russia called Lake Paanajarvi, there they continue to grow as a salmon would in the sea. At around 4lb 8oz they become sexually mature, at which stage they ascend the rivers to spawn. Each year some 500 specimens are caught, with top weights exceeding 20lb. After the fish return to the river they behave just like salmon, in that they do not feed at all.

Apart from these migratory trout there were large stocks of grayling and whitefish. I also caught perch, pike and ide, a fish that looks just like our roach, but has a record weight of 11lb. The Finnish bream record is over 24lb, pike over 52lb, perch 8lb, Atlantic salmon over 88lb, sea trout over 40lb, brown trout 32lb, Arctic char 19lb, grayling over 14lb, pike/perch (zander) 35lb, and Burbot – now extinct in the UK – 33lb. I thought these might interest readers who take fishing holidays aboard; anglers are usually willing to travel for the best fishing.

The fishing season is short in Kuusamo: the ice disappears in April, and in autumn the lakes freeze up again, usually in October. The fly fishing season is even shorter than this. The season starts at the beginning of

June and finishes in September. The waters warm up in spring at the end of May, or sometimes at the beginning of June. In autumn the waters start cooling as early as August, and autumn floods are usually at the beginning of September; however, although the season is short you can take full benefit of it because the sun shines throughout the day and night (the 'midnight sun').

Another bad hazard here are the mosquitoes, which are about in billions: they bite through layers of shirts and jumpers, and thick moleskins, too, so you need to apply repellent over literally your whole body to avoid being badly bitten.

It was a great shame that with such marvellous brown trout in the rivers, and with plenty of grayling of around 25cm (10in), why they stocked it in places, and why they moved the grayling size limit from the normal takeable size of 25cm (10in) to 28cm (11in). This made the competition nothing better than a lottery, as I mentioned before, and this really put us off completely. It would be worth going back to Finland just to fish for the big browns when they are in season, and then you could take on the grayling and the other interesting fish which take the fly, mainly white fish, ide, pike and perch.

Recommended flies are the large, heavy Hare's Ears, and weighted Green-Tagged Stick Fly, and in the failing light of the midnight sun use big dry sedges.

In truth, river fly fishing is so fascinating, whether by dry fly or nymph. Inevitably it ends up with you working out how to catch them, and it's all about the take – and the fight, albeit good fun, is secondary to that.

Fishing in Scotland

The locals at Kelso in Scotland value the brown trout fishing on the Tweed very highly: it's almost a guarded secret how good it is for quality. Whilst on salmon trips there, I have occasionally caught a big trout by mistake, and also a few grayling to 2lb 8oz but on brass heavy tube flies, so I didn't really record them. I remember Jack Simpson had one of 3lb, when I shared the best with him on Emsford, but again that was on a tube fly. I mention all this because you can pick up low priced fishing permits for the Junction beats during midsummer. The tributary of the Tweed is the River Till, and this is very good for sea trout, too; also the River Teviot holds very big grayling.

My experience of the River Ness on the Ness Castle beat is over the last five years, and I love this river. You can always tell a good healthy river by the high numbers of salmon parr and brown trout present: this river has these in abundance, and it is so lovely.

Big Laxa in Northern Iceland

I had heard of the fantastic Big Laxa river in Iceland from my good friend Dave Whitrum from Dublin. He is a professional who takes parties to Iceland and other top fly fishing places all over the world. He told me he had sampled the brown trout fishing there above the Hydro Dam, and promised me it was the very best brown trout river in the world. He had caught them up to 8lb, with an average weight at around 3lb 8oz, and dry fly was the best tactic.

I didn't expect ever to get the chance to go there – until my very good friend Jeremy Herrmann got married. He is a very successful angler/fly fisher, and has won every competition possible. After coming back from honeymoon he organized a week's holiday for his ten best mates, chartering a small plane and flying us direct into a tiny airport in the north of Iceland. I had fished in central Iceland, and the south and west, mostly for

Sight Bobs

An American river fly fisherman invented sight bobs for spotting takes when using weighted nymphs in white water rapids – the Americans love this technique. In Europe the top Austrian fly fisher Roman Moser popularized the technique some years ago after demonstrating his skills with a sight bob on a very good video. The method then got used in a different form for stillwater fly fishers in the 'Bung' style (see Chapter 10 about the Irish loughs, and Chapter 1 by Iain Barr about reservoir fishing).

The idea is to present your weighted nymphs to travel downstream completely unchecked, so they are moving at exactly the same speed as the currents. When the sight bob dips under, you strike, and nine times out of ten you have a fish on. You must balance your fluorocarbon leader out at the correct depth so as not to continuously catch up on the bottom. I find red or orange to be the most visible colours to use on your sight bob. Practice makes perfect with this method.

Sight bobs vary in the way they are made: some are stick-on coloured circular shapes, where you just remove the back to show the sticky side, then fold them nearly in half and stick them together over your leader about six inches from your floating fly line. Then others are made from tow fluoro wool, there are little mini floats, and of course the over buoyancy dressed flies, as in the Bung method.

I like to use a sight bob in roughish, turbulent flows where takes are otherwise more difficult to detect. Try one, you will be surprised, and it will increase your catch rate. This applies to grayling and rivers where nymph fishing is allowed. Some high class beats allow only upstream dry fly fishing until autumn.

salmon and char, and had always noticed the quality of the browns we caught.

Jeremy had managed to get our party of all-serious fly fishers a few days on the

FISHING FOR TROUT AND GRAYLING IN RIVERS

Bob playing a fish on the Big Laxa river.

Another quality brown returned.

Bob shows the ghillie, who then took photographs.

Some of the fish were almost black.

Bob returns it.

Big Laxa river, and one day for sea-run char on a close-by river. Suffice to say the fishing was sensational; we caught virtually all our fish on dry fly, and I found the Black Hopper size 10 by far the deadliest pattern. We found the wading quite good, and fished our way upstream; the river was wide, but in the main quite shallow. I really enjoyed the fishing.

I tried to keep a total for the group of all the fish caught: I got up to 187 over 2lb 8oz and up to 7lb, and gave up. We agreed not to do any publicity when we arrived home, and we kept to that, although Jeremy has allowed me to mention the river

Bob netting a good fish on the River Laxa.

in this book. The week was good; I fished with expert fly dresser Oliver Edwards for the sea-run char, and although we only managed a brace each, it was a fascinating day – and they certainly made the best

Two of Jeremy Herrmann's friends hooked these fish simultaneously.

eating! (Back at the lodge the lady chef prepared them in a special way: she marinated them in lemon juice and various herbs, and after twenty-four hours we ate them raw.) The flesh was very soft, similar to the best wild smoked salmon but much better, a sort of gravad lax, and as nice as that is, it beat it by miles.

So if you can get to Iceland, I am sure you will enjoy it. Orri Vigfusson was the main instigator in paying off the estuary salmon netsmen, thereby improving the salmon's lot in all the UK rivers. I met him and he showed me around the whole area: it is truly a fantastic place if you are a fisherman. One evening a few of the party went cod and haddock fishing just offshore, and it was a case of cod to 15lb and haddock to 7lb, at every cast. Everything fishwise is quality, and that includes the people.

The Fly Fisherman's Hat

Before I left Iceland Orri said, 'By the way Bob, you look like you need a new Sherlock Holmes hat. Leave this one with me and I will get a lot for it when I hold my next fishing charity fund-raising auction – as "Game Fisher of the Millennium" and all that, you really are very well known.' So I gave him the hat, which was full of my old flies and was about three years old. I usually buy a new one about every five years. My hat was always my identifying point as I would wear it continuously for all fishing occasions, also my moleskin cravat, all part of my image.

Now here is a little tip on purchasing a woollen hat like mine. Always buy it one size too big, then wash it and leave it to soak for twenty-four hours, and dry it out quickly and you will have the perfect fit through shrinkage – it won't shrink any more, no matter how many times it gets wet while fishing. Always put a few flies in as well, to get a nicer 'I am a fly fisherman' look.

Bob didn't rate bonefish fishing after catching twenty-five in the first morning. Andros Island, Bahamas.

Stephen Church nets a nice rainbow trout on the River Test.

A good quality stockie rainbow trout.

Grayling, Trout and Brown Trout Rivers I have Fished

I will name only the rivers I can vouch for, and tell you how and when to go and fish them: the lovely River Kennet, River Test and its tributary the River Dever – in particular the Junction Pool is good. Most of these rivers are excellent for grayling as well as trout. In Yorkshire, the rivers Wharfe and Ure are very good. The River Itchin is known for its brown trout and grayling. The Derbyshire Wye is known for its wild rainbows, but I have had some nice browns and grayling here over the years.

Just last year I caught six lovely browns on dry fly from the Welsh Dee at Corwen. I knew they were stocked fish, but you could hardly tell the difference between those that had been in the river a fair while, and a wild one. The grayling fishing here is also very good.

List of Rivers

- River Test: rainbow, browns, grayling, salmon and sea trout.
- River Itchen: rainbows, browns, grayling, salmon and sea trout.
- River Kennet: rainbows, browns, grayling, salmon and sea trout.
- River Wye (Derbyshire): rainbows, browns and grayling.
- River Ure: browns and grayling.
- River Wharfe: browns and grayling.
- River Dee (Welsh): browns, grayling and salmon.
- River Ness: browns, sea trout and salmon (produced a new record salmon in October 07, but returned fish after witness saw it, see my photograph).
- River Teviot: browns, sea trout, salmon and grayling.
- River Till: browns, sea trout, salmon and grayling.
- River Tweed: browns, sea trout, salmon and grayling.
- River Dever: rainbows, browns and grayling.
- River Moy: sea trout, browns and salmon.
- River Avon (Hants): brown trout, sea trout, salmon and rainbows.

Iceland
- River Hitera: excellent, salmon, sea trout and char.
- River Big Laxa: massive brown trout.
- River Zog: salmon.
- River Rangi: salmon and brown trout.

Finland
- River Kuusinki: big browns, grayling and whitefish.
- River Kitka: big browns, grayling and whitefish.

I have also fished in rivers in New Zealand, Tasmania, Canada and Sweden, all of which have superb river fishing.

12 Fly Fishing for Pike and Zander

By Mike Green

I expect many people will be wondering why pike should be included in a game fishing book: it is not especially migratory, it has no adipose fin, and it is not even a 'trouty' shape. Nevertheless fly fishing for this predator is simply so productive, fascinating and exciting that both Bob and I feel that it should be thought of as the 'up-and-coming' game fish.

I have written previously that, other than fishing for bonefish, if I could participate in only one branch of our wonderful sport for the rest of my life, then without the slightest doubt I would fish for pike with a fly rod. What is more, my obsession is getting worse! As I write it is mid-June, the time of year I would, in times gone by, be thinking of carp, tench, bream and so on. This year, however, having had such a terrific winter's pike fishing (seven pike over 20lb, the largest 26lb 8oz), I just can't seem to get enthusiastic about anything else! Of course I give them a rest at spawning time (which can vary from late February to mid June), and I don't fish for them at all when the weather really warms up, as this tends to reduce the oxygen levels in the water: an exhausted fish needs plenty of oxygen to recover safely, and the lack of it may easily result in a dead pike. I regret to say that I have lost one nice fish in this way, but do not intend to repeat the event in the future.

My interest in fishing for pike with a fly rod began some years ago when my best friend Ken Heath 'wangled' permission for us to fish a private Cheshire lake for rainbow trout. In brief, I hooked and eventually boated an immaculate 25lb pike on a trout fly. Ken was convinced that it was not a fish at all but a *crocodile*, and refused to go anywhere near it! But the battle with

My personal best fly-caught pike to date at 28lb 8oz, a fabulous fish from the River Nene. This river has been kind to me, with six twenty-pounders so far, four of them taken by fly fishing.

A gravel pit mid-double comes to the boat on fly tackle. Fish of this calibre put up a great fight when caught this way.

that huge fish, and the awesome sight of it lying alongside the boat, is a memory that will never fade.

The indisputable fact is that, generally speaking, if you catch a 6lb or 7lb trout it is perhaps the fish of the season (if not a

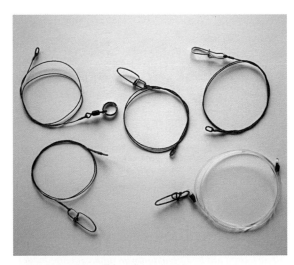

A selection of wire traces and different clips. The bottom right is in fact not wire, but 120lb bs heavy duty monofilament, and I still have to decide which I prefer.

lifetime!), but it would be a rare occurrence not to catch a pike of at the very least 6lb. In the right conditions a catch of ten to fifteen fish up to maybe 14lb is quite possible, with very occasionally a twenty-pounder thrown in. Add a couple of nice perch or chub, and a number of 'on and offs' and 'follows', and it represents a great day's sport that I would heartily recommend to anyone!

The best session I have ever had was in January 2006 with Bob on our local river, which happened to be in perfect order. In a four and a half hour spell Bob landed fifty-six pike, including three 'doubles' to 12lb on a jerk bait I had made for him, while I managed thirty-four pike and a specimen perch all on the fly rod. Certainly that was an exceptional occasion, and please don't think it's always the same: we do have blanks, too – though having said that, not very often!

Compared to spinning and jerk fishing, trying to tempt them on fly tackle has advantages and disadvantages. On the minus side:

M.G. standard pike flies, which will all 'do the business' when the pike are in the right mood.

For your own amusement you can make your flies as fancy as you like, though I really don't think it makes too much difference to the fish!

- It is more demanding and laborious. Fly lines are attracted to bank-side vegetation and snags like a magnet, and it can be really frustrating.
- It is vital to have room for a back cast (fishing from a boat eliminates this problem, of course).
- However competent a fly caster you may be, a jerk bait will cast further and more quickly, covering more water and consequently more fish.

On the plus side:

- There is a certain amount of satisfaction in casting a big fly a long way.
- It's a very pleasant way to fish, even if your efforts go unrewarded (which is rare).

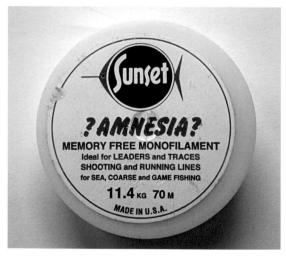

Almost any 15lb to 25lb nylon will suffice for the leader. I have found 'Amnesia' very easy to work with, and have recently been experimenting with 25lb fluorocarbon, which is supposed to be invisible in water.

Decent pike will often snap at a trout fly. This nineteen-pounder took a liking to my 'Jeannette Killer' tin head on a size 8 longshank hook and 7lb leader, third cast on opening day at Ravensthorpe this year. Fortunately it was hooked in the scissors and therefore failed to 'bite me off' during the fifteen-minute battle.

- The 'take' on fly tackle comes straight to your hand, and not via the rod, and is therefore more dramatic: one second you are retrieving a virtually weightless line, and the next there is pandemonium as a toothy monster engulfs your fly with a savage snatch!
- The fight of a pike, unless it is a big 'double', on a jerk rod is a fairly routine affair. As ever the 'pull' is exciting, but a 'billiard cue' of a rod and 50lb braid gives the fish little chance to 'show its mettle'. On fly tackle even a four-pounder will put up a spirited battle, and remember that you will catch a great number of small pike relative to the occasional 'twenty'.
- With a single hook, although it may be a large one, unhooking is so quick and easy, causing minimal trauma to the fish and inconvenience to you.
- Quite often the pike will follow your fly to the rod tip before either taking or refusing, and either way it brings your heart into your mouth. Or again, it may 'come from nowhere' at lightning speed and take the fly almost at your feet, and this is equally enthralling.
- Tackle requirement is minimal, and you can travel really light, with just rod, reel, a packet of flies and traces, and some unhooking pliers. Great distances can be covered in just a few hours' fishing, giving you the chance of showing your fly to many different fish.
- Lastly, and following on from the previous point, it is quite feasible to pop down to your local river or pit for just an hour's fishing, and that could be the very time when a 'big one' is in the taking mood!

Tackle

A start may easily be made with an eight- or nine-weight reservoir rod, provided the fly size is kept reasonably small (size 2 to 2/0). A larger fly of 5in to 7in tied on a 5/0 or 6/0 hook is awkward to cast on such tackle, and I wouldn't recommend it. To project such a creation any distance (and into the wind), a

Another 'gem' of a pike from the Nene, proving once again that big fish will take a fly at times. This one weighed in at 17lb 4oz.

ten- to twelve-weight rod is advised, for both comfort and safety. A number of saltwater fly rods (for Tarpon, Snook and so on) are on the market and will do the job nicely, but I have found none better than Bob's own Champion Piker fly rod. Casts of 20 to 35yd can be made with relative ease, and it will handle a 20lb pike quite adequately, whilst being soft enough to enjoy the fight of a small fish as well. A colleague of mine who recently acquired one to try out this branch of angling actually christened it on a fabulous specimen of 30lb.

As for the reel, almost any reliable wide arbour model will suffice, the large diameter spool helping to reduce possible tangles in the line and backing when you least need them. Pike rarely streak off for the horizon when hooked (though I have to say, a twenty-two-pound reservoir fish I recently caught did distance itself from the boat by forty-five to fifty yards in very short order, and with unstoppable power). I use eleven-weight shooting heads backed with 50 or 75yd of non-stretch braided monofilament running line, though a ten, eleven or twelve weight-forward line would do just as well, and may be preferred by some.

Lines are available in different sink rates, and I myself have four: floater, slow-sink, medium-sink and fast-sink, and use them all at various times. For a beginner fishing water from 5 to 12ft (1.5 to 3.5m) I would say the slow sinker would be the most useful, with the floater as second choice. In clear water pike will come up 10 or 12ft (3 to 3.5m) if they want your fly, and what a thrill it is to witness this. The floater also gives you the option of fishing a surface lure or 'popper' if you so wish (of which more later).

At the business end of the fly line all you need is 4 or 5ft of 20lb nylon and a 12 to 18in wire (or 100lb-plus bs monofilament) trace, with some type of clip at the end to attach your fly. A wide selection of commercial pike flies are on sale now, though I prefer to make my own. I use very strong Kevlar tying thread, 2/0 to 6/0 Aberdeen-type hooks, and I tie streamer-type flies with synthetic materials such as 'Slinky fibre', 'Alien hair' and so on, combined with 'Flashabou', 'Crystal hair', and various 'twinkly' fibres. You can choose your own colour combinations, though I don't believe these make much difference; nevertheless I carry white, yellow, hot orange and black ones, and they have all caught many fish on their day. Bob has a thing for yellow, but there again, he almost *always* uses one, so no surprise that it catches the

Yellow scores again! An immaculate gravel pit double.

And again! They just can't resist it!

majority of his fish! My largest fly-caught pike of 28lb 8oz was taken from the River Nene in January 2006 on a home-tied 6in white fly, whereas the 22lb fish mentioned above took a 4in black one – so you just take your choice.

Personally I like to put eyes on my flies, since they are not really flies as such, but fish imitations. To me they look more attractive with eyes, and I like to think it gives the pike something to 'home in on', though in the past I have to say that I have enjoyed some good catches on eyeless lures. Eyes can be painted on, or sequins may be used and pupils added with black varnish, or you can use ready-made epoxy 3D eyes in various colours. At times pike have been known to attack swim-feeders, bubble-floats, bait rockets and indeed almost

anything that moves, so if you feel that your early efforts at making flies are a bit rough, don't worry: as long as they are tied with supple fibres and with a bit of added 'flash', they will surely work.

Location

Pike must be one of the most ubiquitous fish on the planet. I have caught them in Alaska, Canada, Wales, Scotland and France as well as endless locations in England and Ireland. They flourish in rivers, streams, dykes, drains, lakes, ponds, gravel pits and reservoirs, and, I would guess that, wherever you live here will be pike within a fairly short distance. So long as there is decent quality water and a ready food supply, pike

This superbly conditioned twenty-one-pounder fell to an M.G. white and pearl streamer fly in 25ft (7.5m) of water, fished on a DI 7 fast-sinking shooting head. The thrill of catching such a 'belter' on fly gear can hardly be imagined by those who have not experienced it!

will thrive, and indeed I have caught and witnessed fish of 25lb from gravel pits of just two or three acres. Much of my pike fly fishing takes place in the many scores of such gravel pits we are blessed with in the Midlands. As a general rule they share a depth of 5 to 12ft deep, and are mostly clear. This is very important as, in muddy or algal bloom conditions, the pike can't see the fly, and as it doesn't send out pulses or vibrations, they don't even sense that it is there at all, making it pointless even to try.

As to precise location, the pike can lie literally anywhere in the pit, usually (but not always) close to the cover of reeds or weed-beds, and not too far away from their food supply. In short, try everywhere you can reach, and experience will help you build up a picture of where you are likely to find them at different times of the year. In rivers and streams look for the slacker stretches of water – weirs, backwaters, points where back-waters join the main river, and any obvious features such as reedbeds, submerged tree branches, back eddies. Once again, and most importantly, the water *must* be fairly *clear*. Heavy rain will put muddy water into the river as well as raising the height, and

until it has settled down and cleared, forget the fly fishing, as you will be wasting your time. A smelly old sardine in a back eddy or slack might do the trick, but that is not relevant to this chapter. Ask the match fishermen: they love a bit of colour in the water, as they know that 'bite-offs' will be a rarity. In clear conditions pike often drive them to despair by continually grabbing their roach and 'skimmers' on the way in.

Last winter my local river was in spate for almost the whole time, much to my frustration. Several times I tried to kid myself that it had cleared enough to catch a few fish and gave it a go, but the pike left me in no doubt whatsoever that it was *not* clear enough by pretending to be absent. The next day it would be over its banks and chocolate again! Even in what I think of as perfect conditions, occasionally the fish just will *not* play, and the strange thing is that they all seem to know it. Not a single offer in several hundred yards of diligent and concentrated fishing. The answer? I don't know – maybe we should just forget it and go home, because that's fishing! If we always caught, then perhaps the magic might fade.

A nice fish makes a last big effort to gain its freedom before Bob brings it to the boat. This picture was taken a while ago, before the introduction of Bob's brilliant 'Champion Piker' fly rod. Note that he is using a heavy trout rod and wearing his signature deerstalker!

Here's Bob again looking well pleased with a good gravel-pit pike. As ever he is fishing his favourite Yellow Streamer fly.

Basic Tactics

The ability to cast reasonably well is a definite plus in pike fly fishing. The further you can cast, the longer the retrieve and the more fish you are likely to cover. Having said that, in streams, dykes and small rivers, pike may be lying within two or three yards of you, and many times I have caught one by simply dropping the fly nearby and giving it a twitch. So don't be dismayed if your early efforts seem inadequate.

To execute an effective long cast the technique known as 'double hauling' is more or less essential, as it increases line speed, and therefore distance. Reservoir trout fishers will be familiar with it and I won't attempt a description here. The best bet is to find someone who can do it and get them to give you a quick lesson. It may seem complicated at first glance, but don't be put off, like most things it's very simple when you have learned the timing.

So, having cast out your fly, the next step is to allow it to sink a bit (if applicable), then start the retrieve. The pike will soon let you

259

Other predators often succumb to the charms of our pike flies, and fish like this handsome, bristling perch are always welcome.

Classy chub like this Nene five-pounder frequently figure in the day's catch. The best I have had weighed 6lb 3oz (once more on the 'Yellow Canary'), and that one in fact is my best-ever chub. I was unfortunately fishing alone at the time, and therefore unable to get a decent photo.

know how they want it, so try slow, medium and fast until they start to hit. My advice is to keep on the move, and personally I never cast to the same spot twice unless I have had a 'pull' or 'follow'. Showing it to them once and moving on has proved to be the best way of ensuring a good catch for my friends and I.

To land their fish, many pike anglers carry a large net, either by hand or strapped across their back. This is too cumbersome for me and I prefer to land my fish by gently slipping my fingers into the gill cover and sliding it to safety. A glove is advised for this purpose, though I must confess that I am mostly too lazy to use one (and spend most of the winter with lacerated or scarred fingers to prove it!). Once landed it is usually a simple matter to remove the hook with your spare hand, or with long-nosed pliers if the lure is well back in the fish's mouth.

The only other items you may need will be a weigh sling and scales, and a camera to record your catch should it be a big one, and some kind of line tray. The latter is required to hold the retrieved fly line until you make your next cast. Without one (and even with one, at times!), the spare line is continually tangling in the bank side vegetation, of which the dreaded teasels are the worst culprits, driving me half crazy with frustration! Commercial line trays are available, but I prefer the good old washing-up bowl strapped to my waist, and it has given valiant service for several years now.

A further and essential item is a pair of good polarized sunglasses, which will help you to spot following fish more easily, and perhaps more importantly, will protect your eyes from injury in the event of an accident. Big flies on 6/0 hooks are not the easiest things to cast at the best of times, and in

Surprisingly this is the one and only trout I have caught whist pike fly fishing. It weighed 6lb exactly, and was taken from deepish water at Pitsford Reservoir. Just why we don't accidentally hook more big trout scraping the bottom with pike flies is most mysterious.

adverse windy conditions things can get a bit 'hairy'. Being hit in the face by a large hook travelling at 80mph would be no joke, and could be catastrophic if the eyes were not shielded. Always be careful and try not to overstretch yourself: better, and safer, to put the fly out straight at ten yards than in a heap at twenty.

An alternative method to the floating/ slow sink line streamer fly is to use a DI 7 fast sink line, a short leader of, say, 2 to 4ft (60 to 120cm), and a buoyant fly, the idea being to fish the fly in close proximity to the bottom whether the water is 5 or 35ft (1.5 or 10.5m) deep. Buoyancy is usually incorporated at the head of the fly, and this

Bob and yours truly setting off in the morning haze, hoping for a big Grafham zander.

After an epic battle, Bob boats a magnificent zander of 13lb 3oz. Here, he and Martin Bowler display the fish for the camera.

naturally causes it to rise head first. With the line lying along the bottom, as you retrieve, the fly is pulled forwards and down, creating an enticing up/down 'wiggle', and this can be a very effective technique, especially where the water is not too weedy.

Another choice is the surface lure or 'popper'. Again, the lure has a plastazote foam head, but this time it is fished on a floating line. Stripping it back briskly creates an attractive gurgling or 'popping' effect on the surface, which can be absolutely deadly

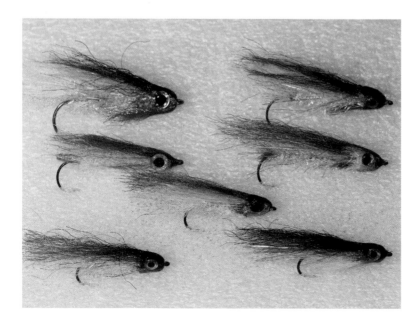

Fry-imitating flies, tied by M.G. to try to tempt those denizens of the deep. Tied on size 2 and 1 long-shank hooks, they worked really well right from the start – those toothy zander just loved them!

Martin holds the net in readiness as I try to bring another good zander to the surface.

Another chunky specimen is hoisted from the net by Martin, to be quickly unhooked and returned without delay. Another victim of the deadly fry fly!

in the right conditions. I have found that shallow water and a flat calm are perfect for this technique to work well, especially when it is dull and overcast, or in the evening as the light begins to fade. A strong heart is a prerequisite if you want to try this method, as one second the fly is chugging its way across the glassy surface, and the next it is engulfed without warning and in a shower of spray by a hungry pike, which often hurls itself into the air in the process. The thrill and excitement of such a spectacle can only be imagined by those who have not witnessed it. Like all fishing tactics, it doesn't always work, but when it does, customers appear to line up to have a go, and sessions can be truly unforgettable.

Conclusion

For the future both Bob and I consider that fly fishing for coarse and sea fish holds endless scope, and will perhaps be the 'way forwards'. As well as pike I have personally taken roach, rudd, perch, chub, eels, carp and zander, pollack, coalfish, flounders, mackerel and garfish all on fly, and have

263

To say I was pleased with this one, my biggest ever zander by a mile, at 2oz under 17lb, would be somewhat of an understatement! After a dogged and prolonged struggle my mouth dropped open when this brute surfaced at the side of the boat. It was truly one of the greatest thrills of my angling life, and one I shall not easily forget!

enjoyed every minute of it. Definitely food for thought!

Lastly, I hope these few words may have stirred up some enthusiasm for this branch of angling, and I strongly urge all pikers to give it a try. Once you have hooked a double-figure pike and experienced the astonishing power and tail-walking acrobatics they can display on fly tackle, you, like me, will not really want to catch them any other way!

I have mentioned above how, when fly fishing for pike, other 'bonus' species are regularly encountered, mainly chub and perch, and perhaps the occasional trout. (With regard to the latter, I can honestly say that in all my fly-piking exploits I have only ever caught one single trout, and that was a

Bob's rod takes on a familiar curve as he bends into a big zander; it has taken a deep-sunk fly in the dark depths of Grafham. Exciting fishing indeed!

very nice brownie from Pitsford reservoir in thirty-five feet of water.) However, recently large numbers of zander have made their presence felt in two of our Midlands reservoirs, namely Grafham Water and Rutland Water, and I have to say that their appearance has been most welcome as far as I am concerned! But how did they get into these waters? You may well ask, and for once I have the answer.

Water is regularly abstracted from the River Nene (for Rutland) and River Ouse (for Grafham) to top up water levels, and baby zander have somehow survived their perilous journey through the pumps and flourished. Bob actually witnessed hundreds of small fish being pumped into Grafham some years ago, fish he at first took to be ruffe, but on closer inspection they proved to be zander. Some were dead, some badly injured, but many obviously made it through unscathed, and they and their descendants are now well into double figures.

Just last week Bob and I caught no fewer than six double-figure zander on fly in two days, the largest being a breathtaking 16lb 14oz, and the feeling is that if there isn't already, there soon will be a record breaker living in Grafham.

I realize that I have digressed slightly from the subject of the chapter, but both Bob and myself felt that this important development should be aired. Big zander are very impressive-looking fish and fight like tigers on fly tackle. Furthermore they will sometimes take a fly quite aggressively, opening up a whole new branch of this wonderful way of fishing to the enthusiast. The popularity of trout fishing on the reservoirs has definitely diminished over the last couple of decades for whatever reasons, whilst there seems to be a fairly ready demand for pike fishing permits. I feel that the relatively new presence of large zander in our local reservoirs may have a major influence on the way things will develop in the near future.

Piking pals enjoying another good day on a gravel pit.

A 30lb Pike Caught on the Fly

Bob Church and I were piking together on one of our favourite gravel pits using my boat Sneaky. The conditions were ideal, mild and calm, and whilst I was gently guiding the boat into our chosen position, Bob had a quick cast with his lure – which was taken immediately. After a spirited battle, Bob's first twenty-pounder of the autumn was boated, weighed, photographed and returned.

A great start, but there was more to come. We started the drift, and after a quick cup of tea, I picked up my fly rod, pulled off some line, and cast away from the boat into twenty-five feet of clear water. Clipped to the wire was a brand new, pearly white fly I had just tied, and, having waited a few seconds for the fast sinking line to get down, I commenced the retrieve.

That virgin fly could not have moved ten feet when it was savagely engulfed by something big, and everything went solid. While Bob prepared the net, I did my best to pump the fish to the surface, but it didn't seem too keen on the idea, and for much of the time my rod tip was well under water. After some exciting and anxious moments, an enormous green flank appeared some six feet down, and soon enough a huge pike was staring defiantly at me from the side of the boat. Bob had it in the net in a flash, and I felt sure I had achieved a long-standing ambition: a thirty-pounder on fly!

With shaking hands we made for the shore, where photos were duly taken, and the scales confirmed my fervent hope: 30lb 4oz, and in pristine condition.

As she sailed off gently back into the depths, I felt a warm glow of satisfaction and excitement. I couldn't fish for another forty-five minutes as my hands were shaking too much, but I was happy to watch Bob as he caught the only other fish of the day, at 16lb. What a result! The only down side is that the rest of my angling life is probably going to be a bit of an anticlimax – but there again, you never know!

Bob looks pleased with his first 20lb pike of the 2007–08 season. This one took a Depth Raider lure first cast on a local gravel pit, an excellent start to a December morning's fishing.

Having netted Bob's fish, taken the photo and repositioned our little boat Sneaky, my first cast with a self-tied fly produced this fabulous pike of 30lb 4oz, and fulfilled a long-held ambition of mine to catch a '30' by fly fishing. The result of the day saw only one more pike come aboard, a sixteen-pounder, but I was 'floating on air'.

Index